Divine Hiddenness

For many people the existence of God is by no means a sufficiently clear feature of reality. This problem, the fact of divine hiddenness, has been a source of existential concern and has sometimes been taken as a rationale to support atheism or agnosticism.

In this new collection of essays, a distinguished group of philosophers of religion explore the question of divine hiddenness in considerable detail. The issue is approached from several perspectives including Jewish, Christian, atheist, and agnostic. There is coverage of the historical treatment of divine hiddenness as found in the work of Maimonides, St. John of the Cross, Jonathan Edwards, Kierkegaard, and various biblical writers. A substantial introduction clarifies the main problems of, and leading solutions to, divine hiddenness. The volume also contains a substantial bibliography on the topic.

Primarily directed at philosophers of religion, theologians, and scholars of religious studies, this collection could also serve as a textbook for upper-level courses in philosophy of religion and philosophical theology.

Daniel Howard-Snyder is Associate Professor of Philosophy, Western Washington University.

Paul K. Moser is Professor and Chairperson of Philosophy, Loyola University of Chicago.

Divine Hiddenness

New Essays

Edited by

DANIEL HOWARD-SNYDER   PAUL K. MOSER

Western Washington University   *Loyola University of Chicago*

CAMBRIDGE
UNIVERSITY PRESS

CAMBRIDGE UNIVERSITY PRESS
Cambridge, New York, Melbourne, Madrid, Cape Town, Singapore,
São Paulo, Delhi, Dubai, Tokyo

Cambridge University Press
The Edinburgh Building, Cambridge CB2 8RU, UK

Published in the United States of America by Cambridge University Press, New York

www.cambridge.org
Information on this title: www.cambridge.org/9780521006101

© Cambridge University Press 2002

This publication is in copyright. Subject to statutory exception
and to the provisions of relevant collective licensing agreements,
no reproduction of any part may take place without the written
permission of Cambridge University Press.

First published 2002

A catalogue record for this publication is available from the British Library

Library of Congress Cataloguing in Publication data
Divine hiddenness : new essays / edited by Daniel Howard-Snyder, Paul K. Moser.
p.   cm.
Includes bibliographical references (p.) and index.
ISBN 0–521–80353–5 ISBN 0–521–00610–4 (pb.)
1. Religion–Philosophy.   2. Hidden God.   I. Howard-Snyder, Daniel.   II. Moser,
Paul K., 1957–
BL51 .D546   2002
212′.6–dc21

2001025496

ISBN 978-0-521-80353-3 Hardback
ISBN 978-0-521-00610-1 Paperback

Transferred to digital printing 2010

Cambridge University Press has no responsibility for the persistence or
accuracy of URLs for external or third-party internet websites referred to in
this publication, and does not guarantee that any content on such websites is,
or will remain, accurate or appropriate. Information regarding prices, travel
timetables and other factual information given in this work are correct at
the time of first printing but Cambridge University Press does not guarantee
the accuracy of such information thereafter.

For our children
William Payne and Peter Edward Howard-Snyder
Anna and Laura Moser

Contents

Contributors

Paul Draper   *Department of Philosophy and Religion, Florida International University*

M. Jamie Ferreira   *Department of Religious Studies & Philosophy, University of Virginia*

Laura L. Garcia   *Department of Philosophy, Boston College*

Daniel Howard-Snyder   *Department of Philosophy, Western Washington University*

Jonathan L. Kvanvig   *Department of Philosophy, University of Missouri*

Paul K. Moser   *Department of Philosophy, Loyola University of Chicago*

Michael J. Murray   *Department of Philosophy, Franklin & Marshall College*

Jacob Joshua Ross   *Department of Philosophy, Tel Aviv University*

J. L. Schellenberg   *Department of Philosophy, Mount Saint Vincent University*

Peter van Inwagen   *Department of Philosophy, University of Notre Dame*

William J. Wainwright   *Department of Philosophy, University of Wisconsin, Milwaukee*

Nicholas Wolterstorff   *Divinity School, Yale University*

Introduction: The Hiddenness of God

DANIEL HOWARD-SNYDER AND PAUL K. MOSER

Many people are perplexed, even troubled, by the fact that God (if such there be) has not made His existence sufficiently clear. This fact – the fact of divine hiddenness – is a source of existential concern for many people. That is, it raises problems about their very existence, particularly its value and purpose. The fact of divine hiddenness is also, according to some people, a source of good evidence against the existence of God. That is, it allegedly poses a cognitive problem for theism, in the form of evidence challenging the assumption that God exists. (Here and throughout we speak of "God" as broadly represented in the historic Jewish and Christian theistic traditions.)

1. Existential Concern

The existential problem often takes the form of a crisis of faith, sometimes leading to a collapse of trust in God. Jewish and Christian theists have committed themselves to the God who, they believe, loves them perfectly. They expect to find their greatest good, their ultimate fulfillment, in personal and social relationship with God. In the Jewish tradition, this general idea finds elaboration in God's entering into a covenant relationship with the people of Israel, who are to respond to God in faithful obedience. In the Christian tradition, the idea sometimes takes a more individualistic turn. To be sure, God enters into covenant relationship with a "people" – namely, the Church inaugurated by Jesus Christ – but Christians often emphasize the importance of each person's entering into a personal relationship with God through Jesus Christ. There are, of course, differences in interpretation and emphasis between and within the distinctive traditions of Judaism and Christianity. Nonetheless, the general initial expectation remains the same: God's reality, including His love for people, will be made sufficiently well known precisely because He loves them, and their flourishing as persons created in the image of God depends on their relationship with Him.

The potential for crisis arises here. Jewish and Christian theists believe that their flourishing as persons depends on their being in a personal and social relationship with God. For many such theists, however, there is no such discernible relationship. God is hidden, if not in fact at least in their experience. Perhaps their existence has no personal guidance from God after all. Perhaps their lives simply blow with the winds of an impersonal nature. If God exists, God seems not to care for them. God seems too hidden to care at all. So the world appears as an uncaring, inhospitable place. Despair over life itself is, then, a natural result of divine hiddenness.

The Hebrew psalmists lament as follows:

My God, my God, why have you forsaken me?. . . . I cry by day, but you do not answer. . . . (Psalm 22:1–2, NRSV)

But I, O Lord, cry out to you; in the morning my prayer comes before you. O Lord, why do you cast me off? Why do you hide your face from me? (Psalm 88:13–14, NRSV)

Psalm 10 complains about God's hiding, as follows: "Why, O Lord, do you stand far off? Why do you hide yourself in times of trouble?" (Psalm 10:1, NRSV; cf. Job 13:24). Psalm 30 laments God's hiding after a time when the psalmist had confident security. "When I felt secure, I said, 'I will never be shaken.' O Lord, when you favored me, you made my mountain stand firm; but when you hid your face, I was dismayed" (Psalm 30:7, NIV; cf. Psalm 104:27–29). Psalm 44 expresses outright annoyance at God's hiding, suggesting that God's hiding is actually morally irresponsible. "Rouse yourself! Why do you sleep, O Lord? Awake, do not cast us off forever! Why do you hide your face? Why do you forget our affliction and oppression?" (Psalm 44:23–24, NRSV).

The subject of God's hiding is no merely theoretical matter in the Hebrew Psalms. It cuts to the core of the psalmists' understanding of God and of themselves. Thus at times it prompts sincere lament from God's people. Isaiah 45:15 likewise sums up a central Jewish view of God: "Truly you are a God who hides himself, O God of Israel, the Savior." God's hiding is sometimes a response to human disobedience and moral indifference toward God (Deuteronomy 31:16–19, 32:19–20; Psalm 89:46; Isaiah 59:2; Micah 3:4), but this is not the full story behind divine hiding. The Jewish-Christian God hides at times for a range of reasons, not all of which seem clear to humans.

Saint Anselm, eleventh-century archbishop of Canterbury and author of the famous ontological argument for God's existence, complains to God as follows:

I have never seen thee, O Lord my God; I do not know thy form. What, O most high Lord, shall this man do, an exile far from thee? What shall thy servant do, anxious in his love of thee, and cast out afar from thy face? He pants to see thee, and thy face is too far from him. He longs to come to thee, and thy dwelling place is inaccessible. He is eager to find thee, and knows not thy place. He desires to seek thee, and does not know thy face. Lord, thou art my God, and thou art my Lord, yet never have I seen thee. It is thou that hast made me, and hast made me anew, and hast bestowed upon me all the blessings I enjoy; and not yet do I know thee. Finally, I was created to see thee and not yet have I done that for which I was made.

Anselm continues:

Why did he shut us away from the light, and cover us over with darkness? . . . From a native country into exile, from the vision of God into our present blindness, from the joy of immortality into the bitterness and horror of death. Miserable exchange of how great a good, for how great an evil! Heavy loss, heavy grief, heavy all our fate! (*Proslogion*, sect. 1)[1]

Anselm believes he gets a divine answer to his prayer of complaint: the famous ontological argument! Even if it is a sound proof, however, it is a far cry from the explicit personal love from God for which he longs. It is as though panting for water he receives a stone.

For many theists, the sense of God's hiding is no fleeting affair. Even devout mystics of Jewish and Christian persuasions languish in what Saint John of the Cross (d. 1591) called "the dark night" of the soul. In a similar vein, many post-Holocaust Jewish writers speak intensely of "the silence of God," something their biblical ancestors experienced painfully. (See, for example, the Hebrew prophetic literature, particularly Isaiah, on divine elusiveness.) For many Christians, the difficulty is exacerbated by the fact that their Lord has promised, "Seek, and you will find; knock, and the door will be opened for you" (Matthew 7:7). Having sought and knocked (and knocked again and again), they still fail to find, and no one answers the door for them. Resisting the natural slide into despair, priests and pastors counsel, "The Lord did indeed promise us, *but* we must. . . ." Well-intentioned counselors promptly fill in the blank with various provisos: For example, we must wait patiently, or we must be more attentive in a certain manner, or we must change certain questionable conduct. Even so, attempts to fill in the blank often seem lame, if not contrived. Sometimes they lead to further frustration and, eventually, to bitterness and despair. Trust in God then crumbles, along with any hope anchored in God's providence. Giving up the struggle to trust the hidden God often seems the only reasonable option as well as the only avenue to psychological well-being. Hence, even devout theists can face an existential crisis from divine hiddenness.

2. Evidence Against God's Existence?

Many nontheists regard the hiddenness of God as salient evidence that the Jewish-Christian God does not actually exist. Friedrich Nietzsche considered the matter in the following light:

A god who is all-knowing and all-powerful and who does not even make sure his creatures understand his intentions – could that be a god of goodness? Who allows

countless doubts and dubieties to persist, for thousands of years, as though the salvation of mankind were unaffected by them, and who on the other hand holds out fright-
ful consequences if any mistake is made as to the nature of truth? Would he not be a
cruel god if he possessed the truth and could behold mankind miserably tormenting
itself over the truth? . . . All religions exhibit traces of the fact that they owe their origin
to an early, immature intellectuality in man – they all take astonishingly lightly the
duty to tell the truth: they as yet know nothing of a Duty of God to be truthful towards
mankind and clear in the manner of his communications.[2]

Divine hiddenness, Nietzsche suggests, warrants the conclusion that theistic
religion arises from an "immature intellectuality" in people. In addition, his
opening rhetorical questions in the quotation suggest that, given the reality
of divine hiddenness, God could not be good. So it follows from the reality
of divine hiddenness, according to Nietzsche, that the perfectly good God of
Jewish-Christian theism does not exist. We thus have an inference from divine
hiddenness to atheism about the Jewish-Christian God.

A recent, detailed defense of atheism on the basis of divine hiddenness is
J. L. Schellenberg's *Divine Hiddenness and Human Reason* (1993). His core
argument is straightforward. If there were a perfectly loving God, He would
see to it that each person capable of a personal relationship with Him reasonably believes that He exists, unless a person culpably lacks such belief. But
there are capable, inculpable nonbelievers. Therefore, there is no perfectly
loving God.

Schellenberg does not demand an undeniable proof that God exists. His
demand is more lenient:

the reasons for Divine self-disclosure suggested by reflection on the nature of love are
not reasons for God to provide us with some incontrovertible proof or overwhelm us
with a display of Divine glory. Rather, what a loving God has reason to do is provide
us with evidence sufficient for belief. One of the consequences of this is that moral
freedom . . . need not be infringed in order for God to be disclosed in the relevant
sense.[3]

The demand, then, is that a perfectly loving God provide evidence that
removes reasonable nonbelief toward God's reality. This is not a demand for
either a compelling proof or a disarming sign of God's existence. Assuming
that reasonable nonbelief persists, Schellenberg concludes that a perfectly
loving God does not exist. Allegedly, then, divine hiddenness underwrites
atheism about the God of Jewish-Christian theism. Some nontheists would
stop short of atheism and recommend agnosticism on the basis of divine hiddenness. This, of course, would be no real consolation for theists. On either
option, atheism or agnosticism, their theism is under cognitive stress owing to
divine hiddenness.

The constellation of attitudes, passions, and actions comprising the existential problem of hiddenness differs from the ingredients of the cognitive
problem. The existential problem calls for the sort of expertise found in a

skilled and experienced pastor, priest, or spiritual director, one well-acquainted with the turbulent ups and downs of the spiritual life. The cognitive problem calls for the sort of expertise one finds in a skilled and knowledgeable philosopher or theologian, one acquainted with the complex ins and outs of assessing evidence and implications. While recognizing the difference between these two problems, we also acknowledge that they often come together in the life of a single individual. Indeed, it is difficult to imagine what it would be like for one to feel frustrated in one's attempt to find God unless one expected certain things of Him and reflected on the reasonableness and implications of those expectations. Those expectations are the main premises of arguments against theism from divine hiddenness, and those reflections are implicit assessments of those arguments. Hence, the existential problem seems naturally rooted in the cognitive problem. This book focuses largely on the cognitive problem.

The cognitive problem prompts examination of whether a certain sort of argument against theism succeeds. It is sometimes helpful to describe the allegedly problematic phenomenon – divine hiddenness – in terms that do not presuppose the existence of God. Talk of "inculpable nonbelief," for example, is useful at times. The idea is that there are people who lack belief that God exists and do so through no fault of their own. It is perhaps noncontroversial that infants and certain mentally impaired adults, for example, fall into this category. Some philosophers contend that a large number of normal adults are included as well. The latter claim is, however, controversial among philosophers of religion. Our talk of "inculpable nonbelief" does not presume that this controversy has been settled.

Several noteworthy themes have emerged in discussion about the argument from divine hiddenness against theism. We mention the following, in no particular order of importance.

1. The cognitive problem of hiddenness has various connections with the more popular, traditional problem of evil. Analogous practical and theoretical problems of evil have emerged. The latter consists of an argument to the effect that the Jewish-Christian God does not exist, since He would not permit any evil and suffering or at least evil and suffering of the sorts, magnitude, and distribution found in our world. Indeed, one might even think of inculpable nonbelief as a certain sort of evil or suffering – a bad state of affairs – that would not exist if there were a loving God. We might, however, distinguish the problem of evil from the problem of divine hiddenness on the ground that we can imagine scenarios in which each might arise even if the other does not. In any case, even if they are logically distinct problems, they resemble each other in certain respects.

For example, the ways to structure an argument against theism from inculpable nonbelief parallel the ways to structure an argument from evil. We commonly distinguish "logical" ("deductive") arguments from evil from "evidential" ("inductive," "probabilistic") arguments from evil. A logical argument from evil affirms of some known fact about evil that it is incompatible with theism, while an evidential argument does not, either because it affirms that the fact in question is not known but only reasonably believed,[4] or because it affirms that the fact in question is only improbable given theism, not incompatible with it.[5] We can easily distinguish arguments from inculpable nonbelief along the same lines as well.[6]

Similarly, the ways in which one might respond to an argument against theism from inculpable nonbelief parallel the ways in which one might respond to an argument from evil. Of course, one might respond by accepting the conclusion. If we do not accept the conclusion, however, we shall likely respond in one of several ways.

At one end of the spectrum, we might suggest that the concept of *perfect love* used to get the argument going in the first place must be revised. For example, we might revise this concept in such a way that our expectation of a loving personal relationship with God is refined somehow. (Analogously, some process theologians have revised their expectation of what God can do in terms of eliminating evil by revising their concept of the power of God.) In addition, we might take the argument as an occasion for a more radical reconstruction of our concept of God. For example, we might infer that the assumption of a *personal* God is ultimately at fault. Alternatively, we might say that just as the "grammar of God" (or, perhaps, the nature of God) does not allow for evidence against God, so it does not allow for evidence for Him.

At the other end of the spectrum, we might deny the allegedly troubling phenomenon in question, inculpable nonbelief, just as Augustine denied the real existence of evil. A more familiar kind of response (one that parallels a certain response to arguments from gratuitous evil) would be to hold that God would indeed prevent inculpable nonbelief (as He would gratuitous evil). We thus might contend that since one's evidence for theism is significantly better than the evidence for inculpable nonbelief (or gratuitous evil, for that matter), there are, contrary to initial appearances, no inculpable nonbelievers (or gratuitous evils). We might thus try to identify a basis for culpable nonbelief in normal adults.

We can see another way in which certain versions of the evidential argument from evil have been connected with divine hiddenness by reflecting on William Rowe's evidential argument against theism.[7] Rowe asserts that there is no reason for God to permit certain horrific instances of intense suffering. Defending this assertion, Rowe says that, so far as we can tell, there is no such reason (or at least no reason we know of) that involves a good state of affairs weighty enough to justify permission of those horrors (or one that requires their permission). Rowe's inference begins with a claim of this form: "*so far as we can tell*, there is no X," or "there is no X of the sort in question *that we know of,"* and then moves to "there *is* no *X*." Some such inferences may be reasonable, but only under certain conditions. It is reasonable to draw this sort of inference only if the following proposition is acceptable:

If there were an *X*, then we would likely know of it.

In that case, Rowe must be assuming that the following proposition is acceptable:

If there were a reason that would justify God's permission of this or that horror, then we would likely know of it.

One way to know of something is directly: You see it for yourself, or you grasp it mentally as when you apprehend the validity of a simple inference rule, say *modus ponens*. Another way to know of something is indirectly: You see something else and infer from it that the item in question exists, even if you do not see or grasp it directly for yourself. It is difficult to see how to argue plausibly that we would likely know directly of the reason that would justify God's permission for this or that horror; and there are good reasons to be in doubt about whether we probably would. So, many have inferred, Rowe's assumption is incorrect. His inference has evidently been defeated.

The previous assessment of Rowe-style inferences is too quick. It does not take into account the likelihood that we would know of God's reason *indirectly*. This is where divine hiddenness might come into play. It seems that if God's reason for permitting a person to suffer horrifically is not discerned by that person, God would make it clear to the person that there is such a reason by assuring the person of His own love and care. By analogy, a loving parent would assure a young child of the parent's love in similar circumstances, especially when the child cannot understand why his or her suffering is being permitted. For many victims of horrific, intense suffering, however, no assurance is forthcoming. God is silent, so to speak. Regardless of whether the latter claims are true, this is one way that divine hiddenness has been linked to the evidential argument from evil.[8] It allegedly provides a context in which the alleged defeater of Rowe's inference has no force; or, alternatively, it allegedly provides a reason for thinking that Rowe's assumption is correct.[9]

2. We have suggested that the argument from divine hiddenness is rooted in our expectations regarding God, specifically how a perfectly loving being would reveal Himself. Different expectations may be motivated by different analogies. People who emphasize that God would do whatever it takes to prevent inculpable nonbelief frequently regard God's love in analogy with parents who wish to comfort their young children in distress. Others, however, see God's love in analogy with familiar adult love, where the lover primarily wants certain attitudes and behavior to accompany any reciprocation of love

on the part of the beloved. Any old reciprocation won't do. Those pushing the latter analogy will focus on different kinds of human attitudes and motivations that God, in His unsurpassable love, might wish to promote or to prevent prior to bringing the nonbeliever to belief. On this view, it is not belief that God exists per se that is primarily important but rather the attitudes and motivations that accompany belief. On this view, the loving thing for God to do is to bring the nonbeliever to belief in such a way that serves these ulterior divine purposes. If their fulfillment is not in the offing now, God may patiently wait until they are before bringing the nonbeliever to belief.

Another analogy sees God as a benevolent reconstructive surgeon. As such, God will not aim to bring one to belief unless one's volitions are in line with God's purposes in one's believing in the first place. Specifically, God seeks a human's willingness to obey, to serve, and to trust Him, as seems fitting for His being the Lord of all. Mere curiosity, or double-mindedness on the matter of giving oneself humbly and obediently, will not do. Only those prepared to respond appropriately to personal divine revelation are its genuine recipients. For all that, God may well give general revelation sufficient to move people to query about one's relationship with God, but even here volitional matters enter into the picture. The unduly skeptical as well as the modestly indifferent may not appreciate what divine light is given them, owing to their resistance or apathy. Passionate striving and setting aside all else for the pursuit of available divine light are mandatory. God will not trivialize the supreme value of divine light.

In reply, those emphasizing the parent analogy will submit that a perfectly loving God would empathize with the plight of those who seek Him but who, through no fault of their own, come up empty-handed. Would it not be in the very context of an ongoing, developmental relationship with the seeker that God's redemptive purposes are best fulfilled, as in the case of a mother and child? At any rate, we can see that one's operative analogies can make a big difference in what one expects of a perfectly loving being.

3. We have suggested that a response to the argument from inculpable nonbelief might deny that God has failed to make Himself sufficiently known. "What do you mean God is hidden? Just look around you and at yourself. What more could you want?" This response might seek inspiration from some biblical sources. "The heavens are telling the glory of God, and the firmament proclaims his handiwork," declares the psalmist (Psalm 19:1, NRSV). The apostle Paul remarks: "Ever since the creation of the world [God's] eternal power and divine nature, invisible though they are, have been understood and seen through the things he has made" (Romans 1:20, NRSV). Aside from what the psalmist and Paul actually had in mind (itself a matter of ongoing debate), if God is evident through creation, we need an explanation of why many normal people fail to believe that God exists. Some theists recommend their

theism with arguments to the best explanation that have to do with historical events, like the history of Israel or the resurrection of Jesus of Nazareth. Still others insist that God makes Himself sufficiently well-known through more internal means, such as one's conscience.

If God is sufficiently well-known in any of the ways suggested, we need an explanation of why so many people fail to believe. A traditional answer is that, generally, failure to appreciate the evidence of creation and history or to hear the internal witness of conscience is a consequence of a person's sinfulness.[10] This could be taken as a denial of the premise of the argument from hiddenness implying that some people fail to believe *inculpably*. The thesis would be that every (normal adult) nonbeliever culpably fails to believe. Exactly how sin enters the explanatory picture here will vary, some emphasizing volitional vices, others cognitive. An explanation emphasizing one thing may apply to one person but not to another. In addition, different explanations may apply to the same person at different times, and several explanations may apply to one person at one time. Naturally enough, those who find such explanations unconvincing think charges of culpability are best laid elsewhere.

Another suggestion is that every human being can believe that God exists, by *implicitly* believing in Him, even though one does not know that this is what one is doing. This can be done by pursuing a moral life and thus relating to God by way of relating to His chief attribute, goodness. Alternatively, one can implicitly believe by acting *as one would if* one were explicitly to believe in Him. In these ways, one can enter into a developmental relationship with God that will become more fully realized and explicit in the future.

4. Some people grant that God fails to make Himself sufficiently well-known, and that nonbelief cannot be written off to human sinfulness – nonbelief is at least frequently inculpable. The goal, then, is to explain inculpable nonbelief, the fact that many fail to believe through no fault of their own. The general strategy here is to articulate the benefits of God's causing or permitting inculpable nonbelief, as against the benefits of belief that God exists and the attendant availability of a personal relationship with Him. Variations on this strategy include developing and defending one or more of the following:

- God hides and thus permits inculpable nonbelief (at least in principle) in order to enable people *freely* to love, trust, and obey Him; otherwise, we would be coerced in a manner incompatible with love.
- God hides and thus permits inculpable nonbelief (at least in principle) in order to prevent a human response based on improper motives (such as fear of punishment).

- God hides and thus permits inculpable nonbelief because, if He were not hidden, humans would relate to God and to their knowledge of God in presumptuous ways and the possibility of developing the inner attitudes essential to a proper relationship with Him would be ipso facto ruled out.
- God hides and thus permits inculpable nonbelief because this hiding prompts us to recognize the wretchedness of life on our own, without God, and thereby stimulates us to search for Him contritely and humbly.
- God hides and thus permits inculpable nonbelief because if He made His existence clear enough to prevent inculpable nonbelief, then the sense of risk required for a passionate faith would be objectionably reduced.
- God hides and thus permits inculpable nonbelief because if He made His existence clear enough to prevent inculpable nonbelief, temptation to doubt His existence would not be possible, religious diversity would be objectionably reduced, and believers would not have as much opportunity to assist others in starting personal relationships with God.
- Inculpable nonbelievers are either well-disposed to love God upon believing or they are not. The well-disposed either are responsible for being so disposed or not. If not, God lets them confirm their good disposition through choices in the face of contrary temptations before making Himself known. If so, they are well-disposed for unfitting reasons and He waits for them to confirm their good disposition in a purer source before making Himself known. Inculpable nonbelievers who are not well-disposed to love God upon believing and who are not responsible for failing to be well-disposed are given the opportunity by God to change before He makes Himself known.

5. The previous explanations for inculpable nonbelief, among others, will be touched on in the book's essays. One theme that has emerged is that no single explanation may be the whole explanation of divine hiddenness. Different people, given their different stances toward God, might call for different explanations. Moreover, all of the explanations might fail individually for any particular individual and yet, to some extent, apply to a single individual, totaling up to a complete explanation. It thus won't do to object to an explanation that it does not apply to certain kinds of people; nor will it do to object that each explanation fails to apply to each candidate for inculpable nonbelief. An objection to such explanations must invoke something like the claim that they fail, collectively as well as individually, to account for what we take to be, at first glance, inculpable nonbelief. Here a distinctively epistemic problem for the proponent of the argument from hiddenness arises. Human beings are enormously complicated, and it is no easy task to tell whether any particular candidate for inculpable nonbelief possesses or fails to

possess those motivations, attitudes, and dispositions that putatively explain their inculpable nonbelief.

6. One might grant that God does not make Himself sufficiently well-known (especially to inculpable nonbelievers) and admit that we do not know of any good explanation for why He would do that. Perhaps there *is* some reason *we do not know*. Indeed, when we are dealing with the purposes involved in divine permission of some (bad) state of affairs, this seems to be a *plausible* option, not just some remote possibility. Evidently, it would not be surprising if we were unable to explain God's not being more forthcoming about His existence. (The book of Job seems to make an analogous point regarding the existence of evil.)

3.   Summaries and Questions

The contributors to this book discuss many of the themes identified herein. In this section we briefly outline their contributions to the discussion.

Peter van Inwagen, in "What Is the Problem of the Hiddenness of God?" distinguishes the problem of divine hiddenness from the problem of evil by imagining scenarios in which the one but not the other arises. Clearly enough, the world could be such as it exactly is with all its horrors, with the exception that things are also as proponents of the argument from inculpable nonbelief say that it should be. For example, prior to the death of every person God could make Himself evident to all by some miraculous vision; this could be a well-known fact about human experience and as such would render the problem of hiddenness moot. Still, the problem of evil would remain. On the other hand, imagine a secular utopia in which no one suffers even the slightest. It's hard to see how the problem of evil could arise here, but, among such a people, theists might maintain that there is a God and nonbelievers might query why He hasn't made Himself known.

Through an imaginative dialogue between an atheist and a theist, van Inwagen argues that the problem of hiddenness comes to a cluster of questions having to do with why we do not see certain things that we do not see if there is a God, such as signs and wonders. "Can one rationally believe in God in a world devoid of signs and wonders?; under what conditions would it be rational to believe a story that reports signs and wonders?; could any possible sign or wonder or series of signs and wonders make it reasonable to believe in a necessarily existent, omnipresent, omnipotent Creator and Sustainer of the world of locally present things?"

Van Inwagen suggests that theists should meet the challenge of the absence of signs and wonders in a fashion familiar to those who work on the problem of evil. Tell an internally consistent theistic story that is not known to be false that entails the absence or rarity of signs and wonders. Van Inwagen does not construct such a story but rather offers two pieces of advice to those who do. First, he notes that God's desire for *why* people believe in His existence may well be much more important to Him than *that* they believe in Him in the first place. It may well be that God wants people to believe in His existence for certain reasons and not for others, that He prefers that they do not believe at all if the only option is to believe for the wrong reasons. Second, van Inwagen suggests that Christian philosophers who attempt to tell such stories reflect on two texts: Luke 16:31 ("If they do not listen to Moses and the Prophets, neither will they be persuaded if someone should rise from the dead") and John 20:29 ("Have you believed because you have seen me? Blessed are they who, not seeing, believe").

Van Inwagen's emphasis on miraculous "signs and wonders" is arguably misplaced. After all, none of us knows that there are other human persons by way of "signs and wonders." So why couldn't God bring about reasonable belief in His existence and love in ways that are more suitable to developing relationships with God? As for van Inwagen's cluster of questions, suppose we answer "yes," "none," and "no." Isn't there a problem of divine hiddenness that remains nonetheless? It seems so.

J. L. Schellenberg, in "What the Hiddenness of God Reveals: A Collaborative Discussion," articulates and defends a concise argument. The first premise is:

P1. If God exists and is unsurpassably loving, then for any human subject H and time t, if H is at t capable of relating personally to God, H is at t in a position to do so, unless H is culpably in a contrary position at t.

From P1 he argues that since one cannot be in a position to relate personally to God unless one believes that God exists, and since belief is not a matter of voluntary control, it follows that:

P2. If God exists and is unsurpassably loving, then for any human subject H and time t, if H is at t capable of relating personally to God, H at t believes that God exists, unless H is culpably in a contrary position at t.

Schellenberg says that there are clear cases of persons possessing the relevant capacities who inculpably deny or are in doubt that God exists – for example, atheists and agnostics who are honest seekers of the truth. In addition, he claims, there are clear cases of persons possessing the relevant capacities who belong to cultures that are without even any understanding of the idea of a personal God and thus they fail to believe. It follows that there is no unsurpassably loving God.

The crux of the matter seems to be P1. Schellenberg regards it as a necessary truth, reflecting part of the very meaning of "God exists and is unsurpassably loving." What does he have in mind, however, when he writes of (a) "relating personally to God," (b) being "capable" of such a relationship, and (c) being "in a position to" have it? To *relate personally* to God is to interact with Him in the various ways that theistic religious traditions describe: on the divine side, God's guiding, supporting, and forgiving us, for example, and on the human side, our trusting Him, showing gratitude, and worshiping Him, among other things. It would also involve an explicit consciousness of His presence and interaction with us. This relationship is to be conceived of developmentally, and not as something that comes complete and mature. To be *capable* of a personal relationship with God is to have the cognitive and affective equipment required to hold the attitudes and to perform the behavior involved in such a relationship and to possess the concept of God, or at least the materials from which it can be constructed. To have the capacity to relate personally to God is not the same thing as being in a position to relate personally to God. To be *in a position* to relate personally to God is to have it within one's power to do so just by choosing.

With an understanding of its key terms in place, why suppose that P1 is true? Schellenberg argues that it follows from the nature of unsurpassable love and can be supported by analogy with the best sorts of human love as well. An unsurpassable lover would *seek* a kind of close, explicit participation in the life of her beloved for its own sake, as well as for the sake of her beloved, so that he could draw from it what he needed to flourish. This would be especially true in the divine–human case. A close, explicit interaction with God would bestow moral benefits. For example, it would enable one to more easily overcome character flaws and it would provide one with a model for other relationships. Moreover, it would bestow experiential benefits, such as peace and joy, security and support in suffering, and the pleasure of companionship. Of course, God would not force Himself on us, as that would make the relationship a sham. He would leave it up to us to enter into it. This – our own free choice in the matter, as well as the consequences of prior free choices – would be the only thing He would allow to prevent us from entering into a relationship with Him and interacting with Him. Otherwise, He would always be available.

One might argue that while a perfectly loving God would certainly strongly *desire* a personal relationship with each capable person, it is not at all clear that, barring individual culpability, He would *do* everything in His power to bring it about, as P1 implies. Schellenberg argues that He would, on the grounds that one who is unsurpassable in love would *seek* a personal relationship, while respecting the beloved's freedom. But here a question arises: Does one's seeking a personal relationship with another imply one's doing *everything else* in one's power to bring about the relationship? Well, no. As we just noted, unsurpassable love will constrain its pursuit of a personal relationship by respecting the beloved's freedom. Are there other ways in which it might constrain itself? Perhaps. Can't there be inculpably acquired attitudes, feelings, dispositions, and habits a perfectly loving response to which is to *postpone* doing all one can to maintain a personal relationship and to wait for further development, encouraging it in various ways? Analogies with adult love – including the sort of so-called tough love recommended by support groups related to Alcoholics Anonymous and by feminists – support this view. If it is not unloving sometimes to withdraw from a personal relationship in order to facilitate and confirm beneficial change in the beloved, then it need be no spot on one's love if one refrains from *starting* a personal relationship for similar reasons. So it is, one might argue, that there is conceptual space for a perfectly loving God to *seek* a personal relationship with a capable person even if He does less than He could do to bring about that goal, provided He has taken or is taking significant steps in that direction. Schellenberg discusses this and other objections in his essay.

In "Deus Absconditus," Michael Murray defends a "soul-making" response to the argument from divine hiddenness. Suppose that God were to reveal Himself (and the fact that He rewards those who seek Him and punishes those who do not) to capable persons so that reasonable nonbelief was impossible. In that case, these people would be coerced to act in accordance with the revealed information, resulting in good choices and ultimately good characters for which they are not responsible. This flies in the face of God's aim for persons to make free choices toward the development of their characters.

Several questions arise for this view. First, unless we know with certainty that a coercer exists and will carry out his threat (reward), we cannot be coerced to behave accordingly. So, if God informed us of His existence and moral will with something less than certainty – say, in a way that merely prevents reasonable nonbelief – wouldn't there be enough room for soul-making? Second, human experience tells us that divine punishment and rewards are not systematically meted out in the here and now but rather (if at all) in the afterlife. Consequently, wouldn't the motivating effect of belief in punishment and rewards fail to be sufficiently coercive to undermine soul-making? Third, couldn't God make His existence sufficiently clear while keeping the facts about divine punishment and reward under wraps? If so, then belief in God's existence *alone* would not coerce one into making only good choices. It seems that Murray's explanation must be augmented. Fourth, even if some nonbelievers would lose their prospects for soul-making upon coming to possess evidence that put God's existence and the facts about reward and punishment beyond reasonable nonbelief, why suppose that *every* nonbeliever would? After all, believers who assume that their grounds for believing in God and the facts about reward and punishment render nonbelief unreasonable retain the ability to shape their souls. So, at best, Murray's soul-making explanation is incomplete. Murray responds to these and other objections by showing the relevance of different elements involved in coercion.

In "St. John of the Cross and the Necessity of Divine Hiddenness," Laura Garcia sketches and defends John's perspective on the relationship between faith and divine hiddenness. In the main, faith is a volitional surrender of one's will to God's will, in which union with God primarily consists. Because of original sin and our own sins, however, the union of our wills with God's will is also a process of purification, of renunciation and self-denial. Purification is not a matter simply of giving up what is seriously sinful and obviously bad. Rather, one must give up created goods, thus coming to prefer God and His will to any created good. This process takes place in three, sometimes overlapping stages. The first stage – "the dark night of the senses" – involves the voluntary, active mortification of one's natural appetites, which tend to interfere with the goal of detaching oneself from created goods. The second stage – "the dark night of the soul" – involves the voluntary, active detachment from our cognitive faculties, which tend to supplant full submission to God with an attempt to understand His nature and ways. So it is that one must give up one's desire not only for sensory goods but for spiritual goods as well. The aim is to concentrate one's appetites and faculties solely on God in such a way that one is not satisfied with any other object. This third and final stage, of concentration, is wrought by God in the willing soul. Then, and only then, will one be in a position to love God as God wants to be loved. Divine hiddenness figures in the process as a way in which one must humbly accept God's will without being able to understand it. The goal is to eliminate our taking pride in what we have achieved and forming a new attachment – this time to a spiritual good, the presence of God – that interferes with a complete surrender to God's will.

John of the Cross assumes that his audience consists of believers who accept the teaching of the Church. Might what he says be extended to nonbelievers? Garcia argues that it can be, at least in part, and takes on several objections to the contrary.

In "Jonathan Edwards and the Hiddenness of God," William Wainwright defends Edwards' rejection of this premise: If a perfectly loving God exists, He would ensure that persons capable of a personal relationship with Him who don't resist it would possess sufficient evidence to bring it about that they believed in His existence and love. That is not to concede that there *isn't* sufficient evidence. On the contrary, according to Edwards, God has provided adequate objective evidence "in the effects and external expressions and emanations of the divine perfections," as well as through direct revelation of "divine things" to the ancient nations and the Jews, which are contained in the Jewish-Christian scriptures. Moreover, God has endowed human beings with the faculties to discern, appreciate, and weigh this evidence, but those

faculties work properly only if they function in accordance with "true benevolence," which consists mainly of an intense desire for truth about God and
for true holiness. So, while there is plenty of evidence, some are not *in
possession* of it because they lack true benevolence.

Aren't there nonbelievers who are truly benevolent, in Edwards' sense? No,
says Edwards. Since the scriptures say that there is "sufficient light for the
knowledge of God," nonbelievers must fail to believe "divine things" owing
to "a dreadful stupidity of mind, occasioning a sottish insensibility of their
truth and importance." This insensibility consists of a "proneness to idolatry"
and a "disregard of eternal things" – dispositions to ignore familiar and
obvious considerations, to be swayed by ridicule and deference to people in
authority, to prejudice against religion, etc. – that impair our ability to reason
properly about God. We bring such impairments on ourselves. One might
object that since belief in God is so important and our faculties so impaired,
God should increase the evidence. Edwards replies that what is needed is not
more evidence but a change of heart, and that without the latter the former
would be inefficacious.

Some pressing questions arise about Edwards' position. First, Edwards
fails to appreciate the evidence for there being nonbelievers who do earnestly
seek the truth about God, who love the Good, who are judicious, and who, if
anything, display a prejudice *for* religion, not against it. Consequently, a lack
of true benevolence leaves unexplained a good deal of divine hiddenness.
Second, why would God permit people to blind themselves this way in the
first place? Third, what can *we* do to get out of our miserable position, especially in light of Edwards' insistence that true benevolence is, ultimately, a gift
of God's bestowed on some and not on others? Fourth, Edwards says the nonbeliever is to blame for her nonbelief. This seems at odds with his insistence
that whether one is truly benevolent is up to God and with the fact that our
dispositions to belief and holiness are almost entirely a causal upshot of our
childhood upbringing and education, and thus are outside our voluntary
control. Wainwright addresses these and related questions in defending what
comes to a modified Edwardsian position.

In "Cognitive Idolatry and Divine Hiding," Paul Moser argues, among other
things, that divine hiddenness is no evidence at all against Jewish-Christian
theism. In fact, divine hiding is to be expected once the loving character of
the Jewish-Christian God is properly understood. God, in His love, would
primarily seek what was morally best for us, and therefore would give us an
opportunity freely to achieve a sort of moral goodness apt for us, one characterized by unselfish love for others and obedient trust in God. If one's believing that God exists on the basis of adequate evidence would not promote
such moral transformation, then bringing one to believe on the basis of such
evidence would not serve God's purposes. So, in general, God would manifest His perfect love by refusing to bring people to belief unless they were

sincerely open to such moral transformation. We have reason, therefore, to expect that God would hide from us.

Who is the "us" here? It is at least people who resist the moral transformation in question. Aren't there nonbelievers who do not resist, who are open to the sort of transformation in question? If there are, suggests Moser, *they* will not insist on a kind of evidence irrelevant to transformation toward God's character. Part of what it is to be open to such moral transformation is to trust God and to let God decide how He will bring one toward Himself. For one to insist otherwise may involve a sort of idolatry, "cognitive idolatry," whereby one exploits evidential standards that amount to refusing to let God be the Lord of one's life, at least regarding proper ways of knowing God.

Two questions arise. Suppose that to *insist* on miraculous signs and wonders or one's favored style of argument is to make an idol of one's preferred evidential standard, and hence constitutes a failure in the sort of openness that God seeks. First, so long as the cognitive idolater is otherwise open to a morally transformative personal relationship with God, would it not serve God's purposes equally well to make Himself known to her and then *in the context of that relationship* try to bring her to repentance? Second, consider one who is open to God and who has no expectations as to *how* He might wish to make Himself known. Might such a person nevertheless properly expect God (if such there be) to make Himself known in God's preferred way *at some time*? Certainly. (Such expectations cannot be written off to "cognitive idolatry" as they do not consist in a specification of a certain kind of evidence without which one refuses to believe, and they are encouraged by the Jewish-Christian view of God's love as well.) What about *now*? After all, she is open to the divine challenge of transformation, and on this account there is nothing else to explain God's refraining from manifesting Himself. Moser addresses these and other questions in his essay, in connection with a discussion of theodicy and evidence for God.

Proponents of the argument from divine hiddenness against theism tend to pose the argument as an "epistemic problem" for theistic belief. That is, they tend to regard divine hiddenness as having sufficient evidential force to move a rational person from theism to agnosticism, or from agnosticism to atheism. In "Divine Hiddenness: What is the Problem?" Jonathan Kvanvig examines this claim. He argues that on a subjective coherentist epistemology, which he is inclined to endorse, just about anything – even belief in scissors – *can* diminish the epistemic status of belief in God, provided the rest of a person's belief system connects the two in the appropriate way. Likewise, just about anything – including belief in divine hiddenness – *can* be in good epistemic standing with belief in God, provided that it is embedded in a belief system that connects the two appropriately. Are there any such belief systems adequate to the task? Kvanvig claims that there are many. One that he sketches explains how God is perfectly loving and yet hidden by reference to the Fall, according to which, ultimately, there are no inculpable nonbelievers since each person rejects God in one way or another. Any such belief system that also recognizes the evidence for inculpable nonbelief can reduce the tension by just adopting skepticism about that evidence, for example, by saying that apparently honest seekers of the truth who are agnostic are self-deceived or possess inflated epistemic standards.

Kvanvig further argues that no factor involved in the hiddenness of God can change the epistemic standing of theism when an objectivist epistemology is assumed. We begin with the assumption that the evidence is *counterbalanced* between theism and atheism. There are only two accounts of the quality of the evidence on such an assumption. Either (1) what is proffered for or against the existence of God is not really objective evidence at all or (2) there is equally good, defeasible objective evidence for and against the existence of God. If (1), since evil would not be evidence against theism, neither would inculpable nonbelief be evidence against theism. If (2), evil is *defeated* evidence against theism (otherwise the total evidence would not be counterbalanced), and so since inculpable nonbelief is a special instance of the problem of evil, the latter of which has already been factored into the total evidence, inculpable nonbelief is not additional objective evidence against theism. If one insists that inculpable nonbelief constitutes a problem of a kind different from the problem of evil and inculpable nonbelief is undefeated, then the sorts of considerations that *in the counterbalanced scenario* defeat the evidential power of evil against theism cannot defeat the evidential power of inculpable nonbelief. This scenario, however, is impossible; that is, it is impossible for there to be a situation in which evil is defeated but inculpable nonbelief is not. So on the only two accounts of the quality of the counterbalanced evidence, hiddenness is not objective evidence at all.

We might question Kvanvig's somewhat cavalier dismissal of the evidential value of hiddenness given a subjective coherentist epistemology. It's not as though the premises of arguments like Schellenberg's and the evidence he adduces in their support are on the periphery of the typical believer's web of beliefs; and whether one's web can survive theodical tinkering at the center will have to be determined on a case-by-case basis. Kvanvig's example is a good case in point. His recommended theodicy of the Fall implies that there are no inculpable nonbelievers, which arguably flies in the face of strong evidence to the contrary. Whether *the implications* of the skeptical attitude latent in rejecting that evidence will adversely affect the rest of one's system of beliefs must be assessed.

Kvanvig's epistemic critique of the objective evidential value of hiddenness assumes that the evidence is counterbalanced. What if we don't make that assumption? How would that affect his argument? Suppose we are unable to make with any confidence even a ballpark guess at the strength of any bit of evidence either for or against theism. In that case, we will not assume that the evidence *is* counterbalanced, nor will we assume that it is *not*. We will have no opinion on the matter. Might we not come nevertheless to view inculpable nonbelief as objective evidence against theism? That would be odd to say the least: to suppose that we are in no position to judge that evil is objective evidence against theism but that we are nevertheless in a position to judge that inculpable nonbelief is. There is another way, however, in which we might have no opinion about whether the evidence is counterbalanced. Suppose we can discern the approximate strengths of various pieces of objective evidence that support theism, on the one hand, and atheism on the other, but we are unable to judge which has the stronger support. In that case, couldn't inculpable nonbelief be objective evidence against theism, even though we don't assume that the evidence is counterbalanced? By way of reply, one might argue (as Draper does) that if we cannot judge which side has the stronger support, adding inculpable nonbelief to the pile will not appreciably change the situation and so will not change our overall epistemic situation.

According to M. Jamie Ferreira in "A Kierkegaardian View of Divine Hiddenness," many people read Kierkegaard's Climacus writings as saying that God refrains from giving evidence that puts His existence beyond reasonable doubt in order to generate intense subjective passion in the pursuit of God or to prevent states that would inhibit such passion. There is in Kierkegaard's writings, however, a more fundamental explanation of divine hiddenness, one that challenges the very idea that there *could be* evidence that puts the existence of a perfectly loving and just God beyond reasonable doubt.

Kierkegaard thinks that there is sufficient evidence for believing that God exists, where "God" is understood in *religiously neutral* terms ("religiousness A"), say, as that portion of "logical space (the qualitatively different) which the understanding reaches in its Kantian striving . . . to know." This is comparable, according to Ferreira, to what Aquinas takes himself to show to exist in his famous Five Ways (see *Summa Theologica*, Question 2, Article 3). Kierkegaard, however, argues that there could not be any evidence at all for belief that God exists, where "God" is understood in *religiously relevant* terms ("religiousness B"), say, as perfect in love and justice. Consequently, there cannot be evidence that puts the existence of a perfectly loving and just God beyond reasonable doubt. The reason is that the concept of God ("B," hereafter) is "absolute" – that is, it is a concept in which the modifiers "perfectly," "unsurpassably," and the like are understood – and "qualitative," not "quantitative" – that is, the concepts of perfect love, perfect justice, and more generally, perfect divinity, are not concepts of something that comes in degrees. Consequently, there cannot be a *probabilistic* or *cumulative* case for the existence of God "because there is nothing comparable in such a case to the way

in which ordinary separate pieces of evidence can accumulate to make a case."
There are no degrees of divinity or aspects of divinity that could be recognized independently of the others and so make the conclusion more probable.
Furthermore, any items of which we might compose a case for, say, something's being perfect in love, would already have to be an example of perfect love. Indeed, there cannot be an objective evidential case *of any sort* for the existence of God. After all, what would it be like for the *absolutely different* to reveal itself as such? What would it be like to have an experience of *God* presenting Himself to us? What sort of evidence could be *nonambiguous enough* to make nonbelief unreasonable? The problem is not that an objective revelation of God by Himself would be misleading. Rather, the problem is that it would not be a revelation of *God* at all.

A few questions arise. First, are the objections to a probabilistic case for God's existence even relevant to either argument to the best available explanation or Bayesian arguments?[11] If probabilistic cases of these sorts work in ways that are not countenanced by Kierkegaard, then the objections may be circumvented. Second, do the rhetorical questions about objective evidence for revelation of God show too much? It might be argued that formally analogous questions that are equally difficult to answer can be asked about objective experiential evidence for *anything* and about *any person* revealing herself. This seems to be a consequence of the underdetermination of theory by perceptual data, not God's being absolute or qualitatively different. Third, as for the rhetorical questions themselves, specific theistic traditions offer well-known answers in their historic narratives, and recent broadly reliabilist epistemologies offer alternatives to evidentialism of the sort in which the questions are framed.

In "The Hiddenness of God: A Puzzle or a Real Problem?" Jacob Joshua Ross follows the injunction "to take religious language *seriously*, but not necessarily *literally*." The evidential problem of divine hiddenness can be dissolved, says Ross, if we reject the "popular," "simple," "ordinary," "everyday," "literal," "anthropomorphic," ways of talking about God that underlie "a more emotional understanding of God's nearness as representing a close personal relationship." Those ways of talking are a hangover from ancient polytheism according to which the gods were "something like animated beings or human-like spirits." Get rid of this last vestige of polytheism, says Ross. Stop thinking of God's love and justice by analogy with human ideals of love and justice. Instead, adopt one of the more "judicious," "subtle," "sophisticated," "profound," "mysterious" theologies, old or new. Consider, for example, the trend in Jewish mysticism that refers to God as "the great Nothing," or Maimonides's "ineffable 'One'" that has no personal attributes, or Vaihinger's Kantian "as-ifery" according to which theistic theologies are nothing more than attempts to represent "the religious experience of teleological, meaningful order in the cosmos." And there are more options besides.

If you take up one of them, then all the "inconsistencies and distortions" that attend such a "primitive and unsatisfactory religious conception" as "Biblical monotheism" – of which the problem of divine hiddenness is just another demonstration – will vanish.

What shall we say of this "purification of the idea of God"? True enough, *those* (alleged) inconsistencies will vanish. What, however, will we be left with? Something so content-free that it can be neither affirmed nor denied? (The Nothing?) Something worth worshiping? (The One?) Something that has a chance of sustaining hope and gratitude in the cancer ward? (Cosmic Order?)

"Seeking But Not Believing: Confessions of a Practicing Agnostic," is Paul Draper's account of why he is an agnostic and what that practically means for him. Naturalism – the view that nothing that is neither a part nor a product of the physical universe can affect it – is the only live alternative to theism for Draper. It implies that nothing supernatural exists; so evidence for it is evidence against theism. Draper holds that several facts are more likely to obtain on theism than on naturalism, and several facts are more likely to obtain on naturalism than on theism. Those facts favoring theism include the facts that the universe had a beginning, that there is intelligent life, that we are sometimes free in the incompatibilist's sense (which doubles as evidence for substance dualism), that there is an abundance of beauty, and that powerful religious experiences occur. Facts favoring naturalism include the facts that humans hold neither a spatially nor temporally privileged position in the universe, that all relatively complex living things are the more or less gradually modified descendants of relatively simple single-celled organisms, that conscious states are dependent to a very high degree on physical processes occurring in the brain, that pain and pleasure are systematically connected to the biological goal of reproductive success, that an abundance of tragedies occur, and that many people do not feel the presence of God when tragedy strikes. Draper does not think that these facts are unclear or that they support their respective positions equally. Rather, he is an agnostic because he finds it virtually impossible to determine which side is better supported by the facts in its favor.

Of special interest is Draper's contention that, *contra* Schellenberg, agnosticism is a stable, reasonable position. Schellenberg argues that the ambiguity of the evidence is itself evidence for atheism and against agnosticism. Draper holds that this would be the case "if it could be shown that, prior to considering the evidential significance of ambiguous evidence, naturalism and theism are equally probable." This, however, is precisely what Draper judges cannot be done, owing to the difficulty of comparing the strengths of the different pieces of evidence. Adding this new piece of evidence to the picture does not appreciably change things. Moreover, it is not at all clear to Draper that for some people, perhaps himself included, moral and spiritual development is better accomplished without belief than with belief. That is in no small part because, on Draper's view, agnosticism has difficult practical implications. Since he regards God's existence as a real possibility, he believes it is incumbent on himself to behave otherwise than if he were an atheist. He ought to pray, for example, and, more generally prepare for a relationship with God. He ought also to continue looking for new evidence and reexamining the old.

"Silence is of many sorts," begins Nicholas Wolterstorff in "The Silence of the God Who Speaks." The sort that is his topic is *"biblical* silence," "the nonanswering silence of God in the face of those questions which take into account what God has already said," the nonanswering silence of God that puts biblical faith at risk. One of the things that God has said of each member of the human species is this: May you flourish on earth in society until full of years. This Genesis benediction frequently goes unfulfilled. Some flourish but shortly; some live until full of years but fail to flourish; and some neither flourish nor live until full of years. Although there is a role for suffering within the life of a person who flourishes, suffering frequently exceeds its proper function and becomes unredeemable. So suffering and life duration have gone awry with respect to God's creating and maintaining intent. A simple question arises: "Why have they gone awry? . . . Why all this brevity of life and why all such suffering? But no answer is forthcoming. Listen as we may, we hear no further speech. Only silence. Nonanswering silence."

Wolterstorff considers several popular theodicies but rejects each because it depicts God as intending to permit or cause the suffering and early death of one person for the sake of a greater good for another. This using of one person for the good of another, he says, is not answerable to the biblical speech of God, who says that He intends *each and every* human being to flourish until full of years. So the question persists as does the silence. How shall we live in such silence?, asks Wolterstorff. We shall remain devoted to God, join Him in protesting early death and unredemptive suffering, seize the opportunity to own our own suffering redemptively, and join the divine battle against early death and unredemptive suffering: disease, injustice, warfare, torture, enmity.

One who considers herself answerable to the biblical speech of God might reason that whatever God intends happens, and so if God intends for each person to flourish until full of years, then that is what happens. Clearly enough, however, that is not what happens. So God does not *intend* for each person to flourish until full of years. So God did not *say* that He intends for each person to flourish until full of years. As for the biblical text, don't benedictions generally only imply that the benedictory *strongly desires* the content of her benediction to happen, not that she intends it to happen? If so, then the Genesis benediction does *not* imply that God intended the content of His benediction to happen; but, without this implication, what becomes of Wolterstorff's particular critique of the theodicies he discusses?

Notes

1. Anselm, *Basic Writings*, trans. S. N. Deane. (LaSalle, IL: Open Court, 1962).
2. Nietzsche, *Daybreak*, trans. R. J. Hollingdale. (New York: Cambridge University Press, 1982), 89–90.
3. Schellenberg, *Divine Hiddenness and Human Reason* (Ithaca: Cornell University Press, 1993), 212–13.
4. Rowe, "The Problem of Evil and Some Varieties of Atheism," *American Philosophical Quarterly* **16** (1979), 335–41.
5. Draper, "Pain and Pleasure: An Evidential Problem for Theists," *Nous* **23** (1989), 331–50.
6. For more on the logical/evidential distinction, see Daniel Howard-Snyder, "Introduction: the Evidential Argument from Evil," in *The Evidential Argument from Evil*, ed. D. Howard-Snyder. (Bloomington: Indiana University Press, 1996), xii–xvi.
7. See note 4.
8. See, for example, D. Howard-Snyder, "Seeing Through CORNEA," *International Journal for the Philosophy of Religion* **32** (1992), 25–49, esp. 40–6, and "The Argument from Inscrutable Evil," in *The Evidential Argument from Evil*, 286–310, esp. 305–7. See also William Rowe, "The Evidential Argument from Evil: A Second Look," in *The Evidential Argument from Evil*, 262–85, esp. 274–6.
9. See Michael Bergmann, "Skeptical Theism and Rowe's New Evidential Argument from Evil," *Noûs* **35** (2001), 278–96, and William Rowe's response to Bergmann, *Noûs*, forthcoming.
10. See Stephen K. Moroney, *The Noetic Effects of Sin* (Lanham, MD: Lexington Books, 2000).
11. See, for example, Michael Banner, *The Justification of Science and the Rationality of Religious Belief* (Oxford: Clarendon Press, 1990), and Richard Swinburne, *The Existence of God*, 2d ed. (Oxford: Clarendon Press, 1991).

1

What Is the Problem of the Hiddenness of God?

PETER VAN INWAGEN

What indeed? One possibility is that the words 'the problem of the hidden-ness of God' are simply another name for the problem of evil: The world is full of terrible things and we observe no response from God when these ter-rible things happen – the heavens do not rain fire on the Nazis, the raging flood does not turn aside just before it sweeps away the peaceful village, the para-lyzed child remains paralyzed. And in the works of some writers, it is hard to separate the problem of divine hiddenness and the problem of evil. But if the problem of divine hiddenness just *is* the problem of evil – well, there already exist many discussions of this problem, and I do not propose to add to their number in this essay.

I think, however, that the problem of Divine hiddenness (whatever exactly it may be) is not the same problem as the problem of evil, for we can imagine a world in which the problem of divine hiddenness pretty clearly does not arise and in which the problem of evil is no less a problem than it is in the actual world. Imagine, for example, that to every Jew who was to perish in the Holocaust there had come, a few weeks before his or her death, a vision of a seraph, a being of unutterable splendor, who recited Psalm 91 in Hebrew – and then vanished. The doomed recipients of these visions, comparing notes, found that the visions were remarkably consistent. Learned Jews understood the seraph's words perfectly. Less learned Jews recognized the psalm and under-stood bits and pieces of it, just as they would have if they had heard it recited in a synagogue. Others, less learned still, recognized the language as biblical Hebrew, and said things like, "It sounded like poetry – maybe a psalm." A few wholly secularized Jews did not even recognize the language, but gave an account of the visual aspect of the apparition consistent with everyone else's, and said that the apparition spoke to them in a language they did not understand. (But those victims of the Holocaust who were not Jews according to the Law but were Jews according to the Nazi Race Laws did not experience the vision at all; some of them, however, experienced other visions, of a kind I will describe in a moment.) There were, then, these visions, but that was all. Nothing else happened: Not a single life was saved, not a single brutal incident was in any way mitigated. With the exception of the visions, the Holocaust proceeded exactly as it did in the actual world. And let us further imagine that many other victims of horrendous evil in our imaginary world, victims of horrendous evils throughout all its recorded history, have received, shortly before their final suffering and death, analogous or comparable "signs" in the form of visions incorporating religious imagery – every victim, in fact, who belonged to any cultural tradition that provided religious images he could recognize and interpret. It would seem that in this imaginary world, the problem of evil is no less pressing than it is in ours, but "the problem of the hiddenness of God" does not arise. Or at least we can say this: If the existence of the visions is generally known among the inhabitants of the imaginary world, writers of the sort who in our world speak of "the hiddenness of God" will not use that phrase (they will perhaps speak instead of the "passivity of God").

The problem of evil and the problem of the hiddenness of God are, therefore, not identical. But is the latter essentially connected with suffering and other forms of evil? Would, or could, this problem exist in a world without suffering? I think that trying to answer this question will help us understand what the problem is. Let us imagine a world without suffering – not a world in which everyone enjoys the Beatific Vision, but a world that is as much like our world (as it is at present) as the absence of suffering permits. I will call such a world a "secular utopia," because my model for this world is just that future of gleaming alabaster cities, undimmed by human tears, that secularists yearn for.

In the world I imagine, human beings are benevolent and nature is kind. There is no physical pain, or very little of it (just enough to remind people to take care not to damage their extremities). There is no premature death, whether by violence, accident, or disease. There are, in fact, no such things as violence and disease, and accidents are never very serious. (The inhabitants of this world all enjoy a vigorous old age and die peacefully in their sleep when they are well over a hundred years old – and the fear of death is unknown.) No one is a cripple or mentally retarded or mentally unbalanced or even mildly neurotic. There is no racial prejudice or prejudice of any sort. No one is ugly or deformed. Everyone is provided with all the physical necessities and comforts of life – but great wealth and luxury are as unknown as poverty. Consumer goods are produced in a way that does no violence to nature: the human and non-human inhabitants of the world live in perfect harmony.[1] Everyone has interesting and rewarding work to do, and this work is appropriately rewarded with respect and, if appropriate, admiration. No one covets anyone else's possessions. There is no lying or promise-breaking or cheating or corruption – there is in fact nothing for anyone to be corrupt *about*, for there are essentially no government and no laws and no money. If there is any unhappiness in this world, it arises only in cases like these: Alfred has fallen in love with Beatrice, but Beatrice is in love with Charles; Delia has devoted her life to proving Goldbach's Conjecture, and Edward has published a proof of it when Delia had a proof almost within her grasp. And even in such cases, everyone involved behaves with perfect rationality and complete maturity, thereby keeping the resulting unhappiness to an irreducible (and usually transient) minimum.

Now let us suppose that, as in our world, some people believe in God – in a necessarily existent, omniscient, omnipresent creator and sustainer of the world. (The theists of our invented world would have trouble formulating the concept of "moral perfection" – but, if you could get them to understand it, they wouldn't hesitate to ascribe moral perfection to God, too.) And, as in our world, some people believe there is no such being. Could someone in this world, perhaps one of its atheists, raise the problem of divine hiddenness? Perhaps we can imagine a brief dialogue in which the problem is raised, a dialogue "purer" than any that could be imagined to take place in our world, purer because neither of the participants has ever known or heard of any horrendous evil.

Atheist: This God of yours – why does he hide himself; why doesn't he come out in the open where we can see him?

Theist: Your question doesn't make any sense. God is omnipresent. That is, he is totally present everywhere and locally present nowhere. A thing is locally present in a place (that is, a region of space) if it occupies or takes up or fills that place. And God occupies neither any particular place (as does a cat or a mountain) nor all places (as the luminiferous aether would, if it existed). He is totally present everywhere in that the totality of his being is reflected in the sustaining power that keeps every spatial thing everywhere in the physical universe in existence from moment to moment. Similarly, we might say that Rembrandt is locally present nowhere in "The Night Watch"[2] and totally present in it everywhere. (But the analogy is imperfect, since the human figures and inanimate objects and spatial relations in the painting are fictional, whereas the ones in the physical universe are, of course, real.) Only a locally present thing can reflect light, and thus only a locally present thing can be visible. Only a locally present thing can exclude other things from the space it occupies, and thus only a locally present thing can be tangible. Someone who wants God to 'show Himself' just doesn't understand the concept of God. Asking for that is like demanding that Rembrandt "show himself" in a painting. The complaint, "I can't find God anywhere in the world" is as misplaced as the complaint 'I can't find Rembrandt anywhere in the painting.'

Atheist: Well, if he can't show himself by being present in the world, why can't he show himself by his effects on some of the things that *are* present in the world?

Theist: You haven't been listening. Everything in the world is his "effect." He "shows himself by his effects" in the world just as Rembrandt "shows himself by his effects" in The Night Watch.

Atheist: That sounds good, but I wonder if it's any more than words. What I want is not "general effects" but, if I may coin a phrase, "special effects." Given your picture of God's relation to the world, everything will look just the same whether or not there is a God – wait, stop, don't tell me that that's like saying that "The Night Watch" will look the same whether or not there is a Rembrandt! I couldn't bear it. Let me put the problem this way. I have bought one of the modal telescopes invented by the great metaphysicist Saul Kripke, and I have looked into other possible worlds. In one of them I caught a glimpse of the following argument, in a book by a man named Thomas Aquinas (evidently a sound atheist like myself):

> *Objection*: It is, moreover, superfluous to suppose that what can be accounted for by a few principles has been produced by many. But it seems that everything we see in the world can be accounted for by other principles, without supposing God to exist. For all natural things can be accounted for by one principle, which is nature; and all voluntary things can be accounted for by one principle, which is human reason or will. Hence, there is no need to suppose that a God exists.

Surely this argument is unanswerable? Surely one should not believe in the existence of an unobservable entity unless its existence is needed to explain some observed phenomenon?

Theist: So what you are looking for is a particular event, an event that is not caused by any human action, whose occurrence resists any natural or scientific explanation, and which is evidently the work of someone trying to send human beings a message or signal whose content is that there is such a being as God. How about the stars in the sky re-arranging themselves to spell out 'I am who am'? Would that be satisfactory?

Atheist: It would.

Theist: You don't want much, do you? But it happens I can supply what you want. My own religion is called Julianism, after its founder, Julia, the great prophetess and author of *The Book of Julia* and the forty volumes of sermons we call *The Words of Julia*. Julia's message was so important that God granted her three times a natural span of life, as a sign of his special favor and to ensure that her teachings would have a chance to put down deep roots. Julia lived 326 years. And every physiologist agrees that it is physiologically impossible for a human being to live 326 years. Therefore, Julia's preternaturally long life must have been a sign from God.

Atheist: Well, that would be pretty impressive if it actually happened. But when did Julia live, and how do you Julianists know that she really did live that long?

Theist: Julia lived about two thousand years ago. We know of her long life and lots of other things about her because the facts of her biography are meticulously set out in the Holy Records of the Julian Church, which originally derive from the testimony of eyewitnesses.

Atheist: Forgive me if I'm skeptical. Stories can become distorted as they pass from mouth to mouth. As stories are passed from one teller to another, people unconsciously fill in or change minor details in the story. These minor distortions can accumulate, and, given long enough, the accumulation of minor distortions can change a story till it's no longer really the same story. We know that this happens. Just last month, there was a rumor in Neapolis of a terrible tragedy somewhere in Asia – a woman had actually lost a *finger* in an industrial accident! The whole town was in an uproar. But when the dust settled, it turned out that what had really happened was that the Asian woman had got her finger badly mauled in a piece of machinery while she was daydreaming. The finger, of course, healed perfectly within a week. Now since we know from experience that stories can become distorted in this fantastic way – the very idea of someone's losing a finger! – and since we know from experience that no one in our modern record-keeping era has lived even 150 years, the most reasonable thing to suppose is that, although Julia may indeed have lived to be remarkably old, she certainly did not live to be 326; the reasonable thing to suppose is that what experience tells us often happens happened this time (that is, the story grew in the telling; it certainly had plenty of time to grow) and that what experience tells us never happens did not happen.

Theist: What you are saying seems to come down to this. You demand that God, in order to make his existence believable, cause some particular, unmistakable sign to occur somewhere in the world of space and time. But when you hear a story of some event that would have been such a sign if it had actually occurred, you refuse, on general epistemological grounds, to believe the story.

Atheist: My position is not so extreme as that, or so unreasonable as you make it sound. Take your first, hypothetical example. If the stars in the sky were suddenly rearranged so as to spell out 'I am who am', I'd believe in the existence of God then, all right. That would be a good, clear case of what I'd call "God's coming out of hiding." In such a case, God would be making it evident to human beings that Reality contained another intelligence than human intelligence – and not just any kind of intelligence, but an intelligence grand enough to be a plausible candidate for the office "God." And, obviously, this – or something along the same lines – is what such a grand intelligence would do if it wanted us to believe in it. If, *per impossibile*, the figures in "The Night Watch" were conscious beings and aware of (and only of) the objects in their little two-dimensional world, what reason could they have for believing in Rembrandt but something he put specially into the painting that was not a part of the natural order of things in the painting (his signature, perhaps). If he didn't do that, how could he blame the denizens of "The Night Watch" for not believing in him?

Theist: Let me make two points. First, these signs you want God to place in the world would have to recur periodically, or, after a few generations had passed, people like you would say that the stories about the signs had grown in the telling – perhaps from the seed of an astronomical prodigy that, remarkable as it was, had some purely natural explanation. Secondly, even the "I am who am" story wouldn't make the existence of *God* evident to a sufficiently determined skeptic – for even the (apparent) rearrangement of the stars could be the work of a lesser being than God. We can imagine no sign that would *have* to be the work of a necessary, omnipresent, omnipotent being. Any sign you might imagine you could also imagine to be the production of a contingent, locally present being whose powers, though vastly greater than ours, are finite. I should expect that someone like you would say that if two hypotheses explain the data equally well, and if they are alike but for the fact that one of them postulates an unobservable infinite being and the other an unobservable finite being, one should always prefer the latter hypothesis, since it does the same explanatory work as the former, but is, literally, infinitely weaker.

Atheist: Well, perhaps you're right when you say that to be convincing the signs would have to recur periodically. I don't see why I shouldn't ask for that, and I don't see that it will weaken my argument if I do. And the more I think about it, the more inclined I am to accept your second point as well. Your argument has convinced me of something you didn't foresee: that you theists have imagined a being whose existence no one could possibly rationally believe in, since the hypothesis that He exists is necessarily infinitely stronger than other hypotheses that would explain any possible observations equally well. And if you haven't "imagined" Him, if He really does exist, even *He* couldn't provide us – or any other finite beings He might create – with evidence that would render belief in Him rational. If He exists, He should approve of me for not believing in him, and disapprove of you for believing in Him.

Let us at this point leave our dialogue and the secular utopia in which it was imagined to occur, and return to the real world. The lesson of the dialogue is that in a world that lacks any real suffering, the problem of the hiddenness of God is a purely epistemological problem, or a cluster of epistemological problems: Can one rationally believe in God in a world devoid of signs and wonders? Under what conditions would it be rational to believe a story that reports signs and wonders? Could any possible sign or wonder or series of signs and wonders make it reasonable to believe in a necessarily existent, omnipresent, omnipotent Creator and Sustainer of the world of locally present things?

These epistemological questions obviously have the same force in the real world as in our secular utopia. We might say that in the real world, the problem of the hiddenness of God has two aspects, a moral aspect and an epistemic aspect. But it would be better to say that there are two "problems of the hiddenness of God": a moral problem and an epistemic problem, or a cluster of moral problems and a cluster of epistemic problems. The cluster of moral problems is collectively called the problem of evil. The cluster of epistemic problems, I have laid out in the above dialogue. I have said that I shall not in this essay discuss the problem of evil. But I want to draw some analogies between the two problems, for they are similar in logical structure. Each is the problem of meeting a challenge to belief in the existence of God that has the general form, "If there were a God, the world would not look the way it does." In the case of the problem of evil, the challenge takes this form: It tells us that if there were a God, we should not see certain things that we do see: vast amounts of horrendous suffering. In the case of the epistemic problem, the challenge takes another form: It tells us that if there were a God – at any rate, a God who cared whether we believed in him – we should see certain things that we do not see: signs and wonders. (Or at least that challenge is one part of the epistemic problem; as we have seen, there is also the problem whether even repeated, ubiquitous signs and wonders would be sufficient to render belief in God rational.) Since the two problems are similar in logical structure, it is natural to wonder whether the techniques that theists have used to respond to the problem of the presence of evil could be applied to the problem of the absence of signs and wonders. The main technique that Christian philosophers (and Jewish and Muslim philosophers) have used in their treatments of the problem of evil is that of story-telling: They tell stories that fall under two headings, *defense* and *theodicy*. A "defense" in the weakest sense in which the word is used is an internally consistent story according to which God and evil both exist. Sometimes the following two requirements are added: The evil in the story must be of the amounts and kinds that we observe in the actual world, and the story must contain no element that we have good scientific or historical reasons to regard as false. A theodicy is a story that has the same internal features as a defense, but which the theodicist, the person telling the story, puts forward as true or at least highly plausible. Students of the problem of evil will know how this story-telling technique has been applied by various authors and the kinds of problems and arguments it has generated.

I want to suggest that the epistemic problem be approached in the same way. Christian philosophers – or other theists who are philosophers – should meet the challenge raised by the absence of signs and wonders in the following way: They should tell stories that entail the following proposition:

The world was created and is sustained by a necessary, omnipresent, omniscient, omnipotent, morally perfect being – that is, by God. There are rational beings in this world, and God wants these beings, or some of them at some times, to believe in his existence. The world is devoid of signs and wonders – of "special effects." Or if the world contains any such events, they are so rare that very few people have actually observed one or even met anyone who claims to have observed one. (In the latter case, among those people whom God wants to believe in his existence are many of the people who are distant in space and time from any of the very rare signs and wonders.)

Such stories, of course, must be internally consistent, and they will certainly be of more philosophical interest if they contain nothing that is known to be false on historical or scientific grounds. Philosophers who present such stories may present them as defenses or as theodicies, according to their philosophical purposes, just as in the analogous case of the problem of evil. (The root '-dicy' in the word 'theodicy', when this word is used in connection with the epistemic problem, may be taken to refer to what may be called God's "epistemic justice": For many will argue, with our imaginary other-worldly atheist, that it would be "epistemically unjust" of God to expect us to believe in his existence without evidence – 'evidence' being appropriate signs and wonders.)

In discussions of the problem of evil, the kernel of every defense and every theodicy is a *reason* (or a set of reasons), God's reason or reasons for permitting the existence of evil. So it should be with discussions of the epistemic problem: The kernel of every defense and every theodicy should be a reason or reasons, God's reason or reasons for not providing the human species (some of whom, at least, he wishes to believe in His existence) with ubiquitous signs and wonders.

I will not in this essay attempt to construct a defense or a theodicy. I will say just two things; I will give two pieces of advice to anyone who sets out to construct a defense or theodicy. First, note that the proposition: *God wants people to believe in His existence* does not entail the proposition: *God wants people to believe in His existence and He does not care why anyone who believes in Him has this belief.* The former proposition, in fact, is consistent with the proposition that God would value the following states of affairs in the order in which they are presented:

(1) Patricia believes, for reason A, that God exists.
(2) Patricia believes that God does not exist.
(3) Patricia believes, for reason B, that God exists.

It is, for example, consistent with God's wanting Patricia to believe in Him that He regard (1) as a good state of affairs, (2) as a bad state of affairs, and (3) as a bad state of affairs that is *much* worse than (2). (And this would be consistent with reason B's being an epistemically unobjectionable reason for belief in God: reason B might be, from the point of view of someone interested only in justification or warrant, a perfectly good reason for believing in the existence of God.) And this is no idle speculation about a logical possibility. Most theists hold that God expects a good deal more from us than mere belief in his existence.[3] He expects a complex of things, of which belief in his existence is a small (although essential) part. It is certainly conceivable that someone's believing in him for a certain reason (because, say, that person has witnessed signs and wonders) might make it difficult or even impossible for that person to acquire other features God wanted him or her to have.

My second piece of advice is directed at Christian philosophers who attempt to construct defenses and theodicies. I recommend serious and sustained reflection on the possible meanings of two texts: Luke 16:31 ("If they do not listen to Moses and the Prophets, neither will they be persuaded if someone should rise from the dead"), and John 20:29 ("Have you believed because you have seen me? Blessed are they who, not seeing, believe.").

The burden of this essay is this. I recommend thinking of "the problem of the hiddenness of God" not as a single problem but as two distinct problems, a moral problem – what has always been called the problem of evil – and an epistemic problem. But I have argued that the two problems are similar in their logical structure, and I recommend that, because of this similarity, theists who attempt to solve the epistemic problem employ the same methods and techniques – *mutatis mutandis* – that theists have generally employed in their attempts to solve the problem of evil.

Notes

1. Those who think that the sufferings of nonhuman animals that are unrelated to the acts of human beings are relevant to "the problem of the hiddenness of God" should feel free to imagine that our invented world is one in which animals in the state of nature never suffer. It is not easy to imagine in any detail a biologically rich world without animal suffering unless one imagines it as a world of ubiquitous miracles – a world in which, for example, fawns are always miraculously saved from forest fires. The imaginer had better take care to make these miracles "unnoticeable," at least in those epochs in which there are human beings to notice them, for if the ubiquitous miracles were *obviously* miracles, this would defeat our purpose in trying to imagine a utopia in which "the problem of the hiddenness of God" could be raised.
2. In our secular utopia, Rembrandt has apparently painted a picture called "The Night Watch" that is not the picture that actually bears that name; there would of course be no such thing as an armed company of men in the secular utopia.
3. James 2:19: "You believe that God is one. You do well; the demons also believe, and they shudder."

2

What the Hiddenness of God Reveals: A Collaborative Discussion

J. L. SCHELLENBERG

In a dialogue, the *name* of a character may be expected to give something of the flavor of his or her contribution. So what is to be made of my 'C' and 'S'? S will not be *smug* or *stultiloquent*, surely. *Scrupulous*? Perhaps. *Sophisticated*? No doubt, but remember that the epithet need not be complimentary (or the attribute complementary). *Skeptical*? So it would appear, but concerning what? Might his researches have *serendipitous* results? We shall have to wait and see. And C? Is she *conservative* or *countercultural*, *Catholic* or (what is not after all so far distant) *Calvinist*? Does she aspire to *captivate* as she *conjures* up objections to S's arguments? More than a *counterpoint* or *counterpoise*, perhaps *Cleanthea* is her proper name. I incline, however, toward the more humble *collaborator*, and I hope that S is listening; for there may be larger realities to deal with here than can easily be captured by any of our divisions or names.

I

Sitting across the aisle from each other in a university lecture theater, with no one else present, C and S at last strike up a conversation. Before long, a question is uncovered concerning which our two philosophers are not agreed, and, in good philosophical style, they proceed to settle the issue through reasoned debate.

S: Looks like we've been stood up.
C: I'm *sure* this is the room. I read it in the Convention Guide – Room 3: 'The Philosophy of Property Rights'.
S: I'm sure this is the room too – but I think it said Room 2.
C: You're S?
S: That's right.
C: A philosopher of religion?
S: Right.
C: You've done something on the hiddenness of God.
S: Obviously there's no hiding from you.
C: A defense of atheism, as I recall.

S: Well, I didn't set out to write an atheistic apologia, if that's what you're thinking. I just wanted to know what kind of epistemic problem the hiddenness of
God represents and how serious it is.

C: I never could understand why you atheists see a problem there. I mean, virtu-
ally everyone in theology and philosophy admits that the ultimate nature of
God is a mystery. 'Hiddenness' is just the human side of the divine mystery.
End of story.

S: Is that an invitation to discussion? It's 1:15, so I suppose there's not much
point in trying to take in one of the other lectures now.

C: As a matter of fact, it's 1:20. I think we can safely say that nothing's going to
be happening here. So do you agree that what you call the 'hiddenness of God'
could all be chalked up to the inevitable *mystery* of God?

S: I'm not so sure about that. But we really need to deal with this concept of the
hiddenness of God – it's a little mysterious itself. Do you mind?

C: I guess not.

S: O.k., the basic problem is this: When we use the words 'hiddenness' and
'hidden' (or other words from that family) in their usual, literal, senses, we're
talking about something that – though inaccessible to us – *really does exist*.
Lots of ordinary language examples could be introduced to support this: 'Jake
is hiding from Sarah'; 'The statue stood off to one side, hidden from view'.
. . . But then it seems that the state of affairs we're calling the hiddenness of
God can be admitted only by *theists*, for only if you believe that God exists
can you say that it obtains! And by the same token, then the idea that someone
who admits divine hiddenness should be led in the direction of *atheism* is
absurd. This can seem to support the kind of suggestion you're making.

C: I've noticed that those discussing your work have been calling your argument
an 'argument from divine hiddenness against the existence of God'. That's
really a contradiction then, isn't it?

S: Given the usual construal of those terms, yes. That's why I didn't want to call
it that. But maybe we can develop an understanding of the notion of hiddenness that accommodates their (apparently nonliteral) usage.

C: So what's your suggestion?

S: Well, it gets a mite complicated at this point. Here's what I wrote down yes-
terday when thinking about this: 'God is hidden' can be seen as equivalent to
the (inclusive) disjunction of the following claims: '(A) Some *theistic experience* – a state of affairs consisting in someone apparently becoming aware of
the presence of God in some way – that could obtain or is desirable if God
exists is *unavailable* to someone (perhaps each of us). (B) Some *theistic proposition* – some proposition equivalent to, entailing, or probabilifying theism, or
bearing one of these relations to a full or partial explication or theological
development of theism – is *epistemically nonsecured* or *epistemically indeterminate* for someone (perhaps each of us): that is to say, either not known (or
not reasonably believed) to be true, or not known (or not reasonably believed)
either to be true or to be false.' (Of course, (A) and (B) here are related in inter-

esting ways – maybe, for example, removing hiddenness of type (A) would at the same time be a way of removing hiddenness of type (B), for some more specific fillings of (A) and (B) – but I'm not going to get into that now.) Reducing the disjunction of (A) and (B) to something more manageable, we could define 'God is hidden' this way (and on my sheet 'H' symbolizes 'human subject or set of human subjects'; 'e', 'theistic experience'; and 'p', 'theistic proposition'): *'God is hidden' = df. 'There is some H and some e such that e is unavailable to H, or some H and some p such that p is either epistemically non-secured or epistemically indeterminate for H.'* Here, have a look. As you can see, the definiens – the defining expression – is put quite generally and schematically, and is really waiting to be filled out by reference to particular subjects, experiences, and propositions. It's important to recognize that Divine hiddenness, thus understood, may be instantiated in many ways – there are many ways in which 'God is hidden' can be true; many specific claims whose truth is sufficient for the truth of the general one. To be a bit more precise: If we accept this schema, there will be as many ways of making a hiddenness claim as there are ways of filling out one or other (or the conjunction of both) of its disjuncts. (Of course, it's also the case that someone might wish to assert only the truth of the schema *as schema*.)

C: Interesting.

S: This seems to fairly represent, and to provide a way of expressing, various assertions I've found in contexts of 'hiddenness talk'. And if it's accepted, then I suppose talk of divine hiddenness, despite contrary appearances, would not commit anyone to theism. Someone might then have in mind only that a certain proposition, 'God exists', is not known, or not reasonably believed by someone. Or she might be suggesting that there is a proposition (say, 'If God exists, God is hidden'), put forward in a theological account of the nature of God, that someone cannot reasonably assess as either true or false. Or she might be thinking of some such thing as the absence of a sense of the presence of God in the experience of someone dying of cancer. Of course, if theism *is* true, then the relevant hiddenness situation, whatever it is, is intended or permitted by God; and so the literal notion – the notion of God existing and hiding (or being otherwise hidden from us) – applies as well. And I suppose that a theist might therefore sometimes speak of the hiddenness of God with this extra element in mind, and even use it in developing a theological interpretation of divine hiddenness *non*literally construed. But since *everyone* seems to like the expression, and since not everyone can use it unless it's interpreted in such a way as not to imply theism, I say let's take it that way. That is, let's take the truth of the disjunction I mentioned earlier as a necessary and sufficient condition for the truth of 'God is hidden.' How does that sound?

C: For now let me just be quite compliant, like one of the interlocutors in Plato's dialogues, and say, "That sounds very good to me, S." But excuse my impatience: What was your reply to my point about mystery? I think all this talk about us knowing God in detail can be shown to be way off the mark.

S: Well, having cleared up one mystery, maybe we can deal with the other. Suppose that by 'God' we mean a transcendent and unsurpassably great source of all things, who works through all and is in all. That would seem to be an understanding your theological and philosophical 'Everyperson' could agree to. Now such a God could not be fully known by us, certainly not in this life and with these puny powers of comprehension. No doubt there are here many propositions (or perhaps just one) impossible for us to so much as formulate. Mystery, in this sense of *incomplete knowledge of the nature of God*, is unavoidable. I'm going to concede this. *But* – and you knew there was a 'but' coming! – it doesn't follow from this in any way I can see that there aren't experiences of God we don't have but could have, and might *expect* to have, or truths about God's nature or existence we don't know but *could* know and might *expect* to know (or at any rate reasonably believe), if God exists. (Notice that all theists who believe in revelation already hold that some truths of this general character *have* been divulged to at least some human beings.) Even if we can't understand *everything* about God, it doesn't follow that we can't understand *anything*. And maybe some of the things we don't understand or believe we *would* understand or believe if there really were a God. This has often been overlooked in the history of philosophy. Where questions concerning the experience of God or God's nature or God's existence have resisted resolution, philosophers have usually been inclined just to suspend judgment. But something is being missed here: *That very fact* – the fact that God is in one way or another not revealed to us – may *itself* be evidentially relevant and need to be taken into account. Indeed, what we *do* know about the nature of God – that God is necessarily all-powerful as well as good or just or loving, for example – may help us put this together. If persuasively developed, this suggestion clearly would represent a serious problem for theism, an *epistemic* problem, in this case, since it threatens to remove the reasonableness of believing that theism is true. No doubt there are other problems of divine hiddenness worth exploring – for example, practical or spiritual or pastoral problems of the sort encountered by one who, believing in God, wishes to draw closer to God, but feels something obstructing the experiential state of affairs she seeks. These problems, however, are well known and much discussed. The epistemic problems are not.

C: But think for a minute about what is involved in saying that we should *expect* to know truths about what God is up to in the world, or *expect* knowledge of the reality of God to be made available to all. Even if in spite of mystery it's possible for us to know such things (and I'm still not at all sure how far I'd go along with you here), surely we get into the old problem of the pot telling the potter what to do if we expect God to produce such knowledge: God is under no obligation to do any such thing.

S: So you think my talk of 'expectation' betrays hubris. Well, maybe you've misunderstood what I meant in using that language. It's not the sort of thing where someone says, "Hey, I'm so great, you ought to do this for me," if that's what you're thinking. It's the kind of expectation you yourself referred to when you said we might expect God to be mysterious – remember that? What you meant, I suppose, is that our information about human nature and the nature of any God there may be is such as to provide justification for the claim that a God would seem mysterious to creatures such as we are. Well, just so, I would say, it might seem to someone who reflects on the nature of God and the world that her information justifies, for example, the claim that if God exists, this or that question is cleared up for everyone (or for everyone who satisfies certain conditions). And maybe reflection makes it apparent to her that the consequent of this conditional is false – that the question in question is still a question! Then, surely, such an inquirer has the materials from which to construct an argument supporting the nonexistence of God. (Notice that this may be the case even if a God would have no *obligation* to clear up the relevant question – even if the action would be a work of supererogation or, for that matter, if it makes no sense to speak of these moral notions where God is concerned at all.) Since we all have the responsibility of thinking carefully about what our information justifies us in believing, I really don't see how hubris need be involved here at all.

There's another thing, too – and this is important because it's so often overlooked or ignored: The arguer who is troubled by hiddenness of type (B) – propositional hiddenness, if you like – need not claim, as you suggest, that we should expect *knowledge* of this or that truth to be made available to us; perhaps the provision of *evidence sufficient to sustain reasonable belief* is all that her information warrants us in expecting. Now perhaps we *might* expect knowledge – I'm not denying that that will ever be the case. My point is rather that even if this is *not* the case, it doesn't follow that there is no problem here. Even if knowledge of some theistic proposition is theologically or for some other reason ruled out, maybe there's an argument to show that we should expect *a more limited sort of evidence* of its truth that does not in fact obtain, in which case there's still a problem. You can see where I'm going with this.

C: Yes, I can see – and it troubles me. Let me try to clarify why. O.K., maybe hubris can be avoided by someone who tries to turn the hiddenness of God into the nonexistence of God, and maybe no obligation claim need be involved here. Still, how on earth is the relevant evidence to be provided? By some spectacular miracle? Maybe God organizes the stars into words expressing the proposition in question? There's something almost childish about such an idea. Notice that even if such events occurred and removed all doubt, they would at the same time remove all *moral freedom*. Considering themselves to be observed by the all-seeing eye of God, human beings would do only what they considered God's will, out of fear of divine wrath. Here's another problem: The whole idea has a decidedly *patriarchal* feel to it: God as the Father who knows best and will take care of all our needs, and see to it that we never have to experience any troubling emotions or think things through for ourselves. A mature theology and one sensitive to the concerns of women will reject this. And I still haven't seen any reason to suppose that God would *want* to give us evidence of the truth of propositions that may now seem doubtful; you need to provide more evidence of your own that this is the case, or there's not much point in discussing the idea any further. To sum up: There are points that, if added to the 'information' of the arguer you describe, may reduce its force; and further, it's not clear what that information is in the first place.

S: You came prepared, didn't you? Let me address your concerns. Starting with the first: again, you seem to be thinking of evidence that would – as you in fact say – *remove all doubt*; spectacular events that would leave us absolutely convinced, with overwhelmingly supported and unquestioned *knowledge* of the relevant proposition(s). Not all requests for hiddenness to be removed are asking for this, and so to keep talking about it in such a general, all-or-nothing, way is to take a rather uncharitable approach to the atheist's position. Don't we teach all our first year students to avoid this sort of thing? Moving on to a related point: Miracles probably do not represent the only epistemic possibility available to unsurpassable greatness. So even given that *that* possibility, if realized, would be freedom-removing, it doesn't follow that God must remove our freedom in removing hiddenness. More specifically, not all the ways available to omnipotence of making true theistic propositions concerning God's nature accessible to us would entail *revealing* an all-seeing God. We need to use our imaginations here. God could – just for example – gift the world with many more theological geniuses; or give us all a greater natural capacity for formulating and recognizing necessary truths. We wouldn't all immediately or even upon reflection believe that there is a God if this state of affairs obtained. (And in case you're inclined to think that this would unacceptably limit the scope of possible inquiry, and thus our *intellectual* freedom, notice that if God is indeed unsurpassably great, then no matter how much we come to know of the nature of God, there will always be more to learn.)

C: But what if the thing God is expected to make accessible is *theism itself* – that is, the very *existence* of God? You seem to be ignoring that here.

S: Even then, I would argue, evidence could be provided in a way that need not be unacceptably freedom-removing (either because it is not significantly freedom-removing at all, or because it brings with it compensating or outweighing goods). Here I would prefer to explore the epistemic and religious appropriateness and effectiveness of religious experience. (As I suggested earlier, removing experiential hiddenness might be a way of removing some kinds of propositional hiddenness.) I can't get into the details, but suffice it to say that many of my critics are independently convinced, on the basis of impressive recent arguments, that religious experience can provide epistemic justification for religious belief. Surely it isn't hard to see how more people could be blessed with it. And if, as these critics presumably believe, religious experience of the sort that *is* available isn't seriously problematic, from a theological point of view concerned to preserve our freedom, why should we suppose that there *would* be a problem had it been made *more widely* available?

Actually, all of this vastly oversimplifies the issues here: We need to consider, more generally, (1) what *types and amounts of evidence* are *relevant* here (that is, what amounts of evidence would be needed to remove to the extent desirable the various forms of divine hiddenness, and what types of evidence could do it); (2) what *types of freedom* are *valuable* here (we've already mentioned a distinction between moral and intellectual freedom, though no doubt they are also related); (3) what types of freedom would be *threatened* by the relevant evidence concerning God's nature or existence, and to what extent and under what circumstances; (4) what *other* types of freedom (and more generally, what offsetting or outweighing goods) would be made *possible* by such evidence, and so on. You can see that the one who says that evidence of the relevant sorts and amounts could not be provided or must inevitably – and *regrettably* – be freedom-removing has a big job on her hands.

C: I guess I can see that. I'll have to think about it some more. Whatever the case, let's assume for now that there is at any rate some significant sort of hiddenness that could be removed without the removal – or at any rate the regrettable removal – of a significant measure of freedom. What about the other problems I mentioned?

S: Right. Let's look at them. A mature theology (and philosophy of religion) will indeed reject the childish desire to have a great Father in the sky who removes everything emotionally troubling from our experience and never makes us work for intellectual (including theological) results. But it's not as if an atheist arguing from divine hiddenness has to *endorse* such a desire. If this is the theist's reply, there are rather obviously a lot of holes in it.

C: Why don't you just give me your arguments and I'll count the holes myself, O.K.?

S: Fair enough. We need to notice, first of all, that one who argues from Divine hiddenness may avoid patriarchal assumptions altogether, wishing to distance herself, in particular, from the confused idea that the unsurpassably great source of all things is literally male or exclusively masculine. Indeed, we have *less* reason to believe God would be distant and aloof if, with the feminists, we reject patriarchy, not more – a God who values relationship and is comfortable with love is, on the face of it, *less* likely to be hidden than a ruggedly individualistic and independent 'male' God! Further, even if this or that theistic proposition were known to us or reasonably believed by us – even if, for example, we had reason enough to believe that God were real – life wouldn't, just like that, be turned into a cakewalk: Many relational difficulties and sufferings in the face of disease and horrific car accidents and plane crashes (and so on and so on), due to our finitude and fragility, and the capriciousness of the world in which we live, would continue to beset us and present emotional challenges. (Don't theists suffer?) Now, again, it may be thought that someone who argues that the hiddenness of God should be removed is advocating something more theologically unrealistic – some sort of more wholesale removal of ignorance concerning Divine things or continual, 'in your face', presentation of divine majesty and goodness. But as I've already said, this is not the only possibility. And those, including myself, who are suggesting that there is a problem of divine hiddenness are asking for no such thing. We need to look at the arguments that are actually being made.

C: Fine. That is, indeed, why I asked you – in my last point – to provide more detail as to what such arguments might look like. That's where I think we should go next. Let me put it this way: Which hiddenness claim do you think is most problematic for theism, and why?

II

Having cleared the ground for more serious discussion by defining its subject and discovering reason to question some of the more obvious and popular objections to the very idea that there could be a strong argument for atheism from divine hiddenness, our philosophers now prepare to consider the details of S's attempt to provide such an argument. But before S can begin his exposition, a somewhat dishevelled, clearly agitated individual bursts into the room, shouting something about Room 318, and then just as quickly disappears, leaving our thinkers bemused and wondering.

S: Who the heck was that?

C: That was C.S. You know, the popular religious writer who likes to take on philosophical questions – the one they say is suffering from some kind of psychological disorder.

S: That sure narrows the field!

C: Yeah, right. No, really. Some kind of an identity crisis – first an atheist ridiculing theism and then a theist ridiculing atheism; something like that.

S: Did you catch the words? Sounded like 'Room 13'.

C: No. I'm sure I heard 'Room 383'. Hey, I'll bet that's where the lecture is. We've been in the wrong room all this time!

S: I'm certain it was 13.

C: Well, why don't we go find out who's right. Let's try your idea first. (13 is closer anyway.) It'll be nice to get moving after sitting all this time. Maybe we can talk as we walk.

S: Sounds good. As I recall, just before C.S. disturbed us you were asking which hiddenness claim I think is most problematic for theism, and why. I was going to say that that sounds like an essay question on a philosophy exam. Let me try to answer it now. You'll have to tell me how I do.

C: Oh, don't worry; I will – and the results may not be what you expect!

S: I guess I'll have to learn to live with that if it happens. Well, in my view, it is the hiddenness of God's *existence* that is most problematic. Using terms I introduced before, we could put it this way: What I consider most problematic is the fact that the theistic proposition 'God exists' is epistemically nonsecured for so many of us. To see why, think of this: 'If God is unsurpassably great, then God is unsurpassably loving'. What we've got hold of here is a proposition that qualifies as a necessary truth if any does. Love – real love – is one of the most awesome qualities of personal being we know of (and even that may be an understatement). How could God exist but lack it? If God lacked it, God would *not* be unsurpassably great. (And of course, as you know, many religious traditions on their own grounds endorse this idea of God as necessarily loving.) Now what sort of love are we talking about here? Much could be said and has been said, but let's focus on this often neglected point: the best human love – the best love of parent or spouse or friend – involves seeking *meaningful personal relationship* with the beloved. It seeks a kind of *closeness* between itself and the beloved. The lover clearly wants this for its own sake – she reaches out to the one she loves naturally and spontaneously and without depending on some calculation of advantages and disadvantages for either party. But instrumental value comes into the picture too. The lover, being – as the best and truest lover must be – benevolently disposed toward the beloved, will also seek relationship *so that* she may offer opportunities for *explicit participation in her life*; she will allow and indeed encourage the beloved to draw from this relationship what he may need to flourish. Would you say that the seeking of personal relationship is, for such reasons, to be thought of as an essential part of the best human love?

C: Well, that sounds right. And you think all of this has implications for our understanding of God's love?

S: Yes, I want to bring God back into the picture. Clearly God, too, must value personal relationship for its own sake if God is loving. That's just a conceptual point. And just *think* of all the value that would be realized in the life of someone personally related to God. Now suppose God loves *us* with an *unsurpassable* love. This *must* mean that God seeks to be personally related to us! I think we have been prevented by our familiarity with the hiddenness of God and much theologizing within this context over many years, and perhaps by our use of the 'Father' model together with the commonness in our experience of distant or absent human fathers, from appreciating the full force of this point.

C: But God isn't *like* your parent or your friend in being available for personal relationship. Precisely because God *is* unsurpassably great – not 'on our level' – all this talk of personal relationship seems inapplicable, even mildly blasphemous. I mean, you can't just buttonhole God and start talking . . . Well . . . I guess there *is* prayer.

S: That's right. A personal relationship with God might indeed be *different* in many ways from other personal relationships we experience, but that doesn't mean the notion is inapplicable. Even if we think it best to avoid the 'chummy' talk of, say, some forms of evangelical Christianity, we're just disagreeing with the way the relationship is *described*. Clearly we *can* still speak of, for example, prayer, and the observation of God's work in our lives, perhaps

42   J. L. SCHELLENBERG

thinking of the latter as in some way causally related to prayer. All theistic traditions speak of such things as divine guidance, support, or forgiveness, and –
on the human side – trust, gratitude, and worship. And what are these if not
forms of personal interaction? Even if we prefer to speak of mystical experience of the divine, spiritual disciplines, and the gradual diminishment of the
ego's influence, talk of personal relationship applies. For here we have persons
consciously orienting themselves toward God and feeling the effects of this in
their lives, which they attribute to a consciousness of God's presence. If God
really is present to them, and they respond to this presence, and if the nature
of their response varies with the nature of the felt presence, and vice versa, is
this not personal relationship? The common meaning here, or as we might say,
the *relevant content* of personal relationship is a pattern of reciprocal activity:
a giving and receiving directed towards (among other things) a deeper knowing
and being known, in which both terms of the relation participate and which
both find valuable.

C: I guess if we take 'personal relationship' that broadly. . . . But what makes you
  think that everyone is going to be *capable* of this sort of interaction with God,
  or *open* to it?

S: Well, I *don't* think that. That's why I would add, as a sort of filling out of
  what I've already said, that God, if loving, will pursue personal relationship
  with those of us who possess the cognitive and affective equipment required
  to hold the beliefs and exhibit the attitudes and do the actions *involved* in
  personal relationship with God (but notice that this includes virtually everyone: Virtually everyone is, for example, capable of feeling and expressing gratitude, and possesses either the concept of an unsurpassably great source of all
  things who works through all and is in all, or the materials from which it could
  be constructed or emerge under the influence of argument or experience). I'd
  also add – and this takes care of your second suggestion – that God would not
  coerce anyone into (or toward) personal interaction of the sort I've described.
  This is just another implication of love, as we can see from human examples.
  It is a truism that love respects the freedom of the beloved. So we can be sure
  that those who have the relevant capacities but fail to respond to God's overtures or completely shut themselves off from God will not be harried by the
  hound of heaven! But that still leaves us – here, let me write it out for you –
  that still leaves us with reason to believe *this*:

  P1 If God exists and is unsurpassably loving, then for any human subject H
     and time t, if H is at t capable of relating personally to God, H is at t in
     a position to do so (i.e. can at t *exercise* this capacity just by choosing
     to), unless H is culpably in a contrary position at t.

  Take a look. God – I'm saying – will see to it that the only thing that can
  prevent us from interacting with God is our own free choice (whether it is the
  free choice to ignore a God we are aware of, or to take steps to remove that
  awareness, and so to remove ourselves from that place where we are in a posi-

tion to relate personally to God). This is what I should be taken to mean when I speak of a loving God *seeking* personal relationship with us.

C: Wait a minute. You're slipping something new in here with that phrase "at any time t". Why suppose a relationship with God must *always* be possible for us – isn't this sort of continual awareness of God something that has traditionally been thought to be available only in the afterlife? We have to be careful not to get greedy here. And you say we have "reason to believe" what you're saying. That's a little vague, wouldn't you agree? What *kind* of reason, and how *powerful* are you supposing it to be?

S: Good questions, and I'll try to answer them. Am I 'greedy'? I don't think so. I'm just working out as best I can the meaning and implications of the claim that God is unsurpassably loving, or more specifically, that God unsurpassably loves human beings. This has nothing to do with what we might want or deserve or any such thing: It has to do with the nature of Divine love. Again, I think that, due to a variety of social and religious factors, we have got used to thinking of even *God's* love in a limited and limiting fashion, contrary to what the usual philosophical methods for working out an explication of the divine nature would indicate. Why suppose that, if God exists, there will be times (other than times when we ourselves culpably take a hand in things) when personal relationship with God will not be possible for those of us capable of it – when we will not (as I put it earlier) be *in a position* to relate personally to God? While a perfectly good and loving parent might occasionally stand to one side and let her child make the first move, and refuse to suffocate a child with her attentions, or even withdraw for a time to make a point, these are moments *within* the relationship, which *add* to its meaning. The *possibility* of *some* form of personal interaction with the parent will (insofar as she is able to ensure it) always be there. What loving parent would ever willingly allow this possibility to be taken completely away? Parental love will not permit this to occur when it can be prevented. And similar points apply to love as it occurs in the context of friendship or marriage relationships. So the *possibility* of some form of personal relationship is always going to be there. Now someone might say that we have to understand talk of God's love differently here. But quite apart from the other problems that sort of move runs into, I think such a claim forgets that these features of love are precisely those (or among those) that we consider to be great-making. As such, they can hardly be excised from our concept of divine love!

C: Well, I can see that your points have some force. *But* – and you knew there was a 'but' coming! – I still have a worry or two. In particular, what do you make of the point that you're unacceptably blurring the theological distinction between this life and the next, and the possibilities for awareness of God in each?

S: I'm glad you brought that up again. It might be thought that I'm asking for something like the beatific vision in this life. But a closer look will dispel that illusion. The 'personal relationship with God' I'm talking about, like any personal relationship, is to be understood in developmental terms. Were it to obtain, it would admit of change, growth, progression, regression, and so on. It might be shallow or deep, depending on the nature of our response to God. Caught up as most of us are, most of the time, in the toil and change of earthly life, it would normally lack most of the features of the so-called beatific vision. Which allows me to make an important point. Life is tough, and so in a certain sense the relationship to which I refer *belongs* in this life. *Now*, in the midst of earthly pain and suffering and bewilderment, is when we need divine guidance, support, consolation, forgiveness. When in the afterlife of traditional theology are we going to need these things? Because of the evil we face and the evident frailties of our natures, the proper picture of humans in this life is not (as traditional theology sometimes supposes) a picture of mature adults: We are instead like children still immature, still needing a home – in particular, still in need of parental support and encouragement in the development of a character and self-esteem able to withstand the pressures toward fragmentation and despair life represents, a character and self-esteem that will make the achievement of our full potential possible. It seems to me, therefore, that the contrast between this life and the next, if it shows anything here, shows only that, if God exists, we may expect the *nature and circumstances and perhaps intensity* of our awareness of God to be different in each; it does nothing to support the claim that such awareness would be *unavailable* to us at any time in this life. If we add to this the fact that love looks not for excuses but for opportunities, that unsurpassable love by its very nature would rejoice in each moment in which it could express itself, we can see that there is no reason to resist the all-inclusive claim in question. Quite the contrary.

C: That's quite a little sermon. Looks like you came prepared too.

S: Well, I do find myself needing to preach to the converted sometimes.

C: I can see that most of the objections I've been raising seem to you to have fairly convincing answers. And I must admit they don't have as much force as I was inclined to think they had. But remember (way back when) I suggested that your claim that we have *reason* to affirm all this needed to be filled out. Maybe you could address that now. I mean, supposing these objections I've been raising are unsound, what are you left with? Are you claiming, in that case, to *know* the conditional in question – that if God exists and is perfectly loving, those of us with the relevant capacities will always be in a position to relate personally to God?

S: Unless . . .

C: Unless we are culpably in a contrary position? Or maybe you think it can be proven to be *probably* true? What is it? Where are you going with this? And how does it all relate to the alleged badness of the proposition 'God exists' being, as you say, epistemically non-secured for us? That's what this is ultimately all about, right? How can such an item of knowledge or belief, an event or state in the mind or brain, be so significant where relationship with God is concerned?

S: Right – but one thing at a time. Let me first explain the support we have for the conditional in question, and then I'll clarify the link with the other matter.

It all goes back to the discussion of human love at its best. This, I would argue, together with the points that emerge when we apply it to God (points about the lack of human *limitations* in God, for example), constitutes a prima facie good or justifying reason to believe the conditional in question, which I define as a reason sufficient to justify belief of that conditional in the absence of available undefeated – undermining or rebutting – defeaters. (This way of putting it doesn't reflect any hesitation on my part about the conditional. A prima facie reason may also be an ultima facie reason. I just think that one should treat all one's beliefs and all one's reasoning as fallible.) And though we don't have time for a thorough analysis here, perhaps you'd agree that no relevant defeater is *available* to someone if she has looked hard for defeaters and thought carefully about all the defeaters known to her but is convinced by none of them?

C: I'd be inclined to agree. But I need more clarity about something. What is your view of justification anyway? Clearly what it takes to have a prima facie justifying reason for believing something is going to depend on what justification *is*, right? I've noticed that many epistemologists, including many of your critics, seem inclined to accept a deontological view here, saying – how does that go? – H is justified in believing a proposition p at a time t if and only if there is nothing contrary to epistemic duty in H's believing p at t. Something like that. What you've said so far – especially about 'available' defeaters – suggests that you've got something like this in mind. Is that true?

S: Well, yes, I'd be willing to go along with that – though, as I'm sure you realize, a lot more would need to be said to flesh it out properly. One thing we need to recognize is that what gives a prima facie good or justifying reason that status will vary from context to context. There are, after all, different sources of justification and different forms of reasoning, and so on. So we have to look at *our* situation. What are the standards of correct reasoning *here*? And I'd say that what gives our justification prima facie status is basically that its reasoning instantiates an intuitively very plausible and widely accepted way of determining the meaning of divine attributes – namely, extrapolation from mundane examples of the relevant properties. When thinking of what it means to say that God has knowledge, most philosophers suppose we are using the word in its ordinary sense, while making such adjustments as are required by certain relevant differences between God and ourselves which our background knowledge or belief concerning the nature of God suggests ought to be taken into account (and so, for example, God is said to know *all* true propositions, not just some). Likewise, when discussing the *goodness* of God, most philosophers assume that we are using an ordinary term in its usual sense. In discussion of the problem of evil, for example, it is widely agreed that a good God, like a good human being, might well have a reason for permitting evil to occur, while – again like a good human being – necessarily resisting what is seen as *unjustified* evil. (Adjustments here include the observation that God, being, unlike ourselves, omnipotent, can be said necessarily to *prevent*, and not only to resist, what is seen as unjustified evil, and, being omniscient, will always see it correctly.) Given the force of what we say about human beings in such cases – that is to say, because discussions of human beings and their interactions represent the primary contexts in which the relevant terms are used and acquire their meaning – we would have to be given a very good reason indeed to suppose that 'divine goodness' and 'divine knowledge' are to be otherwise understood in order (reasonably) to be prevented from applying what is true of human knowledge and goodness in fixing their meaning. In other words, what we know of how these terms are used in human contexts provides a prima facie good reason for believing that talk of God is to be understood in the same way.

What follows? Well, it would seem, then, that what we know of human love at its best and the nature of God must provide a prima facie good or justifying reason for believing that God, if loving, seeks personal relationship with us (where this conditional includes everything I put into it earlier). Since a perfectly loving human being wouldn't ever willingly be prevented from making personal relationship available to her beloved, and since our background knowledge concerning the nature of God suggests that God does not suffer from our limitations (for example, restrictedness in time and space), limitations that sometimes nonetheless *do* prevent humans from seeing to it that their beloved is in a position to relate personally with them – given that all this is the case, we are permitted to affirm the conditional in question in the absence of defeaters. Indeed, we are *required* to do so. If upon careful reflection we can find no reason to suppose that our human examples have not been correctly understood or do not apply in all the ways we have supposed to God, then we are surely justified – in a manner identical to what we find in other cases of reflection on divine attributes – in believing that the conditional I have put forward is true.

C: Identical? Are you saying that your conditional is *necessarily* true? That's what's going on in the other cases, you know. When, for example, we say that God would, if perfectly good, resist unjustified evil, we mean this is a necessary truth. Its necessity stares us in the face. What you're saying about love and personal relationship – especially the availability of personal relationship at all times – just doesn't seem to fall into the same category.

S: Well, remember that not *all* necessary truths may be expected to stare us in the face (there are plenty of examples of nonobvious necessary truths in philosophy!) And when we are able to identify – as I've suggested in this case we can – sociological or other causes that may prevent candidates for necessary truth from appearing obvious, their lack of this property of being obvious to everyone is obviously no evidence that they are not necessary. We have to look at what the arguments show. My arguments are out there, and I suggest that they provide a familiar sort of (defeasible) a priori justification for my claim. Let me say this, too: Even if it should – contrary to my expectation – turn out to be implausible to suppose that my conditional is necessary, that wouldn't remove its usefulness in an argument for atheism unless the conditions cited in the proof of non-necessity obtained in the actual world. Unless this were so, we could continue to affirm that the conditional were *true*, even if not necessarily true. Indeed, as we've seen, there are circumstances in the actual world – evil, etc. – which suggest that here *especially* we might expect an unsurpassably loving God to be available for relationship. All of this seems to me, however, to be unnecessary maneuvering because of the arguments for supposing that my conditional reflects part of the very *meaning* of 'God exists and unsurpassably loves human beings'.

C: Wow! That's a bold claim!

S: Well, bold perhaps, but is it true?

C: O.k. I think I see a little better where you're coming from now. So let me suggest a problem! Mightn't there be reasons concerning the well-being of the *beloved* that deter a lover from seeking personal relationship? It is at any rate *conceivable* that someone might think it better for the one she loves not to know about her or be able to relate to her, at least for a time. Take, for example, someone who's just coming out of jail and whose child, unaware that his biological mother is alive, is relating wonderfully to a newly acquired step-mother, or alternatively, is going through a really difficult time right now, his plate full, not needing his whole world to be turned upside down by this rather large new piece of information. Can't you just hear the psychologist say to the mother: "In my considered opinion, it would be better for you to wait with this disclosure until later, when your child will be in a better position to respond positively?" Since a loving mother would want the *best* for her child, surely she would remain hidden in such circumstances.

S: This isn't clear to me at all. Suppose the child's well-being would, at least at first, be negatively affected – by turmoil or bad feeling of some sort or other. And suppose that the mother, expecting this, remains hidden. Is this love at its best? It seems we might say that in such a case, while one of the *necessary conditions* of love – namely, a certain measure of benevolence – is retained, love *itself*, which by definition involves seeking personal relationship, does not exist: The fuller, deeper state that alone deserves the name of love has indeed been *given up* in order to achieve a more benevolent benevolence. To support this, we could point out that one who loves will not treat the goodness of personal relationship with herself as just one among many goods that it would be fine for the beloved to possess: She wants the beloved to have *this* good, and she wants to in some measure share with him the difficulties and the joys that life presents. And although the beloved may choose at some time to take a different path, he will do so recognizing that he could have preserved relationship with the lover instead. The lover would not remove herself from the life of the beloved or fail to appear in it in the first place just because some incompatible good as great as or even greater than personal interaction with herself over that period of time happens to present itself. There is indeed something quite contrary to the spirit of love in someone who acts this way. If I know you can have a good life with me, then I will be a *poorer* lover if, aware of someone with whom you might well be happier still (or of other circumstances requiring my absence attractive in one way or another) I leave the relationship or fail to pursue it in the first place. (This, by the way, shows how inapt are those suggestions I continue to hear about a loving God forgoing personal relationship in order to facilitate some good or other – courage in aloneness, say, or responsibility for the religious belief of others – that our well-being and the well-being of the universe simply does not require, functional equivalents of which can indeed – through myriads of other circumstances calling for courage and responsibility and so on – be made possible even if God's existence is revealed! A God who hid in such circumstances might still be benevolent but would not really care about *loving*. Such a God would have to be afraid of loving, or, perhaps through watching overly many movies portraying fathers of the 1950s, under some misapprehension about the nature of parenting.)

Of course, even if benevolence of the timid sort we've been talking about is not misguided and represents genuine love, so that the woman in your example *can* exemplify human love at its best even if she remains hidden, we still need to notice that this would no longer be an example of love *were the relevant human limitations to be removed*, as they must be when we begin to speak of God. Indeed, there is a sense in which such examples are just not relevant to our understanding of God's love, since the goodness, the contribution to our well-being, represented by the possibility of choosing to become personally related to God, even for a time, is so very great. We would no doubt do a poor job of appreciating it, but just *think* of the intrinsic value we're talking about when we refer to personal relationship with the unsurpassably great source of all that is!

C: Just wait – I'm seeing something here. . . . Yes, this is it! There's also the matter of how likely it is that the possibility you're talking about will be *realized* – how likely it is that individuals will *make* the choice in question. If God sees that it's not likely at all, then what, really, is being given up? Indeed, if we take this a little further, I *can* say that something as good as personal relationship with God – namely personal relationship with God! – might in such circumstances be lost unless God remained hidden.

S: What? That's not clear at all.

C: Here – let me back up a bit and clarify this point in the context of my earlier example and what you said about it. First of all, surely if the anticipated harm were *very great*, both the mother and God, if loving, would remain hidden. Surely – as you've admitted – the best love must include *some* benevolence! Against this, you'd presumably say what you said earlier: that a lover may be expected to be more concerned about the absence of relationship than about the loss of other (perhaps, to an outside observer, roughly comparable) goods.

But now these two points can be connected – can be seen to support what is really the same conclusion. Here's how: What if revealing herself now and making relationship available now means the mother sacrifices *relationship*? Suppose, for example, that the child may be expected to react so strongly and negatively as to set up an emotional state of affairs incompatible with meaningful present *or* future relationship. What then?

S: That's an interesting thought – but there's still a certain unclarity in our discussion here. Even if a harm is such as to make a certain period of my life seem bad, it may be ameliorated or absorbed in my life as a whole. I think for your first point, your *general* point about harm, to get off the ground we have to suppose that the lover has reason to suppose the harm will *not* be such: Only then would we have clear reason to consider her love deficient in benevolence. Taking your other point into account too (and it really does have independent force, doesn't it, since God's seeking of relationship is not just about creating benefit or avoiding harm?), we might put things together this way: The best lover will not disclose herself to the beloved at a time t if she can see that in so doing she would likely produce a harm that could not be sufficiently ameliorated or absorbed in the beloved's life as a whole, *or* that in so doing she would likely prevent personal relationship for a significant period beginning at t or some time after t. Does this principle express what you're saying?

C: Close enough.

S: All right. Suppose that it's true. I'd say it's unclear that your human lover would ever have reason to believe with any degree of confidence that revealing her existence would cause such a radical harm, or prevent significant relationship now or in the future. So much here depends on circumstances and choices that cannot be predicted. Love is a risk. A lover takes the risk. Furthermore, the more committed a lover is to being the best lover she can be, and the more faith she has in her beloved's ability to make *good* choices, and the more encouragement she provides for such choices, the more likely she is to believe that the future is bright. And are these not precisely the attitudes we expect to find in the best lover? (Notice also – and this is important – that if the threat to relationship is not that of harmful choices made in normal circumstances of freedom, but of some psychological condition the beloved is powerless to control, then we have a situation in which the beloved is *incapable* of relationship – *and so an example irrelevant to our discussion*.)

Turning to God, again I have to emphasise that *whatever* the case may be where human love is concerned, things will be different here. That is, even if human lovers cannot expect to bring good out of evil, or to make it possible for the life of the beloved to be a great good to her on the whole, or to turn a relationship problem into a possibility, *God can*! Part of what would make divine love so great is what we might expect to be its infinite resourcefulness in addressing human need. Surely a theist can't deny this without contradicting what she believes about the greatness of God! You're no doubt aware of the testimonials of those who claim that precisely *through* relationship with God all manner of ills of the sort that might be introduced here – such as initial resistance to God or fear of God – have been defeated and indeed turned into good. Whatever we may think of the truth of their reports, wouldn't we consider the implicit assessment of God's resourcefulness here to be correct? It seems unreasonable, therefore, to say that the disjunctive antecedent of your principle so much as *could* be true when it is applied to theism. So even if the *principle* is true, it poses no threat to my claim – or so it seems to me.

C: Well, suppose we give you that one.

S: And there's another problem with your principle, too: It suggests (though it doesn't imply) that we're imagining a loved one for whom the self-disclosure of the lover represents, as we might say, a cognitive and emotional *disruption*. But notice that if God seeks relationship in the manner of P1, then there is *never* a time when we are capable of relationship with God but not in a position to enter into such relationship. (At the dawn of the relevant capacities, the conditions of being in a position to *exercise* those capacities are also there.) The same oversight, it seems to me, appears in the comments of *all* those who say that God might not become revealed to someone capable of relationship at a certain time (and inculpably ignorant of God) because she may not at that time be *ready* for relationship. This *presupposes* that God has not sought relationship in the manner of P1 instead of justifying or explaining it, and so can provide no defeater for my claim about P1. (In this connection you might also want to notice that even if the conditions of being in a position to relate personally to God are always satisfied for those capable of such relationship, and they *do* relate themselves to God, there is all kinds of room for withdrawal and fresh disclosure *within* the relationship. Indeed, it's interesting that this sort of hiddenness-within-relationship requires the *absence* of the sort of hiddenness of which the advocate of my argument complains. So if you think you have reason to value the former – the 'dark night of the soul' which is held by theists to be *part* of relationship with God – and especially if (as I would argue if we had more time) this sort of hiddenness can accomplish much, perhaps all, of what believers sometimes say the *latter* hiddenness is designed to do, you have reason to accept my view on the latter.)

C: O.k., o.k.! As I said before, I'm ready to give you that one! The principle I suggested earlier may not fly as effortlessly as I thought. But it seems to me that we still haven't clarified the connection between all this and belief in the existence of God, which you seem to think should be evident to us.

S: I'm getting to that. The connection should really be quite easy to see now that we've got clear about the sort of relationship we're talking about. It is this: A personal relationship with someone – whoever that is – entails *the belief that that someone exists*. This goes for personal relationship with God too. How can I hear God speak to me or consciously experience Divine forgiveness and support or feel grateful to God or experience God's loving presence and respond thereto in love and obedience and worship *if I do not believe that there is a God*? This is a *logical* point: As I say, how *can* I? It's logically impossible. Because belief is involuntary, it follows that while in a state of nonbelief I am not in a position to relate personally to God. But then, given what we've seen about God seeking a personal relationship – a relationship with such features as I just mentioned – we can infer that God will ensure that so long as I'm capable of personal relationship and don't resist, I am never in a state of nonbelief. (In doing so, notice again, God is not *forcing* us into relationship or any such thing, but simply satisfying one of the necessary conditions of *seeking* personal relationship with us.) So if we have prima facie good reason to believe that God will do the one thing – seek personal relationship – we have prima facie good reason to believe that God will do the other – ensure belief. What we have arrived at, more precisely, is prima facie justification for a new claim (let's call it P2) – and here, let me write this one out as well:

P2   If God exists and is unsurpassably loving, then for any human subject H and time t, if H is at t capable of relating personally to God, H at t believes that God exists, unless H is culpably in a contrary position at t.

If I had more time, I'd develop this a bit – clarifying the term 'believes' and the notion of degrees of belief, discussing the sort of evidence required here, and so on. (Even without that, I think we can see that it is simply evidence sufficient to make nonbelief culpable or unjustified or unreasonable, in a sense that can be worked out by reference to the deontological notion of 'justified belief' you mentioned earlier – no need for knowledge or making God's existence *evident* here. And by 'sufficient' I mean 'causally sufficient': The evidence would be such as to produce belief in anyone inculpable in the relevant respects.) For the sake of discussion, let's reduce the consequent of P2 to this: 'God's existence is *beyond reasonable nonbelief*.' So we have: 'If God exists and is loving, then God's existence is beyond reasonable nonbelief.' Add now that the consequent of this conditional is false (as surely it is, there being clear cases of persons possessing the relevant capacities who inculpably deny or are in doubt about the proposition 'God exists', or who without even any *understanding* of its content fail to believe it), and you can see how we have here an argument for the nonexistence of God: an argument that goes through in the absence of considerations defeating the prima facie justification for its main premise we've been talking about.

C: Very interesting. So everyone who doesn't resist belief will be provided with it (and so, for example, all those who sincerely and wholeheartedly desire to be personally related to God will believe) – not just so that they have this extra bit of information or to force them into personal relationship with God, but because otherwise personal relationship would not be so much as *possible* for them, which is incompatible with what we have prima facie good reason to believe an unsurpassably loving God would bring about.

S: I couldn't have said it better myself.

C: O.K. But in thinking about the argument, I find myself still wondering whether there isn't an alternative to what you've emphasised here in talking about belief. Couldn't someone be responding to God (and so in a sense in a relationship with God) *without knowing it* – by engaging in serious moral inquiry, for example, and thus connecting up with goodness (ultimately instantiated by God), or more generally, by acting as it would be appropriate for them to act if they believed? We could call this, as Karl Rahner does, *implicit* belief, and say that such individuals are responding to God all right, without recognizing that they are.

S: Well, I suppose inculpable nonbelievers might have to settle for that *if there were reasons for God to permit reasonable nonbelief.* In other words, this point does not solve the problem: It too *presupposes* a solution. For surely implicit belief is an extremely distant second best when compared to explicit belief and all it facilitates. Any measure of real belief here makes literally a world of difference. One's whole picture of the nature of things, of what is and will be, changes. Without belief one is not in a position to *feel* God and to experience the greatest intrinsic good there is. Think, for example, of those who once believed but now do not, even though they *want* to. Saying that implicit belief will do in their case, or would be thought by an unsurpassably loving God to be good enough in the absence of any special reason requiring it, is like saying that there is nothing out of the ordinary in a loving parent abandoning her child and providing evidence that causes the child reasonably to think that his mother might very well have been an imposter, and to wonder at night whether she was ever really there. No, this argument from implicit belief is a nonstarter; I almost want to say it is an insult to the unsurpassable love of the God it is intended to represent.

C: Well, I must say your arguments have a certain appeal – I didn't think I'd be saying this, but I'm starting to find them persuasive. I suppose you'd not have much use for the move of a Christian or Muslim or Jew who says that the doctrines of his tradition provide an answer to some of this – say, to your claim that there *is* inculpable nonbelief ?

S: What doctrines might we be talking about here?

C: Oh, say, the Calvinian idea that all nonbelief is due to sin – the sin of the nonbeliever, who is resisting God in some way?

S: Well, that claim just seems to me to be falsified by empirical evidence. You could think about conscientious doubters here – some of whom are actually practicing members of religious communities, who are willing to act-as-if, despite the absence of belief, hoping that belief may come to them. Do you see any resistance there? Or you might consider those who are growing up in a nontheistic or antitheistic tradition of one sort or another – who fail to believe in God or believe there is no God as naturally as someone growing up in an evangelical Christian family in the American Midwest or in an orthodox Jewish family in Israel will believe that God is real. (If the truth of theism isn't even an *issue* – maybe because you haven't even heard of or thought of the God-concept – and you've been raised that way, how can there be *resistance* to it of a sort that could produce culpability?) Examples could be multiplied, and among them are people who live as unselfishly as your most exemplary theist.

Of course, if you suppose that you have weightier independent evidence for a doctrinal package including the proposition that all nonbelief is due to sin, you will think that the empirical evidence must be misleading. I myself cannot imagine holding on to such a doctrinal package in the face of the evidence for inculpable nonbelief, especially when dropping the view that all nonbelief is due to sin *does not entail dropping the rest of the package*, or even the view that nonbelief is *sometimes* due to sin. In any case, it's only if there's *incredibly powerful* support for the *whole* package that this move can work. I surmise it will be a rational option for few.

C: You're pretty negative about the 'sin' view! Doesn't it have *anything* going for it? We are fairly murky creatures, you know, acting many times on deeply hidden selfish motives and blind to truths that should be obvious.

S: For sure – I fully agree. Indeed, the 'sin' strategy we've been talking about could be said to instantiate its own sort of 'blindness', an ideologically based blindness to the good of (some) others and inability (in some contexts) to perceive sincerity and blamelessness. It looks a lot like a lack of openness to love, for love reserves judgment on matters like this as long as possible, and is inclined to form its views of the other on the basis of personal interaction. The kind of blindness and judgment in the absence of personal closeness we seem to see here does a lot of damage in the world, and is in any case inconsistent with the humility and charity that is advocated by those religious people whose intellectual commitments reflect it. How could I be humble and charitable while, even after noting that all the other evidence is against it, judging your basic spiritual state negatively on the basis of a theological interpretation that has *theological* alternatives! (The behavior of Jesus and his interaction with ideology blinded individuals comes to mind here.)

But there's another point too. If the package we've been talking about (that whole conjunction of religious beliefs) is true, then *God exists* – the proposition 'God exists' is *one* of the beliefs in the package, and indeed, a presupposition of most of the rest. Why, then, we may well wish to ask, wouldn't someone thinking of the sin strategy you mention, and recognizing strong evidence against the view that all nonbelief is culpable, drop it in favor of the following equally effective strategy: the strategy of arguing that, because of relatively very weighty independent evidence supporting *the existence of God*, we have reason to believe what the latter proposition entails, namely, that – though we may not be able to put our finger on what it is – there is *something* wrong with the argument from divine hiddenness? One would expect that, having both strategies open to them – both the more specific 'sin' strategy and this more general move – and recognizing the empirically questionable and *uncharitable* features of the first, convinced theists would choose the second. But often they don't.

C: Well, it could be that persons using the 'sin' strategy are strongly convinced by the very arguments you have defended for the view that if there were a God, God's existence would not be hidden from anyone who fails to resist the evidence. In that case, even if they felt they had good reason to believe in God, they might very well stick to the 'sin' strategy.

S: Maybe – that's an interesting suggestion. Someone who lacks strong independent reason to believe in God is clearly not in the same boat: She can affirm both that if God exists, God's existence is not hidden from anyone without culpability, *and* that for some it is inculpably hidden. I myself would appear to be in that position. But if I *were* in their boat and had to affirm just one of these propositions, would I affirm the former? To me it seems obvious that I should not – and it wouldn't just be a matter of not accepting while still believing either. While I believe both those propositions, it seems clear to me that the evidence I have for the latter is stronger than the evidence I have for the former. So if I believed that they couldn't both be actually true and believed as well (on what I considered good grounds) that God exists, I would take my total information as clearly supporting the view that there is some reason, unknown to me, for God to remain hidden from some people. It's interesting to note that the Calvinist philosophers who advocate the sin strategy are not at all averse to using the 'God's reasons are inscrutable' strategy for the problem of evil. Indeed, they have championed it. So why is it so hard to adopt here? And would it still be hard if they properly acquainted themselves with the full range of allegedly inculpable nonbelief? Surely their ignorance here provides the basis for a defeater they could only hope to defeat after acquiring the knowledge it says they lack.

III

Having taken (as philosophers discussing among themselves are wont to do) nearly an hour to make their way from Room 3 (or 2, if you accept the word of S) to Room 13, and – thinking that perhaps C had discerned the words of C. S. correctly – from Room 13 to Room 383, and being by this time too deeply engrossed in the discussion to worry about correct location, our thinkers linger for a time by the doorway of Room 383 in order to seek some conclusion on the matter at issue between them.

C: Can I ask you to clarify, then, how exactly you think we are positioned with regard to your argument? Should we take it to be sound (I gather you don't think there are, in addition to the defeaters we've considered, others that are more successful)?

S: Actually, there is in my view no one position in which we all find ourselves. As usual, there are various epistemic possibilities, given that we're talking about different persons and different bodies of evidence and different argumentative contexts. There *are* other available defeaters, especially defeaters suggesting reasons God might have for permitting reasonable nonbelief. But as I have sought to show in the discussion you mentioned at the beginning, none of these defeaters are themselves undefeated. (Some alleged defeaters are, indeed, just question-begging. They skirt such arguments as we have surveyed for the claim that God would put the divine existence beyond reasonable nonbelief and tell stories about reasons God might have for doing otherwise which, it is said, are true *for all we know or justifiedly believe.* Unfortunately, this *assumes* that the aforementioned arguments are unsuccessful instead of showing it, for if they *are* successful, *this itself* provides justification for believing – as an entailment of their conclusion – that all such stories are false!) Now suppose you accept this view – and note that as part of this we're assuming that the 'sin' strategy is unsuccessful. You have, then, what seems a powerful argument against the existence of God. Must you conclude that God does not exist? That depends. As I suggested earlier, if you're a theist who reasonably supposes that the relevant independent evidence provides even *more* weighty support for the *existence* of God – and I'm thinking of 'evidence' broadly here, so as to include such things as a priori arguments or religious experience – you will reasonably conclude that the argument does not succeed: There must be *something* wrong with it though you cannot see what it is.

C: So the argument needn't have any effect on theists like me? Why, then, am I *feeling* its effect?

S: We have to beware of misunderstanding here. Not all theists will find themselves in the epistemically privileged position I've just described. Indeed, given that the argument is valid and that its premises entail the nonexistence of God, if a theist is inclined upon considering various defeaters to *believe* those premises, she would need in her independent evidence some *other* valid deductive argument (or arguments) *for* God whose premises she is *more* inclined to believe (or else religious experience or probabilistic arguments for theism, which, perhaps together with the former deductive arguments, produce the same doxastic state) in order reasonably to view that evidence as more weighty, and so to use *it* as a defeater. And of course, this higher degree of belief would have to be one that could reasonably be sustained when considerations supporting the *non*existence of God that are included in the independent evidence (evil, etc.) are taken into account. In light of these facts, not just anyone starting out as a theist will reasonably remain so after considering an argument from the hiddenness of God. A theist might very well come to be in a position where the independent support for theism seems only *as* weighty as the (now expanded) support for atheism, or where it seems *less* weighty. In that case, one's theism could reasonably be turned into agnosticism, or even atheism.

C: I'm not certain *where* I'm at right now. But continue.

S: Now suppose you come into the discussion not as a theist, but as an agnostic. Let's say you consider the existence of God to have, on the independent evidence, a probability of .5. What must you conclude upon finding the argument from divine hiddenness persuasive? Clearly, that there is no God. When you see the implications of the weak evidence that makes you an agnostic, then (lacking the defeater that might be provided by strong independent evidence for theism) you have reason to cease being an agnostic! That weak evidence is, as we might say, *itself* evidence for atheism.

C: O.k. But what if you're one of those agnostics who think *there's no way of telling* what the independent evidence shows? Would such an agnostic have reason to go over to atheism upon finding your argument persuasive?

S: What sort of difference are you hinting at here?

C: Well, the latter sort of agnostic could argue as follows: "If the independent evidence available to me provides a *lot* of support for theism, then the prima facie justification S is talking about is defeated by my total evidence. But I do not know or reasonably believe anything with regard to whether this is so. Therefore, I do not know or reasonably believe anything with regard to whether I have this defeater. But if I don't know or reasonably believe anything with regard to whether I have this defeater, then I don't know or reasonably believe anything with regard to whether S's argument is sound. Therefore, I am no further ahead given his argument and should remain an agnostic." What do you think of that?

S: Yes, I suppose one could try such a move. Unfortunately, however, it seems incorrect to say that when I'm unable to get clear about what the independent evidence for and against theism shows, that evidence may nonetheless provide me with a defeater for a new and persuasive argument for atheism. (In other words, your argument's interim conclusion does not follow from your first two premises.) Supposing that in some objective sense that evidence 'shows' the existence of God or does not, we may say that in that objective sense it also either defeats my argument or does not. But this is not to say that perhaps I *have* a defeater here. To have the defeater in question, one must know or reasonably (and very firmly) believe a proposition – namely, 'God exists' – that an agnostic clearly does not know or believe. For only then is one in a position to infer in this way that the argument is unsound. (We'd have to say that perhaps the agnostic *does* reasonably believe theism to say that perhaps she has this defeater; but that's just confused.) Lacking theistic belief, the agnostic *lacks* the defeater. There is no 'perhaps' about it.

C: O.k. But I still think there is a defeater in this neighborhood. Maybe what the independent evidence shows can't furnish a defeater since this cannot be determined, but maybe *that very fact* – the fact that the evidence is not definitely assessable – *does* provide a defeater! At least there seems to be an extreme case in which this would be true. I mean, if the rational agnostic construes all the independent evidence for and against theism probabilistically and can't make up her mind what some of the relevant probabilities are, then your new deductive argument, if persuasive, is going to turn her agnosticism into atheism. But there's also the possibility represented by someone who thinks there are plausible *deductive* arguments on both sides. To simplify this, take someone whose independent evidence consists of exactly two arguments – a deductive cosmological argument and the deductive argument from evil –

and who finds *both* powerfully persuasive. Someone reduced to agnosticism by *this* state of affairs will not reasonably be removed from it by *another* argument for atheism, *even if it is persuasive*. I may be inclined to believe to be sound ever so many deductive arguments for atheism, but if I am *equally* strongly inclined to believe sound a deductive argument for *theism*, I will quite reasonably languish in uncertainty as to whether theism is true or false. Deductive arguments do not – at least not in this context – have cumulative force.

S: Well, even if you're right about that, it is, as you say, an extreme case. How many agnostics have a hard time with the independent evidence *construed deductively*? Most seem to be worried about probabilities, or find *no* deductive arguments persuasive. And of course there's the fact that arguments like the deductive cosmological argument can't really be set alongside arguments like the argument from evil or arguments from divine hiddenness in the way you suggest in the first place: The conclusion the former can validly reach is usually not that *God* exists, but that there is a first cause or a necessary being or a creator or a cosmic designer or some such thing. To oppose the latter arguments, they would need to support the claim that something with *other* properties of unsurpassable greatness as well – like perfect love – exists. This is one of the reasons that theistic philosophers have taken to construing the evidence reported in the premises of cosmological and other such arguments *probabilistically*, as evidence in some sense supporting, though not entailing, the full claim of theism. And of course with probabilistic arguments come all of the problems of that dark domain. So – this is the long and the short of it – your extreme case may not be a realistic case at all. Either way though, whether it is or it isn't, it seems clear from what we've seen that in the vast majority of actual circumstances the argument from divine hiddenness, if persuasive, is capable of (reasonably) turning agnostics into atheists.

Just to add a further complication or two, let me point out that the argument from divine hiddenness, as I have developed it, is only one among several arguments focusing on the hiddenness of God's existence that ought to be explored here. Even if my argument, which refers to reasonable nonbelief in general, were to fail, it would always be possible to mount an argument referring, more narrowly, to the nonbelief of *this or that subclass* of reasonable nonbelievers. (Broad is the way that leads to destruction, or so it is said; it might therefore be good for anyone interested in divine hiddenness to recognize this narrower alternative!) Take, for example, those famous nonbelievers who have diligently sought for God and who would love to believe – who perhaps even live *as though* God is real – but without being provided with any experiential or other grounds sufficient for belief. It's not hard to see how considerations we have already discussed could be used again, and even more powerfully perhaps, to support the view that *such* nonbelief would not exist if there were a loving God. Not the least important feature of such an argument would be its ability to repel such counterattacks as the 'sin' strategy, and the objections of those who consider divine hiddenness necessary to preserve a certain kind of moral or intellectual freedom. I will say no more about this here. Suffice it to note that it is a possibility.

Another additional form of argument presupposes that at any rate some agnostics (and perhaps some one-time theists, too) may reasonably be driven to atheism by one or other of the arguments we have discussed and comments on something remarkable about that fact, which may provide yet further support for atheism – support which could negatively affect even the theism of those theists apparently unaffected by the previous arguments. I will only mention its main point, and leave you to consider it. Isn't it interesting that the only persons who clearly have the resources to defeat the arguments previously mentioned are individuals who *already believe*, and that some of those who are earnestly seeking to know and follow God, and who might have continued to do so as agnostics, are instead reduced by these arguments to the belief that there is *no* God? Put otherwise, the main point of this approach is that, for some conscientious agnostics, no defeaters for these arguments are available. Is this what we should expect if a loving God exists, given that this reduces the agnostic to atheism *and apparently removes any basis for theistic religious practice*? (If we add that some of these former agnostics were former believers, who indeed at one time took themselves to be in a personal relationship with God, we have a disturbing chain of events indeed.)

C: Yes, these are troubling considerations. And given the many possible formulations of the basic hiddenness claim, no doubt there are other arguments from divine hiddenness that have themselves not yet been revealed! It does seem that, given the content of our discussion, in some quarters not much hope for reasonable theistic belief remains.

S: Do you find yourself in one of those quarters?

C: I'm not so sure.

S: You seem distracted – what's going on?

C: Look, I know we've been at this for quite a while, but I want to run by you this idea that has been emerging as we talked today – I really just became fully conscious of it now. It's an idea that puts this whole hiddenness discussion into a different perspective. If it works, it may, among other things, cast enough doubt upon what you've said about the relation between talk of human beings and talk of the Divine to constitute a defeater for those claims.

S: By all means. Be my guest.

C: We have been assuming that much of the nature of God is known to us through reflection on what is great or good in human beings. Specifically, we have assumed – and it would seem that *any* argument from divine hiddenness as you've defined it is going to have to do this – that what is unsurpassably great is a nonhuman *personal agent*: a consciousness and agency separate from ourselves but in at least those respects similar to ourselves, and thus in some significant measure accessible to us and expressible by us. You have assumed this, with a large part of the tradition of reflection on such matters, all the way through – especially in your talk of a necessary connection between unsurpassable greatness and a self-revealing love of the sort we know in human persons. And while I started us off talking about mystery, I, too, have time and again slipped into thinking of the 'main facts' about God as known to us: God is the eternal and personal creator, omnipotent, omniscient, omnipresent, perfectly good and perfectly loving; and while there may be more to know about God, we've already nailed down the main items with this list!

S: So what's wrong with that view. Isn't it just a natural filling-out of the definition of 'God' we started with: a transcendent and unsurpassably great source of all things who works through all and is in all?

C: Well, that definition already makes a disputable assumption with its introduction of the little word 'who'. I know that most theologians who appeal to mystery still tacitly accept a personal God, and so long as they do, your argument can be brought to bear. But suppose we left out the 'who', and allowed for the possibility of an understanding of 'source' and 'working' that really had nothing to do with a separate consciousness and agency exercising thought and power as we presently know these things in human persons. Wouldn't we still want to say we had described something properly called 'God'? You've been nothing if not persuasive today, and I think your arguments may show the nonexistence of a personal God, as that notion is generally construed; but maybe for all of that they do not permit us to drop our concern with 'God'. Perhaps, indeed, they prompt us to enrich and deepen that notion, or at least to consider whether this may not yet be possible. Maybe this is what the hiddenness of the personal God will ultimately help to accomplish in the religious life of humankind.

S: Interesting. But I think we've left unsurpassable greatness behind if we drop the idea of a personal God. And without unsurpassable greatness, the attitudes of worship appropriate to belief in God are just out of place. What I mean is that I don't think you're talking about *God* anymore. And what about all those religious experiences apparently of a personal God?

C: To think that you should be defending such experiences!

S: I just mean we rightly take account of them when figuring out how God-language should be understood.

C: But surely you're aware that not all of the experiences of persons who take themselves to be in contact with God are of the personal sort! And as for unsurpassable greatness and worship: I think it may be – this is at the heart of my idea – that we have just left the idea of an unsurpassably great *personal* God behind (or at any rate opened ourselves to other options) if we consider the route I'm suggesting. Who's to say that what is unsurpassably great is personal? Not all traditions have thought that. Do we know enough to say that? Maybe we're just dead wrong about what belongs to unsurpassable greatness and someone else has got it right. Or maybe none of us can have much more than the formal idea of unsurpassable greatness. Maybe what fills it in is quite beyond us – at least where we're at. Sure, we can say, if we suppose God is a separate agent and has beliefs, like ourselves, that God's unsurpassability consists (in part) in God having the most effective agency possible, as well as absolutely impeccable beliefs and belief-forming processes, but this begs the huge question of whether unsurpassable greatness includes separate agency and belief *in the first place*! Since our own capacities are so evidently limited, how can we say with any confidence that the deepest facts about *unsurpassable* greatness do not in some manner inconceivable to us surpass even what we admire most about ourselves?

S: All right, suppose you're onto something here. Someone who considers this a possibility might nevertheless say that at each stage, we have to go with what seems to us to be essential to unsurpassable greatness *then*, and maybe, depending on what that is, we end up with an uncompromising atheism. Who knows, maybe there are other 'levels' of understanding where we'll change our minds, but as I say – who knows?

C: That's really my point – you seem to have got it now! – and it suggests a different way of looking at this: Maybe right now, at our present level of intellectual and spiritual development, by taking unsurpassable greatness seriously enough and nurturing the sort of humility and love of truth that are favored both in philosophy and in (mature) religion, we will find ourselves with *agnosticism* as to the precise content of 'unsurpassable greatness'– and, yes, as to whether the best human love really is a reliable guide to how God would be related to us. (Call this *theological* agnosticism.) Maybe, if God exists, opening ourselves up to this is the highest intellectual service of God we can render. Notice that one who takes this course need not also be agnostic about whether there is a God at all. Maybe because of certain experiences or arguments she feels that something than which nothing greater can be conceived exists, while – perhaps precisely because of the nature of the experience – not being willing (at least when uncorrupted by philosophy or theology) to say much about what that something is. We could call this position *qualified* agnosticism, I suppose, to distinguish its adherents both from theological agnostics who are also agnostic about whether God exists (call the latter position *total* agnosticism) and from those individuals who are agnostic about whether God exists but not theological agnostics (because of the prevalence of their position, we might call it *common* agnosticism). I won't call anyone 'traditional' for there are traditions – some better known than others – corresponding to all these positions. Now I'm thinking *here* primarily of someone who (whether in some minimal sense a believer or not) utilizes the possibility I've described as a way of engendering doubt about whether the properties we commonly ascribe to God in fact apply to God, if God exists. And such a person I will continue to call simply a theological agnostic.

S: All right. That's clear enough.

C: Now a theological agnostic could concede that the arguments you have developed may show that a loving personal God – where 'love' and 'personal' are given their usual meanings – does not exist. But maybe God exists and is not loving or personal, or at least not personal in the usual sense. This is not to say that we now ascribe to God features of *non*personal items in our experience: We simply, with due humility (and, perhaps, with respect for the unprobed regions of the imagination), suspend judgment on the matter. In so doing, we free ourselves from an assumption of your arguments – that God must be loving in your sense, if God exists – and this by taking even *more* seriously what led you to say that in the first place: the idea of unsurpassable greatness. And now we can at one and the same time say both that your argument may succeed – that reasonable nonbelief appears to show the nonexistence of a personal God – and that God may exist for all we know, leaving us free to pursue religious inquiry in the spirit in which it ought to be pursued. It's fascinating to consider, isn't it, that God may be hidden even more from believers of certain kinds than from agnostics? Maybe even common agnosticism is sometimes more purely religious than belief. Maybe this very awareness is itself a special sort of experience of the real God. These matters are surely worth thinking about. And maybe the reason we have for supposing them worth thinking about is at the same time reason enough to be suspicious of whatever it is that you take to support that critical presupposition of your argument concerning the love of God, and so a defeater for it.

S: Well, I must admit that there is something attractive in what you say, but . . .

C: Hey, look! Down the hall. Someone just went in that door.

S: Looks like we passed the room where everybody's meeting. Why don't we go see what's up?

C: Sure.

S: Will you look at that. It was Room 313, not 383 or 13 as we thought.

C: They've got a banner. Quite a colorful banner. What does it say? Can you see from here?

S: I can only make out the main words – 'philosophy' and 'poverty', I think.

C: That's right. I see them now: 'poverty' and 'philosophy'. Did we read the *title* of the discussion incorrectly too?

S: Who's that holding the banner? Wait a minute, isn't that C.S.?

C: I think I'd like to go get a closer look.

S: Sure, why not?

And so one by one our two philosophers enter Room 313. The Room itself they find to be much larger than might have been inferred from the low and narrow door. Indeed, they notice immediately that it has no discernible spatial limits. The door to the Room remains open after they walk through it, for it is always open. On its back, where no one has ever seen it, is a plaque upon which are engraved these words:

> hidden not from strong and weak
> from those who find and therefore seek
> this Room though One can hold us all
> none here is great and none is small

3

Deus Absconditus

MICHAEL J. MURRAY

> Awake, O Lord! Why do you sleep?
> Rouse yourself! Do not reject us forever.
> Why do you hide your face?
>
> Psalm 44:23–4

It is no surprise to discover that few (if any) have found the existence of God to be an obvious fact about the world. At least this is so in the sense in which we normally use the word "obvious," as when we say that it is *obvious* that the World Trade Center weighs more than a deck of cards or that it is *obvious* that Van Gogh is a better painter than I. Despite St. Paul's claim that God's eternal power and divine nature "have been clearly seen, being understood from what has been made" (Romans 1:20), few (if any) think that such is as "clearly seen" as the book you now hold in your hand.

This fact has raised troubles of at least two sorts for the theist. First, it leads the theist to wonder why God postpones that time at which, according to Christian tradition, we will see God "face to face." Since, at that time, God *will* be as clearly seen as the book you now hold in your hand, what accounts for the delay? Why is there this period of the earthly life where God's reality is less than obvious? Second, the theist has to confront the fact that God's hiddenness seems to lead a number of people to reject God's existence outright and thus to be a contributing cause to what the traditional theist would regard as a great evil: unbelief. For some, the route to atheism is indeed found in the fact that there is, in the famous words of Bertrand Russell, "not enough evidence." But more recently, some have argued that the hiddenness of God provides positive, in fact decisive, evidence in favor of atheism. J. L. Schellenberg, in a recent work, argues that if the God of Western theism exists, he would provide evidence of this fact sufficient to render reasonable unbelief impossible. Since, however, such evidence is not forthcoming, such a God does not exist.

Theists in the Judeo-Christian tradition have often argued that the hiddenness of God finds its explanation in the Fall and subsequent Curse. Sometimes, the passage immediately following the one from St. Paul's epistle to the

Romans cited above is taken as evidence that hiddenness should be explained in just this way, at least for the Christian, since Paul there goes on to claim that "For although they knew God, they neither glorified Him as God nor gave thanks to Him, but their thinking became futile and their foolish hearts were darkened" (Romans 1:21). Yet, while the Fall may play some part in explaining the hiddenness of God, the Judeo-Christian theist would be hard pressed to lay the full explanation for hiddenness here. The reason is simply that the Judeo-Christian Scriptures seem to teach that even prior to the Curse, there is a measure of divine hiddenness already. Even in Genesis 3, one finds that Adam and Eve think that they can somehow escape the presence of God by hiding from God in the garden (Genesis 3:8–10). Although it is Adam and Eve that do the hiding here, still the presence of God, while still obvious to them in a certain sense, is escapable in a way it seems not to be when one looks at descriptions of the beatified state as described, for example, in Revelation 22:1–5. In what follows I will offer an account of divine hiddenness that attempts to allay the two types of concerns raised above.

I. Divine Hiddenness and "Morally Significant Freedom"

In an earlier essay I argued that at least one of the reasons that God must remain hidden is that failing to do so would lead to a loss of morally significant freedom on the part of creatures.[1] The reason, in brief, is that making us powerfully aware of the truth of God's existence would suffice to coerce (at least many of) us into behaving in accordance with God's moral commands. Such awareness can lead to this simply because God's presence would provide us with overpowering incentives which would make choosing the good ineluctable for us.

I will flesh out this account in some detail below, but before doing so, let's take notice of the overall strategy being pursued here. Theists have often argued that morally significant freedom is a good (indeed, a very good) thing. Thus, in creating the world, God would seek to establish conditions that would permit the existence of such freedom. A variety of such conditions are necessary, but among them is that there not be overwhelmingly powerful incentives present in the environment which consistently coerce or otherwise force creatures to follow a particular course of action.

Theists have, at least of late, lain a great deal of explanatory weight on the need to preserve creaturely freedom. Here I will attempt to lay the explanation of divine hiddenness there. Others have sought to lay the explanation for all (or at least much) of the evil that the world contains there as well. In such cases, the argument is roughly that morally significant freedom is an intrinsic good, and that though evil is a necessary consequence of allowing creatures to have freedom of such a sort, the intrinsic goodness of freedom outweighs evils liabilities.[2] The evil in question might not only be of the (moral) sort that we read about in the headlines of the newspaper, but of the (epistemic) sort in view in this essay, namely, the unbelief of great numbers of people due to the lack of evidence entailed by God's hiddenness.

But there is something odd about laying all this freight at freedom's doorstep; and it is an oddity that seems to be too little noticed by analytic Christian philosophers. We can begin to see what is odd by first noticing that it is not the intrinsic goodness of libertarian freedom *simpliciter* that is at issue here. For if it were, it seems that libertarian freedom simply could not do the work it has been given to do in these accounts. The reason for this is that there seems to be no reason why God could not create a world with libertarian free beings who are incapable of doing evil. If human minds were created in such a way that they were not, say, even capable of deliberating about evil courses of action, it might still be the case that multiple courses of action would be open to them given the history of the world and the laws of nature. No doubt, this would restrict the kinds of behavior that such creatures could engage in (assuming that it must be possible for one to deliberate about a course of action for one to be able to freely choose it). But God surely restricts the sorts of activities we can choose to undertake in all sorts of ways by not only limiting the kinds of things we can think about (by, say, limiting the sorts of cognitive equipment we have), but even by limiting the kinds of things we are physically capable of accomplishing (by limiting the sorts of bodily equipment we have). It is hard to see why similar constraints could not simply preclude deliberation about evil courses of action, while stopping short of full blown determinism. If this is right, libertarian freedom *simpliciter* cannot explain or justify the existence of evil.

It is, then, libertarian freedom *to choose between good and evil courses of action* that is important here. And the theist might argue that this is just what was meant by "morally significant freedom" in the first place. Without the ability to choose freely between good and evil courses of action, freedom would have no moral significance and thus would not be an intrinsic good.[3] What is odd about this story, however, is just how rare this supposed intrinsic good is among rational beings on the Christian scheme of things. For if we consider the sorts of rational beings Christians admit to being aware of, it seems that only one type of being has freedom of this sort, and beings of this type possess it only for an infinitesimally small span of their existence. Traditional Christian theology holds that neither God, angels, nor demons have such freedom, and that of human beings, neither beatified nor damned have it either. Thus, freedom of this sort is found only among human beings during that narrow span of their existence spent in the earthly life.

All of this seems to argue that morally significant freedom of the sort described above might not be best regarded as the intrinsic good many have claimed it to be. If it is such a good, it would be odd, to say the least, that neither God, angels, nor the beatified possess it.

We might, however, look at the worth of morally significant freedom in creatures in another way. Reflecting on the rarity of such freedom as it is described above leads to the question: Why does God allow creatures to pass through this earthly phase of existence in the first place? Since all rational creatures will end up either perfected in the beatific vision, choosing good forever, or separated from God, choosing evil forever, why have them pass through this prior stage during which they stand poised between these two extremes?

When posed this way, I think an answer readily suggests itself, namely, that the function of this earthly life, a time during which we are capable of making free choices between morally good and evil courses of action, is to have the opportunity to develop morally significant characters. Developing characters which have moral significance requires that they be chosen and cultivated by their bearers. And this can only be done if creatures are first given the sort of morally significant freedom we have been discussing heretofore. Philosophers have taken to calling this sort of character development "soul-making," following the phrase coined by John Hick.[4] Thus, we might say that the function of the earthly life on this view is soul-making, and that a necessary condition for soul-making is morally significant libertarian freedom. Libertarian freedom alone simply will not do here since the point of character development is that one has the opportunity to choose to do *good* or *evil*, and by so choosing to become either a lover and imitator of God, or one who "worships and serves the creature rather than the creator."[5]

Thus, even if we have reason to doubt the *intrinsic* worth of morally significant freedom, there is good reason to think that it has significant *instrumental* value as a necessary condition for rational creatures engaging in soul-making. Of course, possessing the capacity for morally significant soul-making is not sufficient. In addition, external constraints on the agent must not preclude the possibility of the agent at least frequently being able to choose freely between good and evil courses of action. What I was claiming above is that among those conditions is the absence of circumstances which provide overwhelming incentives for creatures to choose only good or only evil. For if the moral environment contained such incentives, the creature with the capacity to choose freely would be precluded from exercising that ability and thus blocked from engaging in the sort of soul-making that makes freedom (and the earthly life) valuable in the first place.

The result of all this is that God must remain hidden to a certain extent to prevent precluding incentives from being introduced. Here then we find an answer to the first concern regarding hiddenness. At least one reason why we do not see God face to face from the beginning is that to do so would be to lose the ability to develop morally significant characters. According to the Christian scriptures, God calls his creatures to be "imitators" of him.[6] But to do this in a way that yields moral significance requires that character be to some extent self-wrought.[7] And soul-making of this sort requires divine hiddenness, at least for a time.

As mentioned above, J. L. Schellenberg has offered an argument for atheism on the basis of divine hiddenness. Along the way, Schellenberg critiques a variety of accounts of hiddenness a theist might offer, including a soul-making account of the sort sketched above. In what follows I will develop this account in more detail against the background of and in response to this critique of Schellenberg's.

II. Schellenberg's Critique of the Soul-Making Response

In his wonderfully provocative book, *Divine Hiddenness and Human Reason*, J. L. Schellenberg has presented an extended argument that the extent to which evidence for the existence God is not forthcoming, in conjunction with certain other plausible assumptions, entails the truth of atheism. This argument, which I will call "The Atheist Argument," is presented by Schellenberg as follows:

(1) If there is a God, he is perfectly loving.
(2) If a perfectly loving God exists, reasonable nonbelief does not occur.
(3) Reasonable nonbelief does occur.
(4) No perfectly loving God exists.
(5) There is no God.[8]

After an extended presentation and defense of the argument and its premises in the first half of the book, Schellenberg goes on, in the second half, to discuss various responses theists might lodge against its premises. Specifically, he focuses on theistic critiques of premise (2) since, he argues, only this premise of the argument is open to question. In this section I will examine Schellenberg's critique of the soul-making account and argue that his critique ultimately fails. As a result, the theist has plausible grounds for rejecting (2) and thus for rejecting The Atheist Argument.

Preliminary Considerations

Because Schellenberg recognizes that most theists will want to take issue with (2), he begins his survey of potential theistic responses by discussing what it is that the theist must show in order to defeat the premise. He contends that,

(2) is false if and only if there is a state of affairs in the actual world which it would be logically impossible for God to bring about without permitting the occurrence of at least one instance of reasonable non-belief, for the sake of which God would be willing to sacrifice the good of belief and all it entails.[9]

As noted above, the second half of the book is devoted to explaining and critiquing various theistic attempts to provide accounts which attack (2) in just the way Schellenberg suggests. The first such attempt roughly mirrors the account described at the end of Section I. On this view, the state of affairs that God wants to actualize which logically requires him to permit some instances of reasonable unbelief consists of (i) creatures who have the capacity for acting freely and (ii) a world suitably constituted for the exercise of that freedom. On this view, if God were to make his existence evident to too great an extent, an extent that would rule out reasonable non-belief, we would all become powerfully aware of the importance of not only believing in His existence but also obeying His will. Yet such a powerful awareness of God's existence and moral will would suffice to overwhelm the freedom of the creature in a way that would preclude further morally significant free actions by the creature. Because it would be utterly obvious to us that God, the one responsible for temporal happiness as well as eternal bliss or damnation, exists and wills that we act in certain ways, we would be compelled to believe and act accordingly. As a result, God must keep His existence veiled to a certain extent in order to insure that this sort of overwhelming does not occur.

To know whether or not such a claim is plausible, we first need to know whether God's revealing himself in the way Schellenberg thinks he would (and in fact *must* given the fact that God is a perfectly loving being) could lead to such a result.

It is noteworthy that Schellenberg has only argued that God's loving nature entails that God would make his *existence* known to creatures in such a way that reasonable unbelief is not possible. Schellenberg makes no claims about whether or not God's loving nature would also require that God make known the existence of other facts that might be necessary for human beings to be able to attain ultimate human fulfillment. In one sense, this minimalist strategy helps Schellenberg, since one might think that if God simply made his *existence* clearly known, there is no reason to think that this would introduce any incentives that might serve to derail human freedom. Bare knowledge that God exists simply doesn't seem to have any immediate practical import.

One might, of course, agree that God would make his existence plainly known, but might further argue that God's loving nature further entails that other facts would be made known as well. Many theists claim that ultimate human fulfillment requires not only belief in God, but a number of other beliefs about what it takes to be rightly related to God as well. If loving entails seeking the well-being of the beloved, God would surely seek to make the necessary information for human fulfillment available. As a result, I will assume for the moment (as I think all parties in the dispute must) that, all other things being equal, God's love would lead him to make us aware not merely of his bare existence, but also of all of the other truths needed to obtain our complete temporal and eternal happiness. Surely such a revelation would carry significant practical import. Nonetheless, for those who want to stick to Schellenberg's more minimalist strategy, I will return to address that view shortly.

III.   The Soul-Making Response to (2)

Given my more robust notion of what divine love entails, we can see why there might be good reason for God to remain hidden on the soul-making account. At the end of Section I I noted that introduction of powerful motives to choose either only good or only evil would preclude the possibility of soul-making. Instead, the environment needs to be such that there are, at least in a number of cases, incentives to choose to do good and incentives to choose to do evil, such that neither incentive induces desires that overwhelm all competing desires.

Yet surely a probabilifying demonstration or revelation of God's existence and plan for human well-being as described above would introduce just such incentives. If God were to reveal Himself and His will in the way required to eliminate reasonable nonbelief, any desire that we might have to believe or act in ways contrary to that which has been revealed would be overwhelmed. Our fear of punishment, or at least our fear of the prospect of missing out on a very great good, would compel us to believe the things that God has revealed and to act in accordance with them. But in doing this, God would have removed the ability for self-determination since there are no longer good and evil courses of action between which creatures could freely and deliberately choose. Thus we would all be compelled to choose in accordance with the divine will and would all thereby become conformed to the divine image. However, a character wrought in this fashion would not be one for which we are responsible since it does not derive from morally significant choosing. It has instead been forced upon us. Richard Swinburne, defending a position regarding divine hiddenness summarizes these considerations in the following paragraph, also quoted by Schellenberg:

The existence of God would be for [human beings] an item of evident common knowledge. Knowing that there was a God, men would know that their most secret thoughts and actions were known to God; and knowing that he was just, they would expect for their bad actions and thoughts whatever punishment was just. . . . In such a world men would have little temptation to do wrong – it would be the mark of both prudence and reason to do what was virtuous. Yet a man only has a genuine choice of destiny if he has reasons for pursuing either good or evil courses of action.[10]

Schellenberg emphasizes that on this view, desires for evil would not cease to exist were we to be given such a revelation, it is just that powerful new desires would be introduced, e.g., the desire to avoid punishment, with a strength that overwhelms contrary desires and renders them "inefficacious." He cites coercion as a similar case in which the introduction of a new desire renders all competing desires inefficacious. I may desire, says Schellenberg, to go to the university bookstore to buy a copy of a newly released book. Yet, if some crazy ideologue, bent on keeping scholars from being exposed to the ideas in the book, threatens me with serious physical harm if I go to the bookstore, I won't go. My desire to go is still present, but this desire has been overwhelmed by a newly introduced desire, the desire to avoid the serious physical harm.

Schellenberg thus summarizes the soul-making case against (2) of the Atheist Argument as follows:

(16) In the situation in question [that is, where God reveals himself in such powerful fashion that reasonable unbelief is rendered impossible], persons would have strong prudential reasons for not doing wrong.

(17) Because of the strength of these reasons, it would require little in the way of an act of will to do what is right – there is little temptation to do wrong, contrary desires would be overcome.

(18) Where there is little temptation to do wrong, persons lack a genuine choice of destiny.

(19) Therefore, in the situation in question no one would have a choice of destiny.[11]

IV. Incentives, Coercion, and "Soul-Making"

The remainder of this chapter in Schellenberg's book is occupied with an assessment of (16) through (19). Here Schellenberg contends that there are good reasons to reject both (16) and (17). Before looking at his criticisms of these premises however, it will prove worthwhile to try to fill in a few more details in this argument. How exactly, one might wonder, would probabilify-ing knowledge of God's existence and will for human creatures influence our desires? What does it take for desires to be sufficiently strong to overwhelm competing desires? How does this overwhelming prevent our ability to engage in self-determination exactly? Answering these questions will help us both to understand the force of Schellenberg's critique of (16) and (17) and to see what, if anything, can be said in reply.

Recall that on the soul-making account the trouble that arises in a world in which God is not to some extent hidden is that incentives are introduced which serve to *coerce* otherwise free creatures, in ways which render them incapable of soul-making. Thus, if God were to make himself plainly evident to us in the ways described above, we would find ourselves confronted with what would amount to threats (if God were to reveal disobedience as subject to pun-ishment) or offers (if God were to reveal obedience as a source of temporal and eternal well-being) that would suffice to coerce human behavior.[12] In what follows I will speak generally about the ways in which God's revealing himself in perspicuous fashion can introduce "incentives" which can "overwhelm" competing desires. One can think of such incentives as consisting of either threats or offers, though I will frequently use examples drawn from cases of coercion via threats.

It should be obvious that not just any incentives will suffice to overwhelm our desires for contrary courses of action. The incentive must be sufficiently strong that it outweighs the desires I have for those things which are inconsistent with acting in accordance with it. Let's say that a desired course of action, A_1, renders competing desired courses of action, A_2-A_n, *ineligible* when A_1 is sufficiently compelling that it makes it impossible for me reasonably to choose A_2-A_n over A_1.[13] We can then say that an individual, P, is *coerced* to do some act, A, by a threat when a desire is induced by a threat, which desire is sufficiently compelling that it renders every other course of action except A ineligible for P.[14]

This next leads us to wonder what it is that makes desires induced by threats "sufficiently compelling." One might think that the only relevant variable is the *strength* of the threat, i.e., the degree to which the state of affairs that the threatener is promising to bring about (if the conditions of the threat are not met) are disutile for the threatened in comparison with the disutility of performing the act commanded by the threatener. Thus if a stranger threatens to call me a ninny if I fail to hand over my money to her, this threat would not compel me in the least since I am not a bit concerned about being called a name by this stranger and I would like to keep my money. On the other hand, if someone threatens to shoot me in the leg if I fail to give her my money, I would surely give her the money since I care a great deal about my bodily integrity, far more than keeping the few dollars I carry with me.

However, a moment's reflection should make it clear that threat strength alone does not determine whether or not a desire induced by a threat is sufficiently compelling to coerce me. To see why this is so, compare the following two cases. In the first case, a maximum security prison assigns one guard to each prisoner and gives the guards orders to shoot all who attempt to escape. Here the threat strength is very high. Thus, one can suppose that prisoners in such a situation would find all courses of action which include an attempted escape ineligible. In the second case, prisoners are again being watched by guards who have orders to shoot any who attempt to escape. However, in this case, there are only two guards on duty for the entire prison at any one time, and they are perched high in a tower. While the threat strength is identical for prisoners in both prisons, it seems clear that prisoners in the latter case might find an escape attempt eligible. The reason for this difference, presumably, is that the prisoners in the second case might believe that the probability that the threat could be successfully carried out is quite low. The guards, the prisoner might reason, might be too busy watching other prisoners to notice an attempted escape, or they might miss when shooting from such a great distance. In any case, the prisoner's belief that the threat cannot be successfully carried out significantly mitigates the compelling force of the desire induced by the threat. Thus, in addition to threat strength, another factor, which I call *threat imminence*, is relevant. We can define threat imminence as the degree to which the threatened believes the consequences of the threat will be successfully carried out if the terms of the threat are not met.

But notice that there is more than one way that threats can be imminent or distant as I have characterized imminence. While the sort of imminence described above, which I will call *probabilistic imminence*, is one species of imminence, there are at least two others. First, there is *temporal imminence*. When the threatened understands that there will be a significant lapse between the time that he fails to meet the conditions of the threat and the time that the threat is carried out, the desire induced by the threat is less compelling than when the consequences will follow immediately upon the failure to meet the conditions. Thus, if someone was to threaten to give me a powerful shock that would hospitalize me for two weeks if I failed to hand over my money immediately, this situation would be more compelling than one in which a threatener threatened to poke me with a delayed-reaction cattle prod which would cause me to receive the same shocking sensation fifty years hence, if I failed to hand over my money now. Even though the threat strength is the same, and even though I might have an equal degree of certainty that the threat will be carried out in both cases, I am less compelled by the threat in the latter case than I am in the former.

The final species of threat imminence is *epistemic imminence*. We might say that epistemic imminence is the degree to which the disutility of the threatened consequence is *epistemically forceful* to the threatened. To illustrate the role of epistemic imminence consider the fact that massive advertising campaigns against smoking, drug use, and drinking and driving have been successful in reducing the incidence of these behaviors. In all three cases, no one believes that the purpose of such advertisements is to convey information to the target audience that members of that audience do not already have. Instead, the goal is to make the disutility of engaging in that behavior more epistemically powerful. By repeatedly showing accident scenes strewn with dead or mangled bodies, people become more powerfully aware of how dangerous drinking and driving is.

Yet even these two factors, threat strength and threat imminence, are not sufficient to determine the degree to which threat-induced desires are compelling. This should be clear from the fact that two individuals, in circumstances where threat strength and threat imminence are identical for each, might feel differently about the eligibility of their alternatives. Two prisoners might find themselves under threats of identical strength and imminence and yet one might feel that an escape attempt is still eligible while another may not. One might simply feel that a probability of .5 that he will be shot is a risk too great to bear, whereas the other might think that the same probability makes for a "good bet." This factor, which I will call *threat-indifference*, is the third factor determining the strength of the compelling force of a threat. Some individuals are simply more threat-indifferent than others. Threat-indifference can be described in two ways. One might say that threat-indifference is the degree to which one finds pleasure in taking the risks posed by failing to abide by conditions of a threat. It might also be described as a sense of indifference to one's own well-being in the face of a threat. However we characterize this trait, it is surely relevant since something like it is needed to explain why, when two individuals are in the same circumstances, one is coerced while the other is not.

In sum, there are at least three factors which determine the degree to which a threat-induced desire is compelling: threat strength, threat imminence, and threat-indifference. The degree to which the desire compels me to act in accordance with the threat is directly proportional to the first two and inversely proportional to the third.

V.   An Assessment of Schellenberg's
Critique of (16) and (17)

With this in mind, let us return to Schellenberg's critique of (16) and (17) and see to what extent they are successful. Schellenberg raises two problems for (16) and I will treat each in turn. First, he charges that the only way in which probabilifying revelations of God's existence and moral will could provide strong prudential reasons for not doing wrong, is if the knowledge acquired as a result of this revelation were *certain*.

The situation referred to [by Swinburne] is . . . one in which humans know for *certain* that there is a God and in which whatever reasons humans take themselves to have for doing good actions they consider themselves *certainly* to have. A situation in which the evidence available is [merely] sufficient for belief . . . is, however, not of this sort. . . . In any case, given evidence [merely] sufficient for belief instead of proof, one who is under the influence of desires for what is "correctly believed to be evil" is likely to seize upon the margin of possible error: believing, but not certain of God's existence, or of punishment, she may well move, through self-deception, from the belief that God exists and will punish bad actions to [other beliefs which deny at least one of the two conjuncts]. . . . If self-deception *is* still open to individuals, then clearly they are still in a position to yield so bad desires and so retain a genuine choice of destiny.[15]

Schellenberg holds here that unless we know with *certainty* that a threatener (God in this case) exists and will carry out the threat, we cannot be coerced,

since it is always open to us to deceive ourselves about the truth of propositions we know less than certainly. As a result, it is false that these probabilifying revelations would suffice to provide the recipient of the revelation with
strong prudential reasons for not doing evil (and correspondingly, with overwhelming incentives), since one can always reappropriate ones beliefs in such
a way as to eliminate these strong prudential reasons.

But is this true? We might recast Schellenberg's point as the claim that
probabilistic threat imminence must be maximal if a threat is to be sufficient to
coerce. But clearly that is false. Consider a case in which someone comes up
behind me late at night in Manhattan, sticks a small cylindrical object in my
back, and demands that I hand over my money or be shot. I do not know with
certainty that this threat can be carried out. There is some non-zero probability
that, even if this mugger has a gun, he also has an overridingly strong aversion
to shooting people. Furthermore, there is some non-zero probability that the
cylinder I feel in my back is not a gun but a carrot. One might suppose there
is even some non-zero probability that someone has surgically inserted a
bullet-proof vest under my skin in my infancy that would, in this case, prevent
me from being harmed by this mugger. And yet, while all of these things have
some non-zero probability, none of these things matter in the least. Even if I
thought there was only a .5 probability that the mugger would carry through on
his threat, *I* would be coerced into handing over the money.

And something similar holds in the case under discussion here. Even if I
do not know with certainty that God exists or that He will bring temporal
and/or eternal punishments on me if I fail to believe or act in certain ways, I
can still be coerced into acting or believing in those ways. This is not to deny
that if probabilistic threat imminence falls below a certain point that I will not
be coerced by the threat. Still, the sort of probabilifying revelation that critics
of theism such as Schellenberg have in mind would insure that probabilistic
threat imminence would remain above this threshold.

However, Schellenberg has one further problem with (16), a problem which
also amounts to his only substantive critique of (17). He seems to think that
even if the probabilistic imminence problem is soluble, there is an additional
problem concerning temporal imminence that is not. The recipient of the clear
and evident revelation will believe, he claims, that the punishments attending
failure to believe or act in a certain way will be either temporal, eternal, or
both. That is, the divine retribution may be meted out immediately, or it may
be postponed to the after-life (in hell, say), or both. However, if punishments
are *only* eternal, and, he claims, our experience surely teaches us that this, if
anything, is the case,[16] we again find that threats of such punishment would
fail to produce strong prudential reasons for not doing wrong, against (16).
Furthermore, Schellenberg contends, in his only significant argument against
(17), that even if such strong prudential reasons were to arise, they could easily

be ignored or shoved willfully into the background of our deliberation. As a result, it is false that the desires to do evil would be overwhelmed:

> Human beings, it seems, might very well conceive of God as justly lenient in the moment of desire, and of punishment as, at worst, an afterlife affair, and hence find themselves in a situation of temptation [to engage in evil] after all. . . . As soon as punishment is pushed off into the future, rendered less immediate and concrete, the force of any desires I may have to *avoid* punishment is reduced. . . . If punishment is seen as something in the future, its deterrent effect must be greatly reduced . . . I suggest therefore, that it is only if an individual believes that God's policy of punishment implies that a failure to do good actions will in the *here and now* result in bodily harm or loss of life, that the motivating effect of his belief can plausibly be viewed as great.[17]

No doubt what Schellenberg is pointing to here is the role of temporal imminence in coercion. Greater temporal imminence translates into greater compelling force of the threat.

The adequacy of this criticism depends on how we answer two questions. First, is Schellenberg correct in his contention that the recipient of these probabilifying revelations would come to believe that the punishment for wrongdoing was ultimately to be meted out in eternity alone? If not, then his argument that one would not be coerced by such revelation due to the great temporal distance between performing the evil action and the punishment inflicted for it fails. Second, is it true that if punishment were to be meted out solely in eternity the temporal distance between performing the bad action and receiving the punishment would be great enough to mitigate the force of the threat and leave the creature free for soul-making? If so, then despite the fact that the "threat" will not be carried out until later, the creature will still be left with multiple eligible courses of action, and these will be sufficient to allow him or her to engage in soul-making.

It seems to me that the answer to the first question is certainly no and the answer to the second question is probably also no. Schellenberg argues that even if we were to believe, initially, that punishments for wrongdoing would be forthcoming immediately after an evil act is committed, experience would cure us of this error. Looking at others, or ourselves, it is obvious that there are a number of evils that we "get away with." And this may seem enough to make his point. But is it? Even if there are some evil acts for which we receive no temporal punishment (that we know of), all the theist must hold is that *on some occasions* we believe that evil-doing is met with temporal punishments. That alone can provide sufficient probabilistic imminence to yield coercion. Consider again the case of the mugger discussed above. Let's say that I know that during the recent rise in muggings, police have determined that only half of the muggers in fact have guns, guns which they inevitably use if the victim resists. The other half try to mug victims using mere water pistols. It does not at all seem implausible that this knowledge would make me any less coerced when a mugger approaches me and asks for my money. What this shows is that even if we agree with Schellenberg that experience shows us that negative temporal consequences do not *inevitably* follow our evil acts, our belief that such negative consequences *sometimes* follow evil acts can suffice for coercion.[18]

Furthermore, while it is admittedly true that reducing temporal imminence reduces the compelling force of a threat, it seems unlikely that pushing the threat of punishment for wrong-doing off into the afterlife in this case will suffice for mitigating its coercive force. The first reason for this is that, at least on the traditional Christian view, the punishment described in eternity is so great in magnitude and duration, viz., maximal and eternal, that the temporal distance suggested by the average human life span seems unlikely to mitigate the coercive force of the threat to any great degree. This reply gains even more force when one realizes that, while one's life span may be some seventy or so years, a given life might continue only for a few more minutes or hours. As a result, it is unreasonable to assume that the coercive force of the threat is mitigated by the fact that the punishment will not be realized for some number of years since, for all we know, it might be realized in the twinkling of an eye. We might liken the recipient of this probabilifying revelation to a victim of an extortion attempt who is told, "If you fail to carry out the plan, we will kill you. You never know when – maybe when you least expect it. But sometime, one of us will hunt you down and finish you off." The victim here might assume that it will take them a long time to track him down and so he might refuse to comply. But since the recipient of this threat is unsure how long it will take for the threateners to find him, it is likely that a threat of this sort would nonetheless be coercive, and that is all we really need here. If many people, or even some people, would find a threat of this sort coercive, and the threat implied by the "clear and evident revelation" Schellenberg describes is of this sort, this seems to provide God with good reason for remaining hidden.[19]

At the end of Section II I noted that Schellenberg's official line of argument is that God's love entails that God would make his existence known to creatures. There I argued further that similar considerations should lead us to think that God's love equally entails that God would also reveal to creatures facts relevant to their achieving human flourishing, especially when those facts are accessible only via revelation. Let's call these two positions respectively the weaker and the stronger positions (weaker not being used pejoratively here, but merely to indicate that Schellenberg makes weaker claims concerning what God's love entails about what God would reveal about himself).

Note that while Schellenberg commits himself only to the weaker position, he is, as the discussion in this section makes clear, more than willing to dispute with those who hold the stronger view. Throughout this section we have seen that Schellenberg is willing to make the case that even if the stronger view is correct, the problem of divine hiddenness is no less severe. None of this is a problem for his own position of course, quite the contrary. For if he can show that the divine hiddenness entails atheism on the stronger view, it would *a fortiori* do so on the weaker view as well.

Here I have tried to show that Schellenberg's critique of the stronger view fails. But one can imagine Schellenberg nonetheless feeling unscathed here, since he doesn't endorse the stronger view in the first place. Even if the case against the stronger view fails, that doesn't undermine the original argument, an argument committed only to the weaker view. Can Schellenberg rest comfortably with this response?

I think not, for two reasons. The first reason is that I think that the stronger view is true (even *obviously* so). But even if one disagrees on that score, there is a second reason for thinking the weaker view problematic. To see the trouble, recall that the soul-making response to the problem of hiddenness holds that two bits of information serve to coerce creatures. The first is that God exists, and the second is that he is a rewarder of those who seek him (or that he punishes those who turn from him). Note that the greater the uncertainty about either of these facts, the lower the probabilistic imminence and thus, correspondingly, the lower the coercive pressure. But more importantly, insofar as one of these facts becomes more obvious, the greater the probabilistic imminence and thus the greater the coercive pressure. The result is that if God were to make his bare existence *more obvious* to creatures, he would have to make the corresponding facts about human fulfillment (or misery) based on a relationship with God *more hidden*. The problem here is that it is hard to see how such a scenario is one that could be favored by a loving God at all. Surely it would not be an act of love of God towards creatures to keep facts about human flourishing tucked safely behind the counter simply in order to make his existence clearly known. As a result, the soul-making response carries with it grounds for thinking the stronger view preferable to the weaker one.

VI. "Two Final Points"

Before closing, Schellenberg raises two final problems for the soul-making account. While both of these points are interesting, I will speak mostly to the first, with just a few words reserved for the second. Schellenberg points out that while the discussion up to this point has focused on what might happen if God were to reveal Himself to creatures in a certain probabilifying way, our inquiry need not be limited to merely hypothetical examples:

[My] claims may be tested by reference to real life situations in which people consider themselves to have experienced God and are convinced of his existence and sustaining presence, and of his moral demands. . . . Now such people seem quite capable of doing what they believe to be wrong . . . [which] provides my response to [the soul-making account] with additional support.[20]

Here Schellenberg points out that we have concrete examples of cases where, even though one sincerely believes that God has revealed Himself in a forceful way, that believer still struggles with wrongdoing. He cites the example of the apostle Paul who clams to have been converted through a powerful theophany and yet still struggled with his desires to do evil. Schellenberg seems to understate himself when he claims that this provides his case with "additional support." One might be inclined to think that this is the trump card. If one can cite cases from a theist's own scriptures in which these grand theophanies are given, and yet the recipients are not coerced into believing or acting in accord with the divine will, would this not show the theist decisively that divine hiddenness is not required to maintain the integrity of human freedom, contrary to the claims of the soul-making account?

The answer is yes and no. It does show that *some* individuals can be the recipients of strong, epistemically imminent threats and yet still remain uncoerced by those threats. But it does not show that all, or even very many, people would be able to receive such revelations without being coerced. Recall that the theist is arguing here that God would not reveal Himself in such a way that this revelation would overwhelm His free creatures and preclude them from engaging in "soul-making." And it seems reasonable to further hold that God would want such self-determination to be available to *all* free creatures, not merely some. As a result, while some creatures might be able to receive probabilifying revelations, and still remain free to engage in soul-making, others may not. Thus, the theist ought to argue that God *will* provide such revelations to those who can receive them and still remain free in the required way. As a result, rather than shy away from such biblical examples as Saul on the road to Damascus or the Israelites at Meribah, the theist might actually *expect* that there would be such cases. What the theist can deny, however, is that such powerful revelations would be *common*.

Above I noted that Schellenberg's critique of (16) and (17) amounts to an appeal to the role of probabilistic and temporal imminence in producing coerced behavior. What he raises in this first of his two final remarks is an objection based on the balance between the two remaining factors, epistemic imminence and threat indifference. The fact is that some individuals are more threat indifferent than others. Those who have a high degree of threat indifference can tolerate a revelation implying a threat which has greater epistemic imminence, and still remain free in the way required for soul-making. But since not everyone will have this high degree of threat indifference, we should not expect revelations of high epistemic imminence to be the norm. This gives the theist good reason for denying that God would produce grand scale theophanies complete with parting clouds, lightening bolts and thunder claps, where God proclaims His existence, etc. to all of the worlds inhabitants. The variability of threat indifference across human beings just would not permit *this* sort of business. Still God might make His existence evident to everyone in more subtle ways, ways that mitigate the *epistemic imminence* of the threat involved and thus mitigate the coercive force of the attending threat.

There is, however, an important response available to the defender of the argument from hiddenness at this point.[21] At most, the argument I give above shows that we should not expect grand public theophanies to be common. But that does not prevent God from making his existence known to creatures by way of private religious experience. In fact, a glance at the recent literature in philosophy of religion would lead one to think that this is the way religious believers in fact come into cognitive contact with God in the first place. Wouldn't it at least be reasonable to expect that God would make his existence as evident to each creature as it could be via religious experience, tailoring the epistemic imminence to the threat indifference of each creature so as not to coerce him or her? Nothing said above seems to preclude this. And yet, the defender of the argument from hiddenness could claim, this expectation is frustrated as well. For surely, each individual is not the recipient of this sort of religious experience.

This is an interesting and important response, one that deserves a more extensive treatment than I can give it here. A complete response would require a separate essay, I will only attempt to sketch an outline of a response here.[22]

To respond to the "private revelation" view in detail, we would first have to know a bit more about how its advocate understands religious experience. While much of this is contested territory, I propose that we regard religious experience, like sensory experience, as beginning with a perceiver coming to be in a state of directly perceiving some state of affairs, a state which provides the perceiver with *grounds* for coming to hold certain dispositional or occurent beliefs. But being in possession of the grounds and forming beliefs on those grounds are two distinct perceptual moments. Even in ordinary cases of sensory experience, we are in possession of grounds which are sufficient to lead suitably disposed perceivers to form a variety of beliefs. The process of forming beliefs upon being in possession of certain perceptual grounds is one which is in turn dependent on other dispositions had by the perceiver. And there is little doubt that at least some of these dispositions are under the perceiver's direct or indirect voluntary control.

Thus I can train myself to form true beliefs about the species of plant I am perceiving by forming dispositions that lead me to have certain beliefs when

I come to be in possession of certain grounds (these might be visual, tactile, or olfactory sensory grounds). In doing so I have indirect voluntary control over my belief-forming capacities. Likewise I can exercise direct voluntary control over belief-forming dispositions when I, for example, will myself to be more attentive to my surroundings. When I am told that I need to be careful of poisonous snakes in an area where I am hiking, I can voluntarily heighten my awareness, making me more apt to form beliefs about the presence of snakes than I would be if I were oblivious to the danger.

In the case of religious experience, God can provide the perceiver with certain religious experiential grounds, but whether those grounds will suffice to form true beliefs, or any beliefs at all, will depend in at least some measure on whether or not the perceiver has disposed himself to rightly forming beliefs on the basis of those grounds. It is a significant part of the Christian story of the Fall that one place where we would expect creatures to be especially self-deceived is with respect to whether or not one is properly disposed to form beliefs on the basis of religious experiential grounds. As a result, one should be especially wary when advocates of the "private revelation" view contend that it is obvious that not everyone is the recipient of clear religious experiences.

Schellenberg's final point is an attack on (18). This premise holds that "where there is little temptation to do wrong, persons lack a genuine choice of destiny." Schellenberg points out this is false since even in a world in which there is no temptation to do evil, one is still able to choose between merely doing the obligatory and doing the supererogatory. And this alone should be sufficient for soul-making.

Schellenberg argues here, as others have against this sort of theodicy, that evil is not in fact a necessary condition for soul-making. Is Schellenberg right that the distinction between obligatory and supererogatory acts pulls the rug out from under (18) and, by extension, we might assume, soul-making theodicies in general. I hold that it does not, at least for the Christian theist, because I am inclined to think that the Christian should not endorse the distinction between obligatory and supererogatory acts. One might reasonably hold that the ethical import of Christ's teaching had as a consequence that the supererogatory is, for the Christian, obligatory!

But I tell you, do not resist an evil person. If someone strikes you on the right cheek, turn to him the other also. And if someone wants to sue you and take your tunic, let him have your cloak as well. If someone forces you to go one mile, go with him two miles.[23]

While this view has some strange consequences, there are not as many such consequences as one might think. However, further discussion or defense of this view would require a separate treatment.

VII. Conclusions

From this we can conclude that the argument set forth in (16) – (19) stands. Schellenberg's attacks on (16) through (18) seem to fail once we take into account those factors that determine the way in which incentives give rise to coercion. I have argued that the coercive force of a threat is determined by three factors: threat strength, threat imminence, and threat indifference. Further, threat imminence comes in three species, probabilistic, temporal, and epistemic. Schellenberg has set forth two serious challenges to the argument proposed by the soul-making account. First, he has argued that the probabilistic and temporal imminence of a threat attending a probabilifying revelation of God's existence and moral will for His creatures would sufficiently mitigate the force of the induced desire that it allows freedom of a sort sufficient to engage in soul-making. I have argued that by looking at parallel cases of coercion we have good reason to deny this claim. Second, Schellenberg attempts to show that there are actual cases in which free creatures who believe they have been the recipients of probabilifying revelation are still free in the sense required for soul-making. I have argued that the theist should expect that there would be some such probabilifying revelations but that, given the wide variability of threat indifference across individuals, such revelations would be and are rare.

Notice then that this response to Schellenberg makes for a strong case that divine hiddenness is, in most cases, the only way to go if God hopes to preserve the ability of free creatures to engage in soul-making. On the traditional Christian view, at any rate, the strength of the threat for failure to believe and/or obey is fixed: There will be severe negative consequences – some temporal, others eternal. I have argued furthermore that probabilistic and temporal imminence cannot be attenuated in such a way as to eliminate the coerciveness of such a probabilifying revelation. Finally, a good case can be made that creaturely threat indifference also cannot be mitigated, by God anyway, since it appears to be a character trait that we, in some measure, freely cultivate. To fix this feature of our character would be to interfere in our self-determination in just the way this account argues God ought not. As a result, the only remaining factor that can be attenuated is epistemic imminence, i.e., divine hiddenness, and this, it seems, is what God has done.

Notes

1. "Coercion and the Hiddenness of God," *American Philosophical Quarterly*, Vol. 30, Number 1, pp. 27–38.
2. Although such evil is necessary here only in the sense that there is no world God can actualize which contains free creatures who do not go wrong (at least without a significant loss of overall goodness in the created world).

3. Nothing I have said here actually sustains such a strong conclusion. However, those theists who propose libertarian freedom as an intrinsic good often cite its relation to moral good to ground its worth. Here I am arguing that there is no such intrinsic relation.

4. See his *Evil and the God of Love* (New York: Harper and Row, 1966 and 1977), pp. 255–61 and 318–36.

5. One might argue that this view on the purpose of the earthly life is summed up in the following passage from the second epistle of St. Peter: "Grace and peace be multiplied to you in the knowledge of God and of Jesus our Lord; seeing that His divine power has granted to us everything pertaining to life and godliness, through the true knowledge of Him who called us by His own glory and excellence. For by these He has granted to us His precious and magnificent promises, so that by them you may become partakers of the divine nature, having escaped the corruption that is in the world by lust. (II Peter. 1::2–4)

6. Ephesians.5:1

7. Some Christian readers might fear that an account of this sort positively precludes the role of grace in salvation and sanctification, making it Pelagian *in excelsis*. I have responded to this charge in more detail in my "Heaven and Hell," in *Reason for the Hope Within*, Michael Murray (ed.) (Grand Rapids: William B. Eerdmans, 1998), pp. 298–9. But there is no reason on the view developed here for denying that grace is a necessary condition for soul-making. It cannot, however, be the case that such grace is intrinsically sufficient.

8. J. L. Schellenberg, *Divine Hiddenness and Human Reason* (Ithaca: Cornell University Press, 1993), p. 83.

9. Ibid., pp. 85–6.

10. Ibid., pp. 117–18.

11. Ibid., p. 121.

12. The question of whether or not offers can be coercive is widely disputed in the literature and cannot be addressed here. I have elsewhere argued that offers can be coercive, see, "Are Coerced Acts Free," David Dudrick and Michael Murray, *American Philosophical Quarterly*, Vol. 32, no. 2, p. 116.

13. One must, of course, define exactly what it means to be unable rationally to choose some course of action. I discuss this in detail in "Are Coerced Acts Free?" pp. 116–19. Roughly, the idea is this. Each of us has a certain threshold such that if (i) a threat carries a grave enough consequence and (ii) the act required of the threatened by the threatener, P, is not, relative to the threat, sufficiently grave, then I am unable to deliberately choose to do anything other than P. So, for example, if one threatens to shoot me if I fail to touch my nose, I *cannot*, all other things being equal, choose to do other than touch my nose. Surely other factors might be added to the case that *would* make it possible for me to choose to do something other than touch my nose. For example, we might add that if I touch my nose I will suffer excruciating pain for eternity. Or we might add that I believe I have a bullet-proof vest on. But barring such additions to the case, I contend that *I* simply cannot choose to do other than touch my nose. To put it more strongly, no possible world continuous with a world segment up to that time, as described, contains me performing any free and deliberate action other than touching my nose.

14. The account of coercion here is vastly oversimplified. Unless a good deal is built into the notion of what counts as a threat, this definition will entail that I am coerced any time one course of action is vastly preferred by me over its competitors. Surely such an account fails to capture what is distinctive about coercion. A fully fleshed out account of coercion can be found in "Are Coerced Acts Free?" Op.cit.

15. *Divine Hiddenness and Human Reason*, pp. 121–4.
16. Schellenberg says this explicitly, "Even if the expectation of [temporal] punishment . . . were prevalent in some quarters at first, upon further experience and reflection the understanding of humans might be expected to mature and deepen . . . to the point where such views were universally rejected. Further, those who (unreasonably) expected severe punishment to follow each bad action would soon note that those who did not have this expectation, and so occasionally fell into temptation and did bad actions, were not immediately severely punished." *Divine Hiddenness and Human Reason*, p. 125.
17. Ibid., p. 124.
18. Of course, inevitable negative consequences alone are not sufficient for coercion. High threat strength, probabilistic and epistemic imminence, and low threat-indifference must be present as well.
19. Schellenberg next presents a fallback position that the theist might retreat to in light of his criticisms discussed above. However, since I have argued these earlier criticisms fail, there seems little reason to discuss this weaker attempt to defend (16) and (17) which he proposes. His discussion of this fallback position is found at, Ibid., pp. 126–8.
20. Ibid., pp. 129–30.
21. In conversation, Schellenberg has indicated to me that he thinks this is the the right response, and the one that gets to the heart of the argument from hiddenness. He also discusses this sort of position briefly at the close of section I in the essay in this volume.
22. I provide another response to this view in my "Coercion and the Hiddenness of God," section V.
23. Matthew 5:39–41.

4

St. John of the Cross and the Necessity of Divine Hiddenness

LAURA L. GARCIA

It hasn't escaped the notice of Christian believers that not everyone is a Christian; indeed, not everyone is a theist. This is a cause for alarm for some theists, but only for those who hold the further claim that: (G1) God desires everyone to believe in His existence. If God is omnipotent and omniscient, presumably He could bring it about that every person (or every person capable of understanding and assenting to theism) believes in God. It might be difficult to defend (G1) on purely philosophical grounds, so theism narrowly considered might plausibly escape from the apparent tension here. Christians and some other theists do seem committed to (G1), however, opening the door to a simple refutation of their position by means of the following *modus tollens* argument: If God exists, then nothing contrary to His (ultimate) desires could exist in the world. Something contrary to God's ultimate desires (nonbelief in the gospel message) does exist. Therefore, God does not exist.[1] If nonbelief is not just contrary to God's desires but also evil (or if being contrary to God's ultimate desires entails being evil), then the problem of nonbelief will be an instance of the problem of evil. But it can be considered as a problem in its own right, prescinding from whether or not nonbelief is a species of evil (and what kind of evil it is).

General Assessment of the Argument From Involuntary Nonbelief

Theodore Drange proposes that some version of this argument successfully refutes Christianity, at least any species of Christianity committed to (G1). At first sight, such a claim seems excessively confident, since it is open to Christians who deny Drange's conclusion to construct the following *modus ponens* argument: "If God exists, then nothing contrary to his (ultimate) desires could exist in the world. Widespread nonbelief in the gospel message does exist. Therefore, widespread nonbelief in the gospel message is not contrary to God's (ultimate) desires." Finding out not just what God desires, but what God ultimately desires, might be a rather difficult task, given that we have no direct access to God's desires. Drange offers several arguments meant to show that

many Christians (especially evangelical Christians, for example) are committed to claiming that it is at least one of God's desires that all (or virtually
all) persons believe in his existence. Some of Drange's arguments rely on an
assumption that God's desire for all to be saved (to be united with God eternally in heaven), which is pretty clearly supported by scripture passages,
requires Him to desire that all believe in His existence. These arguments only
succeed, then, if salvation is impossible without conscious and explicit belief
in God, and maybe even without conscious and explicit belief in the gospel
message. However, many Christians deny this claim and the Catholic Church
explicitly rejects it.[2]

Still, one could reformulate Drange's argument so that it does not depend
on the controversial premise. Unless everyone is in fact saved, then there is
something that God wants that does not seem to happen. We have to say here
that it does not seem to happen rather than that it clearly does not happen,
since it is not clear that Christians are committed to the damnation of at least
some souls.[3] Let's assume for the sake of the argument, then, that not everyone is saved. Again, this is a problem for Christian theism only if the salvation of all persons is not just one of God's prima facie desires, something that
might be overridden by logically incompatible and more basic desires, but one
of God's ultimate desires. As Drange puts it, we must assume that God does
not want anything else that necessarily conflicts with His desire to bring about
the salvation of all persons as strongly as He wants to bring about their salvation.[4] Assuming that "strength of desire" can be read in terms of logical
priority, this claim has some plausibility to it. Nevertheless, it remains open
to Christians to employ the *modus ponens* strategy with this argument as
well: Since not everyone is saved, the salvation of everyone is not one of God's
ultimate desires. There is something God wants that is incompatible with all
being saved, and He wants this more than He wants everyone to be saved.

What this competing desire might be is open to debate and speculation, of
course. Some Reformed theologians urge that God's justice is best served by
damning some souls and saving others. More commonly, Christians argue that
what God desires is not just that every person is saved, but that every person
should come to know and love Him, and so to enjoy Him forever, and that
this is not a state of affairs God can bring about directly. If the true good of
human beings resides in surrendering everything to God and loving Him for
His own sake (i.e., if God is our highest good), then presumably what God
wills for human beings is that they should love Him. But genuine love presupposes freedom, since love is a free gift of oneself to another; any psychological states causally necessitated in a person by someone else would not
count as love. If love requires human freedom, then, it is logically impossible
for God to bring about the salvation of anyone who refuses to love Him. This
is why, I think, Drange prefers to focus on belief in God's existence or in the

gospel message rather than on salvation, since beliefs can be produced in many ways,[5] and even if the intellect is compelled to assent to a claim, this needn't undermine the genuineness of the belief. Still, if an explicit set of beliefs is neither necessary nor sufficient for salvation, then it's hard to make the case that one of God's ultimate desires (according to Christianity) must be to ensure that everyone holds that set of beliefs.[6]

Drange anticipates this line of response on the part of Christians, and he finds it unsatisfactory. For one thing, some Christians do commit themselves to the view that explicit belief in God is necessary for salvation, so these Christians must explain why God desires everyone to be saved and yet does not provide conditions strongly conducive to belief in His existence for every person, or for every person equally. Further, even for those who do not see salvation as conditioned on explicit belief in God's existence, believing in God is still regarded as a great good for human beings, providing a feeling of peace about the future and a sense of meaning that is an important benefit even in this life. It is at this point, I think, that the problem of nonbelief begins shading into the more general problem of evil, since it becomes a complaint that God is unjust in failing to induce belief in every person, or in failing to give every person equal access to important truths about Himself that would be good to know.

At least three responses come to mind with regard to this complaint. First, Christians can reply that since we do not know God's plan for the human race in all its detail, it is logically possible that God has a perfectly good reason for providing exactly the level of evidence for His existence that each person has, and that He has an equally good reason for permitting persons to be in different epistemic situations with regard to evidence for His existence and for the truth of the gospel message. It would be difficult to prove that it's logically impossible for God to have such reasons, given the distance between divine omniscience and our finite grasp of God's ends and His means for attaining them. John Schellenberg considers such a theistic response in his treatment of divine hiddenness, but rejects it as unconvincing. Even granting that there are some goods that are (presently) inscrutable to human beings and perhaps some connections between goods and evils and that are inscrutable to us, "how can we know, with regard to the occurrence of reasonable nonbelief, that it is a member of this class?"[7] Schellenberg judges that there is a .5 probability with respect to the proposition that some instances of evil belong to the "inscrutable" class, and that the probability that reasonable nonbelief is one of the group is only about half of the first probability, giving it an overall probability rating of .25, which is "clearly too low for rational acceptance."[8]

There are many difficulties for Schellenberg's argument, however. One is that different assessments of the probabilities in question are possible, even for agnostics and atheists. If the background assumption is that God exists, and if God is conceived of as infinite in knowledge, then the existence of inscrutable goods and inscrutable connections between evils and goods might be very probable indeed. The fact that many of God's purposes involve goods for human beings and that many of these involve some kind of good experiences for human beings does not do much to offset this probability, or so it seems to me.[9] A second problem concerns the calculation of the nested probabilities above. If God exists and if there are some inscrutable goods, then given that we don't see the reason for every instance of involuntary nonbelief, there is strong reason to place these in the inscrutable goods category – indeed it would have a probability close to 1. Thus, for anyone who thinks that it's likely that God's reasons for some things are going to be inscrutable to us, it will also be very likely that involuntary nonbelief falls into this category.

Second, Christians might claim that God has given every person sufficient evidence of His existence already, and that nonbelief often involves some voluntary suppression of the truth, as St. Paul suggests in the letter to the Romans. Where no such suppression is involved, presumably God would know how to act fairly and mercifully with the persons involved. That many nonbelievers aren't aware of suppressing the truth in this way does not show that they aren't in fact doing so, since there is at least some chance of self-deception in these matters.

Finally, Christians can argue that God's ultimate purpose might be a complex one, including not just the desideratum that people should believe in Him, but some further goals with respect to the way this will occur. According to the gospel accounts, Jesus' miracles were not performed for everyone He met, nor did He explain the parables to every person present, nor did He run after those who left His company after finding some of His teachings too strange. This suggests to the average Christian at least two purposes of God that might move Him to permit a significant incidence of nonbelief.

(1) God respects the freedom of His creatures, and refuses to impose on those who do not respond to his invitations to them (whether direct or indirect). That is, those who seek find, and those who remain indifferent or who turn away do not find Him. After all, belief in God is normally more than a cognitive matter, and our volitional stance (especially our attitudes) may be such that God may not give us more knowledge of Himself until we turn toward Him with greater interest and openness. This silence of God could be more for our sake more than for His, of course, since it could be that the requisite attitude of heart is more necessary for our ultimate good than simply acquiring true beliefs. St. James says that the devils believe in God, yet (we assume) they fail to arrive at union with Him.

(2) God might desire that most persons should come to know of Him (and especially of His love for them in Christ) by hearing this message from

others – originally from eyewitnesses of His miracles and His "glory," but later from those who have not seen and yet have believed. This method preserves the relationality of human beings better than the more direct, individualistic methods Drange proposes, and is perhaps a better introduction into the realm of personal relationships that comprises our final destiny and that characterizes even the inner life of God himself (according to the Christian doctrine of the Trinity). A further benefit of this mode of transmission of the gospel message, for example, is that we must trust in the testimony of others in order to come to faith, and we are deeply indebted to those who brought us the message, often at great cost to themselves. For whatever reasons, God does not seem interested in a low-cost strategy for how to engender belief in His existence and know-ledge of His offer of forgiveness for sin and reconciliation. On the Christian view, the fullest revelation of His nature and plans for humankind is the life, death, and resurrection of Jesus, who is God incarnate. That He wishes to draw human beings into this endeavor of reconciling all of humanity to Himself can be puzzling, therefore, in that it seems remarkably inefficient for omnipotence to rely on finite and fallible instruments in this most important mission. But there are surely great benefits for the instruments, and perhaps even for the recipients of the message, in going about things in just this way.

Perhaps the problem of nonbelief reduces in the end to a more general problem of divine providence. God could see to it that various goods and ben-efits result directly from His own actions, so that no one ever suffers (in this life) from an unequal distribution of these benefits. With respect to food, for instance, a divine being could bring it about directly that everyone has enough to eat, and has exactly the same amount to eat as everyone else, and that no one suffers hunger because of another's neglect or selfishness, or because he is born into a situation of want. Similarly with respect to belief in God (or in the gospel), a divine being could bring it about that virtually everyone comes to hold the desired beliefs, and that no one fails to acquire them owing to the failures of others or owing to the circumstances of their birth and upbringing, etc. But even if these beliefs are a more important good than food or life itself, it doesn't follow automatically that a good, omnipotent, omniscient being will do things the way we might do them. There doesn't seem to be a violation of justice involved, since as long as persons are not punished for involuntary unbelief, it's hard to see that God wrongs anyone by failing to provide every person with the same evidential situation. There are goods involved in allow-ing persons to contribute to human society and to meet the needs of others, and there have to be genuine needs in order for this to occur. So even from our limited perspective, we can imagine some reasons why God does not reveal Himself directly to every person or does not give everyone the same initial access to truths about Himself.

St. John of the Cross on Faith and Divine Hiddenness

The literature on divine hiddenness sometimes suffers from a rather narrow understanding of faith and a similarly thin conception of union with God. If the faith that leads to our true end of union with God is largely a cognitive matter, then enabling persons to come to faith should be a relatively straightforward and easy task. As Drange puts it, people naturally want to know the truth and it's a good thing for them to know it, so God should simply tell it to them (or make it obvious in some way).[10] He mentions various scriptural accounts in which God gives some spectacular confirmation of His existence or power to various persons, in a way that does not completely remove their freedom to reject the truth. But it's instructive to recall that in virtually every such instance (the plagues in Egypt, the feeding of the five thousand, the numerous healings performed by Jesus), not everyone came to believe in God or in Jesus as a result. It's hard to see how God could guarantee belief in His existence without removing human freedom with respect to that belief. More importantly, any coerced beliefs about God will not contribute to the goal of bringing persons to faith, and may instead interfere with it.

Similarly, John Schellenberg's argument in his careful and comprehensive treatment of divine hiddenness seems to assume that God could (and should) give everyone evidence such that nonbelief in God's existence would be unreasonable for them. Again, this seems to leave little room for voluntary rejection of belief in God. Schellenberg distinguishes between the cognitive act of belief that God exists with the decision of trust and commitment involved in belief in God, and argues that if God desires the latter state for each person, and that state logically requires the first (cognitive) state, then God should provide for each person sufficient evidence to prevent reasonable nonbelief in the proposition that He exists. This would still leave people free with respect to belief in God, and would enable them to make a more informed decision about whether or not to make the further commitment to follow or obey Him. On the other hand, if what God ultimately wants for each person is the latter state (trust and obedience), then even if a minimal belief in His existence is necessary for it, it doesn't follow that God will bring about that condition for every person regardless of what other conditions obtain with respect to him or her. If the belief is unlikely to occasion the desired response, for example, God may not provide additional evidence for that person. Further, the free actions someone might perform in seeking evidence for God's existence might themselves dispose one for the right response to God if and when He is found;[11] and many other possibilities suggest themselves.

According to a long tradition in Christian theology, faith is primarily an orientation of the will, an act of surrender to God, that includes belief in His existence but is most importantly a response of obedience to God and a gift of oneself to Him. In a treatise on the nature of the Church, Joseph Cardinal Ratzinger explicates this understanding of faith briefly in the following passage:

Perhaps we are now a little better able to comprehend what a turnabout faith entails – to grasp the re-versal, the con-version that it contains: I acknowledge that God himself speaks and acts; I recognize the existence not only of what is ours but also of what is his. But if this is true, if we are not the only ones who choose and act, but he too speaks and acts, then everything changes. Then I must obey, then I must follow him, even when he leads me where I do not wish to go (John 21:18). Then it becomes reasonable, indeed, necessary, to let go of my own taste, to renounce my own wishes and to follow after him who alone can show the way to true life, because he himself is the life (John 14:6).[12]

This understanding of faith means that there are at least two reasons for divine hiddenness with respect to human beings. First, not everyone will be eager to know the truth about God, since it calls for a kind of radical conversion to which most of us will find some level of internal resistance. Recognizing that God exists cannot be easily separated from one's response to God – a lack of freedom regarding belief that God exists, if strong enough, could also lead to a lack of freedom regarding belief in God (at least for some persons at some times). Second, this kind of faith is most operative when the external indications of God's presence or His love are withdrawn, because then our assessment of the evidence (or in the case of suffering, our judgment of the situation) must yield to His if we are to persevere in faith. The faith that takes us into the very life of God involves renunciation and self-denial, and it is just this attitude that God cannot force upon us without destroying its essence.

We might be tempted to assume that those who are closer to God receive greater confirmations of His existence and His providential care for them, so that the life of faith becomes increasingly easy, faith becoming almost as good as sight, so to speak. A long tradition of spiritual reflection suggests that while there is an element of truth in this picture, it can be very misleading. According to one of the giants of Catholic spirituality, St. John of the Cross, what we need in order to be united with God is to be empty of ourselves. When we are filled with our own desires and preferences, our own plans for our lives, God cannot fill us with Himself. Union with God is primarily a union of wills, so entering into His life means coming to will what He wills, in preference to what we ourselves will. Because of original sin and our own personal sins, we tend to seek ourselves and to find our good in creatures rather than God, so the process of unification is also a process of purification. We must be detached from creatures in order to be fully united to God.

St. John sees this as a three-stage process, though the levels of purification can to some degree be taking place simultaneously. He calls each stage a "dark night," as it involves an absence or renunciation of something one is drawn to, even while the competing good (God) remains to some extent hidden. There is no genuine test of faith or commitment when what one is giving up is obviously bad in itself or clearly an obstacle to one's true or highest good. Purification or detachment is not simply a matter of giving up what is sinful, since it assumed that those who seek God are at least attempting to avoid serious sin. Rather, it is a willingness to be deprived even of things that are good if God should will it, thus preferring Him and His will to every created good.

The first stage of the soul's journey to God St. John calls the "dark night of the senses." "Since love of God and attachment to creatures are contraries, they cannot coexist in the same will."[13] Through the voluntary mortification of one's appetites and the willing acceptance of suffering and trials, one is enabled to achieve a measure of self-control and the ability to forego pleasures that would lead one away from God or that are incompatible with His will. It is not that St. John despises pleasure or the body, but he sees many of our natural appetites as interfering both with our search for God and our ability to unite our wills with His. Thus, he says, "there are many who desire to advance and persistently beseech God to bring them to this state of perfection. Yet when God wills to conduct them through the initial trials and mortifications, as is necessary, they are unwilling to suffer them, and they shun them, flee from the narrow road of life, and seek the broad road of their own consolation, which is that of their own perdition."[14] If what we seek from God is consolations and pleasant feelings and the like, then we love Him not so much for Himself as for His gifts; that is, we really love not God, but ourselves. This first stage of detachment, then, already requires a deep level of humility, a willingness to accept God's judgment as to what is best for us in preference to our own judgment. St. John holds out the possibility that one can in time arrive at a state in which one takes joy in the goods of the senses, though this joy is always ordered to the love of God and does not involve setting one's heart on these goods themselves.

The second stage is called the "dark night of the soul," and it involves a detachment not just from our appetites but from our cognitive faculties of understanding, memory, and imagination. The object of faith, which is God Himself, so far exceeds the human mind that we cannot arrive at much knowledge of Him by way of our natural powers. "Faith affirms what cannot be understood by the intellect. . . . If they were manifest [to the intellect], there would be no faith."[15] Commenting on the scriptural advice (in Hebrews 11:6) that one who approaches God should do so by faith, St. John explains: "This is like saying: To attain union with God, a person should advance neither by understanding, nor by the support of his own experience, nor by feeling or imagination, but by belief in God's being. For God's being cannot be grasped by the intellect, appetite, imagination, or any other sense, nor can it be known in this life."[16] Faith requires that we believe in what utterly transcends our natural powers, and that we believe it regardless of whether God sends us inner confirmations of its truth. By inner confirmations St. John has especially in mind a kind of "inner light" or special revelation from God, whether by way of actual visions and voices or by emotions or a more obscure "sense" of His presence. Since we can be misled by these states of the soul, and since they can lead us into spiritual pride or into a new kind of attachment (this time to spiritual goods rather than to material ones), they are not to be sought after, according to St. John. They are not a sure guide to truth, and they can prevent one from taking the only road to union with God – the virtue of faith, which includes a willingness to renounce oneself and one's own ideas about God. The light of faith comes to us by way of darkness with respect to what we can know on our own, so we advance more by "unknowing" than by knowing. "Since the intellect cannot understand the nature of God, it must journey in submission to Him rather than by understanding, and thus it advances by not understanding."[17] This stage involves an active purification on our part, in that we must seek to detach ourselves from our own desires and opinions even in the spiritual realm, so that God may manifest Himself fully to us in faith and contemplation.

The third and final stage of the ascent to God is the passive purification of the soul by God's actions within it. Through this fire of purgation, the soul's appetites and faculties, unable to derive satisfaction in any other object, are withdrawn from everything and concentrated simply upon God: "This happens very particularly in this dark purgation, as was said, because God so weans and recollects the appetites that they cannot find satisfaction in any of their objects. God proceeds thus so that by withdrawing the appetites from other objects and recollecting them in Himself, He strengthens the soul and gives it the capacity for this strong union of love, which He begins to accord by means of this purgation."[18] This frees the soul for the kind of total union with God through love that is the highest good of the human person, both in this life and in the next. The closer one is to this union of love, the more one suffers. "The reason these trials are necessary in order to reach this state is that the highest union cannot be wrought in a soul that is not fortified by trials and temptations and purified by tribulations, darknesses, and distress, just as a superior quality liqueur is poured only into a sturdy flask which is prepared and purified."[19] St. John speaks most eloquently and passionately about the joys of this state of perfected love of God, and reminds us that this is what God seeks for each one of us. "At the evening of life, you will be examined in love. Learn to love as God desires to be loved and abandon your own ways of acting."[20]

Obviously, St. John of the Cross is directing his remarks to those who are already Christians, and especially to those who earnestly seek holiness and union with God. These are assumed to believe in God's existence and in the articles of faith as set forth in the creeds and the catechism of the Church. If St. John is right in claiming that such persons can only advance toward the goal of union with God by way of trials, darknesses, and abandonment, then it is necessary for God to hide Himself from them in some measure or at some points along the way in order to make this advance possible. God's hidden-ness is thus a result of His merciful love, which develops love and persever-ance in His disciples by withdrawing the signs of His presence from time to time. Depending on one's response to the initial trials and aridity God permits for one, it may be that God will send even deeper levels of trial, so that one can advance more quickly along the path toward a total renunciation of self and come to be totally united to Him. Just as nature abhors a vacuum, says St. John, so does God refuse to allow a mere absence in the soul; whenever one is free of a love of self and of creatures, the love of God pours into the soul and transforms it into his likeness. Suffering, including the suffering brought about by God's hiddenness, is necessary to effect this detachment and to lead us to seek our good in Him and to receive everything from Him. There may be other ways of accomplishing this goal, but apparently they seemed less valuable to God, either because of a lessening of our freedom in responding to Him or for some other reason.

What of those who do not believe in God, or who do not accept the teachings of Christianity? Although St. John does not address this question directly, I think his approach can be extended at least in part to these cases as well. God calls every person into communion with Himself, which necessarily involves at some level at least a renunciation of oneself, so we can assume that God sometimes leads persons by a felt dissatisfaction with natural goods to seek a higher, more permanent good. St. Augustine says our hearts are restless until they rest in God, so presumably this restlessness can be a benefit to the extent that it causes us to freely search for God. Schellenberg quotes Pascal at length on this point, and I think St. John of the Cross would find much to agree with in Pascal's remarks about God's "strategy" in making Himself available to us without overwhelming our faculties in such a way as to coerce us into belief and obedience to Him. "God wishes to move the will rather than the mind," says Pascal. "Perfect clarity would help the mind and harm the will."[21]

Schellenberg sees two arguments emerging from these Augustinian reflec-tions. One is the Stimulus Argument, which is that God may hide Himself in order to stimulate us to search for Him more diligently and with greater urgency. The second is the Presumption Argument, which is that God may hide Himself in order to prevent us from reacting arrogantly or pridefully to the rev-elations He gives us, and so to fail to enter into the right relationship to Him. It seems to me that St. John and Pascal would see these as closely related, in that the hiddenness of God which shows us our need for Him can help to induce the kind of humility that is an important condition of a proper response to whatever evidence of God we come to possess. Nevertheless, Schellenberg finds these arguments unconvincing. He suggests that God could reveal Himself to each person by way of religious experiences that would convince them of everything they can learn in the Pascalian way: that they are wretched and sinful and in need of God's mercy, that God is their sole good, that in Him alone can they find peace, and so on. If God can make us aware of these things directly, then the Stimulus Argument fails, since divine hiddenness will not be a necessary condition of making us aware of them. Further, if making us aware of our wretched condition will not necessarily render us presumptuous, then the Presumption Argument fails, since God could prevent pride while still providing us with plenty of evidence of His existence and our need for Him. Further, in cases where God remains hidden from someone because He knows that person will not respond appropriately to further evidence, Schellenberg finds this blameworthy on God's part. It prevents the person in question from making a free moral decision to reject God (or to respond in some other self-destructive way to the evidence) and God ought to respect our moral freedom on this point.

Beginning with this last point, it's not obvious that God has any moral obligations toward His creatures, but St. Thomas Aquinas and others have certainly taught that God necessarily wills the good of His creatures. If so, then presumably He wills the good of each person, and this means that He wills that the person should be united with Him through love, that is to say, freely. If God is desirous that none should be lost, then we can assume that He strives to minimize the number of occasions in which someone has a choice to make for or against Him and chooses wrongly. There are at least two things that God is after here – that we should know Him and love Him – so it doesn't seem obligatory for Him to grant us knowledge, especially by way of direct experiences, in cases where He knows we will respond to it negatively. He may do so, of course, whether in order to permit us to exercise our freedom or for other reasons, but it is hardly evident that God is required to provide everyone with the knowledge we consider sufficient to make a free decision possible. As for the possibility of providing us with religious experiences that will "fill us in" with respect to our wretchedness and the vanity of earthly goods and the like, it's not clear that this is a genuine possibility for God. Here again, the point is not simply that we should acquire some set of information, but that we should learn to deny ourselves, take up the cross of Jesus, and follow after Him, abandoning ourselves wholly into the hands of God. Religious experiences, or any other sort of evidence, that convinced us of the gain for ourselves of the religious life would not suffice here, since they could well lead to a self-seeking and calculating attitude toward God rather than the union of our wills with His that is our true good. Pascal insists that "Self-love and concupiscence, which hold [the soul] back, are intolerable. Thus God makes the soul aware of this underlying self-love which is destroying it and which

He alone can cure."[22] While Schellenberg takes this to indicate that God could make the soul aware of its self-love by way of religious experiences, Pascal's point is that God cannot do this at all, even by religious experiences, without the willing cooperation of the person in question. God will free us from ourselves, if we so desire, but He will not do so without us.[23]

Thus, depending on what God knows about us and about how we will respond, and depending on His other purposes for ourselves and for others, he may give us some special revelation of Himself, but it's not obvious that he can consistently conquer our self-love by this means purely and simply. It could be instead that purifying us of self-love, with our free cooperation, is a difficult task and that it takes different forms with different persons. While it may be that giving every person strong and nearly undeniable evidence of His existence would not necessarily (with logical necessity) remove their freedom to respond negatively to Him, it's certainly possible that there are many persons for whom this would remove their freedom, and many others for whom the evidence would not lead them in the direction of their ultimate good, either because it renders them presumptuous or because self-love prevents them from a true conversion of heart. I submit that only an omniscient being could know with any degree of confidence which of these situations a given person is in. Even the most self-reflective of us probably don't know in our own case exactly how we would respond to such experiences.

With respect to receiving further information, based on special revelations of a more public kind, about God and His purposes and about the life and teachings of Jesus, this is especially entrusted to those who have already received the message and who are expected to share it with others. The individual's union with God is an identification with God's will, and since God wills the salvation of every person, communion with God naturally leads to communion among human persons. As Ratzinger puts it, "The Church is the dynamic process of horizontal and vertical unification. It is vertical unification, which brings about the union of man with the triune love of God, thus also integrating man in and with himself. But because the Church takes man to the point toward which his entire being gravitates, she automatically becomes horizontal unification as well: Only by the impulse power of vertical unification can horizontal unification, by which I mean the coming together of divided humanity, also successfully take place."[24] One way of bringing about these two ends simultaneously, as it were, is to make it possible that those who have not yet encountered God in Christ may still meet Him face to face, by meeting those in whom He dwells and in whom His love is again made incarnate, albeit imperfectly. Christians are called to be "other Christs," Christ passing by. As the Jesuit poet Gerard Manley Hopkins writes, "Christ plays in ten thousand places, lovely in limbs, and lovely in eyes not his, to the Father, through the features of men's faces."[25]

If this sounds inefficient by comparison with direct experiential communications from God to each person, so be it. It's hard to imagine that we can have an informed opinion about what God's overall purposes are for His creation and what are the best ways for Him to achieve those purposes. Much of the discussion on divine hiddenness assumes that, if Christianity is true, God wills a certain end (the salvation of all persons, say) and that one way to achieve that end, or at least to contribute to that end, would be to make His existence very obvious to every person. This much seems relatively uncontroversial. But the rest of the argument is much more tenuous. We are told that God's existence is not obvious to every person, and though many accept this claim, there would be those who would dispute it. But even aside from the issue of the status of the available evidence, divine hiddenness poses a serious problem for Christian theists only if God's overall set of purposes is such that He can only achieve them by making His existence obvious to every person.[26] It could be that God seeks a complex set of goods, some of them good in themselves and some of them instrumentally good for the achievement of others, and that the level of divine hiddenness that exists in our world is part of a total plan for realizing these goods that is as good as any other total plan. Christians are not committed to the view that divine hiddenness is logically necessary for the attainment of some particular end God has in view, nor are they committed to the weaker claim that divine hiddenness is the best way to achieve some particular end. It may simply be one way to achieve some purposes of God, and thus either willed or permitted by Him as part of a total plan for the universe that includes, among other ends, His desire to unite human persons with himself.[27] Divine hiddenness may undermine some of God's ends, therefore, without undermining His purposes generally speaking, just as evil choices on our part detract from one thing he seeks without necessarily thwarting his total plan for the universe.[28] Nevertheless, reflecting on the ways in which God's hiddenness can actually be motivated by his love and mercy toward us may help to alleviate some of the pain we feel when we cry with the Psalmist, "My God, my God, why have you forsaken me? . . . O my God, I cry out by day, but you do not answer, by night, but I have no rest."[29] It might even be that eventually we will find ourselves concluding, as he does, "For God has not despised the affliction of the afflicted; neither has He hidden His face from him; but when he cried to Him for help, He heard."[30]

Notes

1. This is Theodore Drange's statement of the argument in *Nonbelief and Evil* (Amherst, NY: Prometheus, 1998), p. 49.
2. See *Lumen Gentium.*

3. Some may want to make the case that Judas was certainly damned, however, and others may assume that Jesus would not speak of the possibility of going to hell if no one in fact ever goes there.

4. *Nonbelief and Evil*, p. 60.

5. Drange suggests the following: direct implantation of the given beliefs, creating a "belief gene" that would transmit the beliefs from one generation to the next, inner voices, spectacular miracles, irrefutable arguments, and CD's falling from the sky with the relevant beliefs in spectacular graphics. (*Nonbelief and Evil*, pp. 61–3).

6. In a letter, Drange expresses doubts about the claim that even love requires freedom: "Love may be slightly more voluntary than belief, but only very slightly so, at least in my case. . . . We can be no more motivated to become more loving than we can be motivated to grow taller." This seems highly counterintuitive to me, unless one analyzes love as simply an emotional state, having nothing to do with virtues or attitudes of various kinds. Of course, one could assume that determinism is true and therefore that no states of ours are under our control in any strong sense, but most theists will not grant this assumption.

7. John Schellenberg, *Divine Hiddenness and Human Reason* (Ithaca: Cornell University Press, 1993), p. 90.

8. Ibid., p. 91.

9. See Schellenberg's citation (on p. 90) of William Rowe's argument in "The Empirical Argument from Evil," in Robert Audi and William J. Wainwright, eds., *Rationality, Religious Belief, and Moral Commitment* (Ithaca: Cornell, 1986), where Rowe argues that the appeal to unknown goods is not convincing. For a response to Rowe-style objections, see William Alston, "The Inductive Argument from Evil and the Human Cognitive Condition" in Daniel Howard-Snyder, ed. *The Evidential Argument from Evil* (Bloomington: Indiana University Press, 1996), pp. 97–125.

10. *Nonbelief and Evil*, pp. 122–3.

11. On this point, note St. Thomas Aquinas' view on those who do not deserve to be called "heretics": "As Augustine says (Ep. XLII) and we find it stated in the Decretals (XXIV, Q. 3, can. Dixit Apostolus): By no means should we accuse of heresy those who, however false and perverse their opinion may be, defend it without obstinate fervor, and seek the truth with careful anxiety, ready to mend their opinion when they have found the truth, because, to wit, they do not make a choice in contradiction to the doctrine of the Church." *Summa Theologica* II–II, Q. 11, a. 2, ad. 3.

12. *Called to Communion* (San Francisco: St. Ignatius Press, 1996), p. 160.

13. St. John of the Cross, "The Ascent of Mt. Carmel" I, 6, in *The Collected Works of St. John of the Cross*, tr. Kieran Kavanaugh and Otilio Rodriguez (Washington: ICS Publications, 1964), p. 85.

14. "Living Flame of Love," 2, 27 in *The Collected Works of St. John of the Cross*, pp. 604–5.

15. "The Ascent of Mt. Carmel" II, 6, 2 in *Collected Works*, p. 119.

16. Ibid., II, 4, 4, p. 113.

17. "The Living Flame of Love" 3, 48, *Collected Works*, p. 629.

18. "Dark Night of the Soul" II, 11, 3, *Collected Works*, p. 353.

19. "Living Flame of Love" 2, 25, *Collected Works*, p. 604.

20. "Prayer of a Soul Taken With Love" 57, *Collected Works*, p. 672.

21. *Pensees*, Fragment 234, cited by Schellenberg in *Hiddenness*, p. 135.

22. Ibid., Fragment 460, cited by Schellenberg in *Hiddenness*, p. 149.

23. Along similar lines, St. John of the Cross claims that "All the visions, revelations, and feelings from heaven, or whatever else one may desire to think upon, are not worth as much as the least act of humility." *Ascent of Mt. Carmel* III, ch. 9, 4.
24. *Called to Communion*, p. 76.
25. "As kingfishers catch fire," in *Gerard Manley Hopkins: Poems and Prose*, ed. W. H. Gardner (London: Penguin Books, 1963), p. 51.
26. Schellenberg's dialogue on "What the Hiddenness of God Reveals: A Collaborative Discussion" (included in this volume) anticipates many of the objections theists will make to his argument, though his replies often introduce several additional claims that would themselves be contested by the theist. To take one example, Schellenberg's reply to the argument that God's providing certain kinds of strong evidence to a given person might be "freedom-removing" for that person is that the theist must demonstrate with respect to each type of evidence that it would remove a specific freedom of overriding value with respect to other goods, and the like. All the theist needs to show, however, is that providing evidence resulting in immediate belief in God's existence is possibly freedom-removing for some person at a given time, and that God possibly (hence rightly) wills not to provide such evidence. This would suffice to block the logical move from *God exists* to *God will provide evidence to each (nonculpable) person at every moment such that his existence is beyond reasonable nonbelief for that person.*
27. For a discussion of these issues, see the exchange between Daniel Howard-Snyder and J. L. Schellenberg in *Canadian Journal of Philosophy* 26 (1996). Howard-Snyder's paper is entitled "The Argument from Divine Hiddenness" (pp. 433–453), followed by Schellenberg's "Response to Howard-Snyder" (pp. 455–462).
28. To take an example, Theodore Drange argues in *Nonbelief and Evil* that "A god who strongly desires that humanity should love him maximally should not have purposes which he keeps hidden from humanity." And even if we could not understand these purposes, "God could [and presumably should] at least reveal to humanity that the purposes exist." (pp. 226–7). This assumes that God's overall purposes are best served by revealing to humanity what they are or at least by revealing to every person that He has these purposes. It's hard to see how anyone can be confident of this claim.
29. Psalm 22.
30. Ibid.

5

Jonathan Edwards and the Hiddenness of God

WILLIAM J. WAINWRIGHT

If God exists, why isn't His existence more obvious? Why are God's reality and goodness hidden from not only the careless but from so many sincere and honest inquirers? In an important recent book, John Schellenberg contends that in the absence of satisfactory answers to these questions, we must conclude that God doesn't exist. His argument is this:

(1) "A perfectly loving God would desire a reciprocal personal relationship to obtain between himself and every being capable of it."

(2) "A logically necessary condition of such a divine-human reciprocity is human belief in divine existence." Therefore,

(3) If a perfectly loving God existed, He would "ensure that everyone capable of such belief (or at any rate, everyone capable who was not disposed to resist it) was in possession of sufficient evidence to bring it about that such belief was formed."

(4) "But the evidence actually available is not of this sort." Hence,

(5) A perfectly loving God doesn't exist.[1]

In what follows we shall see how one Christian philosopher would respond to Schellenberg's argument. Sections I–V examine Jonathan Edwards' views of revelation and human noetic failure. As we shall see, Edwards accepts Schellenberg's first two premises,[2] but denies the third. Evidence sufficient to bring about a belief in God's existence and goodness in everyone capable of such belief and not disposed to resist it *is* available. It is also intrinsically clear and compelling although sin has blinded us so that we fail to appreciate its force. While these claims are not novel, Edwards' treatment of them is interesting and illuminating. Sections VI and VII will argue that, with some modifications, it is also defensible.

I

There are at least four reasons for believing that God would reveal Himself to humankind. First, "reason shows that 'tis very fit and requisite that the intelligent beings of the world should know something of God's scheme and design in his work, for they doubtless are the beings that are principally concerned in it."[3]

Second, knowledge of God and a "future state of happiness and misery," and how to act to obtain the former and avoid the latter, are necessary for human well-being. But "God takes care of mankind and all other creatures that usually they may not be without necessary means by foresight or something equivalent, for their preservation and comfortable existence, and that in things of infinitely less importance." He will therefore instruct us by "revelation and direct teaching into the right way of using [our] reason in arguing from effects to causes, etc.," in order that we may know Him, our future state of happiness or misery, and what we need to do to obtain the former and avoid the latter. (Misc 1297, T 214–18)

Third, we were given "reason and a capacity of seeing God in his works for this," that we "may see God's glory in them and give him the glory in them." But we cannot do this unless we know what God's design is, "and what he aims at by what he is doing in the world." (HR 521–2)

Finally, it is fit that humankind "should be informed something of God's design in the government of the world because [it] is made capable of actively falling in with that design and promoting of it, and acting herein as his friends and subjects." (HR 521–2)

A divine self-disclosure is fitting, then, and therefore to be expected. And, in fact, God *has* revealed Himself. In the first place, the world provides objectively adequate evidence of God's being and goodness, that is, evidence that should convince any rational being whose epistemic faculties are functioning properly. Indeed, "man's reason was given to him" for this purpose, "that he might know God and might be capable of discerning the manifestations he made of himself in the effects and external expressions and emanations of the divine perfections." (Misc 1340, T 233)

But God did more than provide objective evidence of His existence and goodness, and equip us with reason. Since we would initially have been too preoccupied with survival to concern ourselves with "divine things," we would have arrived at correct ideas about God only belatedly if He had left us to our own devices. And the Fall's impairment of our cognitive faculties made it even less likely that we would acquire correct ideas about God without His help. God did not, therefore, rely on the vagaries of human reason but directly revealed correct ideas of "divine things" to humankind. As a result, the "nations" "had many things among them derived originally from revelation, by tradition from their ancestors, the ancient founders of nations, or from the Jews, which led 'em to embrace many truths contained in the Scripture." (Misc 1297, T 217) Sacrifices, for instance, "possessed" their minds "with this notion that an atonement or sacrifice for sin was necessary. And so" prepared them "for their more readily receiving the gospel." (HR 137) God also holds direct "communication" or "conversation" with humankind through the Bible. (Misc 204)

God has, then, provided adequate objective evidence of His existence and goodness, and supplied us with true ideas of divine things. He has also given us epistemic faculties which are capable of knowing Him. These include not only our reasoning powers but also our affections; for certain affective and conative attitudes are needed to use those powers properly.

Edwards' view is briefly this. "Actual ideas" are ideas that are lively, clear, and distinct. Actual ideas of complex ideas (such as the idea of God) involve actual ideas of the simple ideas that compose them. Actual ideas of things pertaining to good or evil involve suitable dispositions and affections – being appropriately pleased or displeased as the case may be. Actual ideas of the "ideas, acts, and exercises of minds" are "repetitions of those very things." (Misc 238)

Thought has a tendency to substitute "signs" (words, images) for actual ideas. This tendency is useful and normally quite harmless. But it impedes reasoning when "we are at a loss concerning a connection or consequence, or have a new inference to draw, or would see the force of some new argument." (Misc 782, T 115) Since accurate reasoning about a subject matter involves attending to actual ideas of it, one must possess actual ideas of divine things to reason correctly about them. To have an actual idea of God, for instance, one must have actual ideas of the ideas that compose it. One won't, however, if one lacks the right affections. Those parts of the idea of God which everyone has by nature (ideas of power, knowledge, and justice, for example) won't be attended to or, when they are, will fail to elicit appropriate affective and volitional reactions. Other parts of the idea of God will be missing. Without the simple idea of "true beauty" (the radiance or splendor of holiness) one can't understand God's holiness, or the facts that depend on it such as the infinite heinousness of offending Him. And because ideas of affections are "repetitions" of them, one can't understand God's benevolence unless one is benevolent oneself.

"True benevolence" or "the love of being in general" (that is, of God and the beings that absolutely depend upon Him and reflect Him) is needed to reason rightly about the divine and our relation to it. Since the truly benevolent love being in general, and God is "the principal part of being," the truly benevolent attend to the ideas which compose the idea of their beloved – ideas of God's awful majesty, for example, or His infinite knowledge. And because their desires are properly ordered, they have a due sense of the goods or evils associated with God's "natural" attributes and activities. They fear offending Him, for instance, and are grateful for His benefits. They also understand God's benevolence since their own benevolence "repeats" or mirrors it. Finally, the truly benevolent delight in the benevolence in which true holiness consists, that is, they "perceive" or "taste" or "relish" its "loveliness," and so possess the idea of true beauty.[4] Only the truly benevolent, then, are equipped to reason rightly about divine things.

Edwards goes even further, however, implying that the truly benevolent alone are possessed with the desire for truth about God which is essential for fruitful and honest inquiry. The Mind 49 asserts that, because perceiving being loves being, it also loves "being's consent to being," and *"to perceive the things that are."* (My emphasis.) That is, perceiving being loves benevolence to being, and the *truth about being.* A natural implication is that since the truly benevolent love being more, they also love truth more.

The truly benevolent love being more because their love isn't restricted to "private systems" (like self, family, nation, or even humanity), and because their love is purer – not rooted in self-love or natural instinct. The love of being in general is thus both quantitatively and qualitatively superior to the love of private systems. If the sense in which the truly benevolent love truth more is analogous to that in which they love being more, we can infer that they wish to know more (important) truths about being in general, and that their love of these truths is more disinterested – freer from self-interest and the pressure of natural instinct.

Is this at all plausible? Does one who loves x love the truth about x more than someone who doesn't love x? It may be true that a person who loves x loves the truth about x more than one who is indifferent to x. But enmity can also make us more discerning. Hatred gives Roger Chillingworth the eyes to detect the secret sin in the bosom of the Reverend Arthur Dimmesdale. Or consider someone who doubts that God exists but would love to love God? Can't *he* passionately desire the truth about God?

These counter examples to Edwards' thesis aren't persuasive. Love at its best doesn't wish to be deceived about its beloved whereas hatred resists truths about its object which would show that its hatred is unwarranted. For all his acuity, Chillingworth's image of Dimmesdale is distorted. As for the second alleged counterexample, a love of the love of a thing whose existence one finds doubtful is itself a kind of love of that thing when one prizes the love of it for the beauty or splendor of its object.[5]

The results of our discussion are these. God has provided adequate objective evidence of His reality and goodness and revealed true ideas about divine things. He has also equipped us with epistemic faculties which, when properly used, are sufficient to discern the force of the evidence He has provided and the truth of the ideas He has revealed. Those who are truly benevolent function properly. They desire the truth about God and employ their faculties in a manner that enables them to discover it. But why, then, is God hidden from so many of us? We will explore Edwards' answer to this question in the next section.

II

God's obscurity has two causes. The first is that spiritual truths are "high" and "abstract," remote from "the common business of life, things obvious to sense and men's direct view." Since language is chiefly designed to deal with these things, the difficulties attending propositions about God and His "grand design"are only to be expected. Indeed, that mysteries attend revelation is no more surprising than that they attend nature. Nature, too, is "a divine word, "the voice of God to intelligent creatures." Its "principal"end is "to be for the habitation, use, and benefit of mankind." Many aspects of nature can remain mysterious, however, without defeating that purpose. Revelation's power to guide and direct our journey toward God is also consistent with its being attended with mysteries and obscurities. All that is *required* of it is that it provide knowledge of what is needful for salvation. (Misc 1340, T 219–35)

Edwards' reflections on mystery may mitigate the problem of divine hiddenness. They do not solve it. For one thing, he thinks that the difficulties attending theology are no greater in kind (although greater in degree) than those attending other disciplines dealing with "high" and "abstract" matters, such as the mathematics of infinities or the philosophy of mind. (See Misc 1100 and 1340, for example.) The trouble is that our knowledge of mathematics and the human mind appears to be on a surer footing than our alleged knowledge of a God who seems hidden in ways in which mathematical objects and minds are not. More significantly, Edwards assumes that the difficulties attending a divine revelation would not obscure the truths needed for salvation. And yet, surely, even these are not obvious to most. So God's hiddenness still requires explanation. Not surprisingly, Edwards accounts for it by sin.

That "sufficient light for the knowledge of God" *is* available is attested by scripture. It is also implied by God's purposes for humanity. Since "the things of this world" were "made to be wholly subordinate to" eternal things, and we were given understanding "chiefly" in order to know them, there must be "sufficient evidence of their truth." So "if men have not respect to 'em as real and certain things," it can only be from "a dreadful stupidity of mind, occasioning a sottish insensibility of their truth and importance." (OS 149, 157)

This insensibility evinces itself in two ways – humanity's "proneness to idolatry" and its "disregard of eternal things." (OS 147) The first is demonstrated by idolatry's prevalence, and by the fact that even God's chosen people constantly fell into it. Humanity's disregard of eternal things is evident from the fact that even though eternal things are infinitely more important, maxims of prudence that are normally observed in worldly affairs are neglected in religious matters. Edwards asks us to consider "how careful and eagle eyed" the merchant is "to observe and improve his opportunities and advantages to enrich himself," or how easily people are "alarmed at the appearance of danger to their worldly estate," and how "they bestir themselves in such a case . . . to avoid the threatened calamity." (OS 154) Yet in spiritual affairs, we ignore familiar and obvious considerations like "the difference between long and short, the need of providing for futurity, the importance of improving proper opportunities, and of having good security, and a sure foundation, in affairs where our interest is greatly concerned, etc." (OS 156)

This blindness is our own fault. Note first that humans differ from the beasts because they "have *voluntary* actions about their own thoughts." (Mind 59, corollary, my emphasis) One can also have a "strong reason" (intelligence, facility in argumentation, and so on) without having a "good reason" (balance, good judgment, and the like). This happens "not so much from a defect of the reasoning powers as from a fault of the disposition" such as "a liableness to prejudice through natural temper or education or circumstances; or for want of a great love to truth and fear of error." (Mind 68) Faulty dispositions like these impair our ability to reason correctly in spiritual matters. For example, among the causes and types of prejudice Edwards lists in "Subjects to be Handled in the Treatise on the Mind" are ridicule and deference to people in authority. One can argue that, through their operation, the secular academy produces a prejudice against religion in the intellectuals it trains. To the degree that we are responsible for these dispositions, the errors they produce are our own fault. Then, too, God's "ordinary method . . . is to give grace to those that are much concerned about it, and earnestly and for a considerable time seek it, or continue to do things in order to it." (Misc 116b) What is true of grace in general is presumably also true of spiritual illumination. Here, too, God's "ordinary method" is to provide saving knowledge to those who seek it and "do things in order to it." If so, God will remain hidden from us unless we sincerely seek Him; our ignorance will be our own fault.

Ultimately, our failure to discern God is due to (1) our inattention to the ideas we have of Him and signs of His presence, and to (2) the absence of the simple idea of true beauty. Both are consequences of a lack of true benevolence and hence of sin (for sin just is the lack of true benevolence, a voluntary fixation of the will on "private systems" rather than being in general).[6]

Yet is this convincing? Even if we tend to make poor use of the evidence we have, couldn't God have remedied the situation by providing *more* evidence of His reality and goodness than He in fact has? Edwards doesn't address this question directly but two answers to it are implicit in *Original Sin*.

At one point, Edwards quotes from Locke's *Human Understanding*: "Were the will determined by the views of the good, as it appears in contemplation, greater or less to the understanding, it could never get loose from the infinite joys of heaven, once proposed, and considered *as possible*: the eternal condition of a future state infinitely outweighing the expectation of riches or honor, or any other worldly pleasure which we can propose to ourselves, though we should grant these the more probable to be obtained."[7] So to one who objects that neglect of eternal interests is not the result of "madness," but of one's finding the "things of another world . . . of a very doubtful nature," the reply is that even "though eternal things were considered [only] in their bare possibility, if men acted rationally, they would infinitely outweigh all temporal things in their influence on their hearts." That they don't evidences a "sottish insensibility of their truth and importance." (OS 152, 156–7)

The implication is clear. Few of those who argue to God's nonexistence from His hiddenness would deny that there is enough evidence to establish His "bare possibility." If Edwards is right, then, even if the evidence is as ambiguous as these critics allege, it is fully sufficient for the properly disposed to "much concern" themselves about eternal things, "earnestly . . . seek" them, and "do things in order to discern" them.

But of course we are not properly disposed, as Edwards well knows. Couldn't God have broken down our resistance by providing more evidence or a more complete revelation?

The second answer implicit in Edwards' remarks addresses this worry. Critics like Schellenberg consistently underestimate human corruption and sinfulness. Given our perversity, and tendency to idolatry, it is likely that even a fuller divine self-disclosure would be corrupted by us, and would thus not help us. What is needed isn't more evidence or a fuller revelation but a new heart to appreciate the evidence and revelation we have.

Of course, this answer raises further questions, and we will address them in later sections. But before doing so, let us consider another issue.

III

How hidden *is* God? Although the Fall has impaired our epistemic faculties, it has not destroyed them. Edwards says, for example, that "arguing for the being of a God according to the natural powers from everything we are conversant with is short, easy, and what we naturally fall into." (Misc 268) We have forfeited the power to *discover* true ideas about God, but not our ability to see their truth once they are presented to us. It may be "very needful that God should declare unto mankind what manner of being he is," but reason "is sufficient to confirm such a declaration after it is given, and enable us to see its consistence, harmony, and rationality in many respects." (Works 8, 217) The point of these remarks is this. Edwards believes that correct ideas of God have been disseminated to humankind by the gospel and by the traditions of the nations which have preserved "scraps of the truth" "derived originally from revelation" to their "ancestors . . . or from the Jews." Whether there was an original revelation to humankind or not, the important point is that, *whatever their origin*, correct ideas of God (that He is one, all powerful, good, and so on) *are* widely known. In particular, they are known by the atheists who dispute them and the agnostics who doubt them. So if we do have the power to discern the truth of these ideas once they have been discovered, a natural capacity to know the truths of natural religion is virtually universal.

Furthermore, Edwards' discussions of conscience indicate that he thought that not only have we retained our *power* to know truths of natural religion, we have retained some knowledge of the *truths themselves*. Conscience is universal,[8] and testifies to a divine lawgiver who punishes offenses. Thus, Miscellany 353 asserts that conscience "suggests to every man the relation and agreement there is between that which is wrong or unjust and punishment. This naturally disposes man to expect it," and hence to believe in a divine "revenger of iniquity." The clear implication of passages like these is this: In spite of the fact that the Fall has impaired our natural epistemic capacities and marred our epistemic environment, most of us discern the moral law and (at least dimly) recognize its theological implications.

The fact remains, though, that our epistemic faculties *are* impaired and that sinful social structures have created an uncongenial epistemic environment. As a result, "were it not for divine revelation [by which Edwards presumably means "*biblical* revelation"], I am persuaded there is no one doctrine of that which we call natural religion [but] would, notwithstanding all philosophy and learning, forever be involved in darkness, doubts, endless disputes and dreadful confusion." (Misc 350) Natural reason is insufficient for constructing an adequate natural theology (although not for discerning *some truths* of natural theology). Biblical revelation alone forms the basis of all sound philosophy.[9]

More importantly, natural knowledge of God is of no real help in securing salvation. In a sermon entitled "Christian Knowledge," Edwards asserts that "there are many truths concerning God and our duty to him which are evident by the light of nature." But "such are our circumstances now in our fallen state, that nothing which it is needful for us to know concerning God is manifest by the light of nature in the manner in which it is necessary to know it. For the knowledge of no truth in divinity is of significance to us otherwise than as it in some way or other belongs to the gospel scheme, or as it relates to a mediator. But the light of nature teaches us no truth in this matter." (Works 5, 378) Miscellany 837 makes a similar point and concludes: "It signifies nothing for us to know any one of God's perfections unless we know them as manifested in Christ."[10]

A saving conviction of the gospel's truth depends upon our possession of the simple idea of its beauty, and "we cannot have the idea without the adapted disposition of mind," namely, true benevolence or the love of being in general. Spiritual (and hence saving) knowledge depends upon "the practice of virtue and holiness." And "from hence it necessarily follows that the best and most able men in the world, with their greatest diligence and laboriousness, most eloquent speaking, clearest illustrations, and convincing arguments, can do nothing towards causing the knowledge of the things of the gospel. For the disposition . . . must necessarily be changed first." (Misc 123) Since Edwards believes that this change is effected by God, he concludes that saving knowledge is God's gift.[11]

If Edwards is right, the problem of God's hiddenness isn't a problem of evidences or proofs. God *could* convince doubters of the truths of natural religion by providing more internal and external evidence.[12] But (as Schellenberg points out) the primary value of knowledge of God consists in the fact that it is needed to establish a *proper* relationship with Him, and increasing natural knowledge of God *won't further that end.* There is no reason, then, why God should increase it.[13] There *does* appear to be a reason why God would wish to distribute *saving* knowledge more widely. But since saving knowledge, true benevolence, and salvation are logically coextensive, asking why God hasn't made Himself savingly known to more people is equivalent to asking why He hasn't bestowed the gift of salvation more widely. The problem of God's hiddenness is thus not really a problem of evidence but of *grace*: Why does God bestow it on some and not others? We will discuss an aspect of this question in Section VII. Before doing so, however, let us ask how uncommon saving knowledge really is.

Edwards' answer, surprisingly, is that the number of those who savingly know God vastly exceeds that of those who don't.

In *An Humble Attempt to Promote Explicit Agreement and Visible Union of God's People in Extraordinary Prayer*, Edwards asserts that the millennium will involve "an abundant outpouring of the Spirit of God, far greater and more extensive than ever yet has been." (HA 329) In those days "the earth shall be full of the knowledge of the Lord, *as the waters cover the sea*, which is as much as to say . . . there shall be no part of the world of mankind where there is not the knowledge of the Lord." (HA 332) In those days, "divine [and] human learning . . . shall be defused all over the world, and the lower world shall be all covered with light, the various parts of it mutually lighting each other . . . ignorant heathen lands shall be packed with most profound divines and most learned philosophers," and all shall "join the facets of their minds in exploring the glories of the Creator, their hearts in loving and adoring him, their hands in serving him, and their voices in making the welkin ring with his praise." (Misc 26)

The relevance of these claims is this: The millennium is the time in which "Satan's visible kingdom on earth shall be utterly overthrown" (HR 457), "the main season of the success of all that Christ did and suffered in the work of our redemption," and undoubtedly "by far the greater number of them that ever received the benefit of Christ's redemption, from the beginning of the world to the end of it, will receive it at that time." Indeed, Edwards calculates the ratio as, conservatively, about 100,000 to 1![14] (HA 342–3) What proportion, then, do those with saving knowledge bear to those without it? In attempting to determine this, we should remember that: (1) Edwards would have shared the contemporary opinion that the world had been in existence for a comparatively short time, and (2) believed that the millennium was immanent. (In Edwards' later, *and more restrained*, reflections, he expresses doubts as to whether, under even the most favorable circumstances, the millennium would begin before 2000!) Coupling these considerations with his speculations on the vast increase in population during the millennium,[15] it is reasonable to infer that Edwards believed that, in the long run, the number of those who enjoy the light of the gospel vastly outweighs that of those who don't. If so, then God *isn't* hidden from most people most of the time. Furthermore, the true ideas of God the saints have in heaven increase continuously both in quantity and quality, approaching infinity as their limit.[16]

The upshot of these considerations is that human knowledge of God utterly swamps human ignorance of Him. If we add the knowledge of angelic intelligences and God's own self-knowledge, the picture that emerges is of a world that, as Edwards says, is "filled with the knowledge of God as the waters cover the sea." God is thus *not*, on the whole, hidden. And this is important.

The problem of God's hiddenness is a form of the problem of evil, and while that problem is raised by *any* apparently pointless evil, it is aggravated by evil's pervasiveness.[17] If Edwards is right, critics like Schellenberg paint a distorted picture of our actual situation when they imply that God is largely hidden. The pervasiveness of *this* evil should not be exaggerated.

IV

But why is God hidden at all? Edwards is convinced that if "philosophy" (that is, natural reason) is not effectual in practice, while revelation and the interior motion of the Holy Spirit are, then God must have so arranged things for a reason. (HR 398–400) God's hiddenness to unconverted reason must, in other words, be part of His "grand design" – a design whose purpose is human happiness and His own glory; for "the work of providence . . . 'tis but one work," all the parts of which "are united, just as the several parts of one building" or machine. (HR 519) How, though, does God's hiding Himself from the unconverted contribute to this "grand design"?

A History of the Work of Redemption argues that philosophy flourished immediately before Christ's advent to prepare "a handmaid . . . to the gospel," for philosophy can be and was "improved" and used for its purposes. Our age is also an age of learning and this learning, too, can and eventually will be improved "as a handmaid to religion, as a means of a glorious advancement of the Kingdom of his Son, when human learning shall be subservient to understanding the scriptures and a clear explaining and glorious defending [of] the doctrines of Christianity." (HR 277–9, 439–41)

In spite of its splendor, however, and its potential usefulness to religion, ancient learning failed to find truth. This failure of pagan "reason and philosophy . . . in their highest ascent" demonstrated "the necessity of a divine teacher." Something similar is true in our own day. Because it scorns "to submit [its] reason to divine revelation," the world doesn't know God by its "learning and wisdom" but, instead, "wander[s] in the dark," and is "miserably deluded." Yet this failure, too, is part of God's plan. "God was pleased to suffer human learning to come to such a height before he sent the gospel into the world, so that the world might see the insufficiency of all their own wisdom for obtaining the knowledge of God without the gospel of Christ and the teaching of God's Spirit." So, now, when God has again shown us the "insufficiency of human wisdom," there is reason to expect our intellectual "humiliation" to be followed by an immanent "glorious outpouring" of the Spirit, through which He will "enlighten men's minds" "by his own immediate influence." (HR 277–9, 439–41)

Edwards' account of God's purpose in hiding Himself is thus similar to Luther's and Calvin's account of the law. The law was given so that we might exert ourselves to meet its demands and, failing to meet them, realize that our best efforts are useless – that salvation is by grace. The failure of reason "at its height" serves a similar purpose. Philosophy is given so that we might learn that our intellectual efforts are insufficient to find the truth that really matters. Divine hiddenness, in other words, is (at least partly) explained by God's desire to bring us to the realization that wisdom, too, is His gracious gift.

V

Edwards' position, then, is this. God is hidden in two ways. First, although true ideas about God and objectively adequate evidence of His reality and goodness are available to everyone, unbaptized reason typically goes astray by either denying God altogether or manufacturing idols. Second (and more importantly), while natural reason at its best can discern many truths about God, it can't discern the beauty of holiness, and hence can't appreciate the great truths of Christianity. A perception of the beauty of holiness is a function of the operation of a truly benevolent heart and the hearts of most of us are *not* truly benevolent. God's hiddenness is thus more accurately described as human blindness – a blindness that is ultimately our fault.

But God orders all things for good, for God necessarily does what is "fittest and best." Human blindness is good, all things considered, because it demonstrates the futility of human attempts to know God, and because a recognition of this futility leads to the realization that (saving) knowledge depends on God alone. Just as our failure to keep the law is a necessary precondition of the recognition that obedience is a divine gift, so our failure to know God is a necessary precondition of the realization that wisdom, too, is a supernatural endowment. The history of human blindness and ignorance, and of the disobedience which causes it, is merely the background against which God displays the glories of His grace – a grace that is "out of all proportion" to our wrong doing and blindness since, where sin and blindness were "multiplied, grace immeasurably exceeded it." (*Romans* 5: 15, 20)

How plausible is Edwards' view? The concluding sections will focus on one pressing issue – our alleged responsibility for our blindness to God's reality and goodness.

VI

In "The Use of Reason in Matters of Religion," Benjamin Whichcote asserts that nonbelief is unnatural. It falls into three categories. Some are "sunk below [their] nature," and "only [have] reason and understanding to live according to sence [sic] or to pursue . . . animal desires." Others have "affection and choice" to be atheists. These men and women "struggle" with themselves to "keep all thoughts of deity out of [their] mind" so that they may be "free from controul [sic]." The third category includes those affected by a "reprobacy of mind" which they have "contracted . . . by violent and unnatural practice."[18]

Claims like these seem empirically false. Surely, *some* of those who doubt religious truth or disbelieve it have neither sunk themselves in their animal nature nor corrupted their intellect by "violent and unnatural practice." And, far from resisting religious belief, many atheists and agnostics *want* to believe.

Still, appearances may be deceptive. Corruption of the intellect can be more subtle than Whichcote suggests. It can consist, for instance, in an inattention to divine things or a misprision of values that results from immersing oneself in ordinary human affairs. Again, the fact that many agnostics and atheists want to believe in God is consistent with their also *not* wanting to do so. For both can be true of the same person. Indeed, theists themselves often display the same ambivalence. Because they more or less consciously realize what real conversion requires, the desire to live comfortably weakens or distorts their tendency to believe. While they may wish to believe, and even do so, they don't want their belief to become so clear and compelling that they are forced to change radically their way of life.

But the most important point is this. If Edwards and others are right, properly functioning natural cognitive capacities, and an epistemic environment that is appropriate to their exercise, aren't the only things needed for a saving knowledge of God. True benevolence (Edwards) or a hunger for God (Pascal) may also be necessary.

There are several reasons for this. First, God is the Good, and a love of the Good may be needed to know it (Plato). Second, as Edwards points out, we are more attentive to what we love and to signs of its presence, and are more receptive to them. Third, like William James, Edwards thinks that we easily dismiss what we have no apparent use for. If our desires are centered on this life, we may be blind to signs of God's presence. Fourth, James argues that if reality *is* personal, it is more likely to reveal itself to us if we make overtures to it. And, finally, if the gospel exhibits true beauty or the splendor of holiness (as Edwards believes), then a lack of true benevolence would blind us to it. For it isn't "rational to suppose that those whose minds are full of spiritual pollution and under the power of filthy lusts, should have any relish or sense of [its] divine beauty or excellency." ("A Divine and Supernatural Light," Works 8, 16)[19]

Yet even if nonbelief *is* a product of faulty dispositions, it needn't be culpable. If it isn't, then attributing it to our blindness won't solve the problem of divine hiddenness. For if theism is true, and our blindness *isn't* our fault, then God, and not we, is ultimately responsible for it. And this seems inconsistent with His lovingkindness.

Edwards, of course, believes that we are responsible. Our blindness is a consequence of Adam's fall, and Adam's fault is ours. But Edwards' view is problematic for two reasons. First, it implies that we can inherit another's fault.[20] Second, Edwards is a theological determinist. In his view, God's decrees are a causally sufficient condition of Adam's sin. Yet if they are, it is difficult to see how even Adam can be blamed for it. Can we defend the claim that we are responsible for our blindness if we reject Edwards' theological determinism and the belief that another's fault can literally be ours?

It might seem that we can't. Schellenberg argues that there are cases of reasonable, and therefore nonculpable, nonbelief. In his view, A's belief that p is reasonable if and only if p seems reasonable to A, given A's evidence and inductive standards, and A's "evidence, inductive standards, and belief as to p's probability on the evidence have been, in his own view at the time, adequately investigated." (S 61) No doubt some nonbelief *is* reasonable in this sense.

But note that a person's nonbelief can be reasonable in the defined sense in circumstance C and not in circumstance C', where the person in question is *culpable for being in C rather than in C'*. If one is responsible for being in an epistemic environment in which relevant evidence is unavailable, for example, or in which cultivating the appropriate epistemic capacities is very difficult, one may be culpable for nonbelief in that environment even though, given the evidence actually at one's disposal in it, and the inductive standards one has, nonbelief is reasonable and one's investigation upon reflection seems adequate.

Note, too, that one can be scrupulous in amassing evidence, and in investigating one's inductive standards and the probability that one's evidence makes a proposition, p, true, and yet systematically get things wrong. For the problem often isn't with one's evidence or inductive standards but, rather, with one's *general take* on the evidence's overall force. There are no mechanical decision procedures for determining the prior probability of the hypotheses that interest us, the relevance or weight of evidence offered for and against them, or whether, when all is said and done, our positive evidence for them outweighs the negative. These determinations call for judgment, and judgment is affected by our personal histories, temperaments, and other "passional" factors.[21] If this is right, then the fact that nonbelief can't always be attributed to careless investigation, ignorance of obvious facts, logical mistakes, or intellectual dishonesty isn't conclusive. One must also investigate the passional roots of an agent's judgments before confidently asserting his or her epistemic guilt or innocence. If these observations are correct, and both our passional nature and epistemic environment are flawed in the way Edwards and the tradition think, then nonbelief can be an expression of human corruption in spite of its being reasonable in Schellenberg's sense.

But are we *culpably responsible* for our corruption, and hence for our nonbelief? Schellenberg would deny that we are. We do not, for the most part, choose our passional natures or our epistemic environments. So in so far as these determine our nonbelief, we aren't responsible for it; for we are not culpable for nonvoluntary flaws in our performance.

I find this questionable. First, I believe that Robert Adams' notion of involuntary sins should be taken more seriously than Schellenberg does. As Adams points out, we are sometimes appropriately blamed for desires, states of mind, and beliefs which are morally defective but involuntary. For example, a member's Hitler Jugend beliefs about, and attitudes towards, Jews were culpable regardless of how they were acquired. Again, we legitimately reproach ourselves and others for unjustified anger, self-righteousness, a lack of respect for others or a belief that they have no rights, and for other involuntary attitudes and beliefs. "Reproach," however, "is a form of blaming."[22] Second, neither Schellenberg (nor Swinburne upon whom he relies) do justice to the many ways in which we sinfully cooperate with, and thereby reinforce, our corrupt dispositions and the sinful social structures within which we function. We do so, for example, when we fail to resist them, when we implicitly assent to them, or when we fail to critically scrutinize them – faults which are all more or less voluntary. The issue I wish to pursue here, however, is different.

Social (and not personal) sin is often the primary cause of epistemic failure. As Plantinga points out, in order to function properly, it isn't enough that our epistemic faculties be in good working order. They must also be functioning in the epistemic environment for which they were designed. If our epistemic environment has been corrupted, then even healthy and mature epistemic faculties can go astray, and immature ones can be warped. When that happens, epistemic blindness is more the fault of others than our own.

Has our epistemic environment been marred in this way? Paul's and John's use of the terms "world" and "flesh" suggest that it has. The institutions of this world are centered on false values with the result that even the virtues of the worldly are (in Augustine's phrase) "splendid vices." Given that our political, economic, social, and familial structures have been marred by sin, it is not surprising that people are blind to the Good.

This does not absolve humanity of responsiblity for epistemic failure. For insofar as our own guilty choices contribute to the perpetuation of sinful social structures, we are responsible for the blindness they partially cause. In this view, then, we are not only (partially) responsible for our own noetic failure. We are also (partially) responsible for that of others. Noetic blindness *can* be traced back to sinful human choices, but the choices aren't only ours but those of countless others. Human freedom includes the ability to cause significant epistemic harm to others as well as to ourselves.

But would a good God permit us to harm others in this way? Richard Swinburne has argued that the ability to seriously harm others is the price of significant freedom. Does it follow that a capacity to cause *spiritual blindness* is necessary for significant freedom? Schellenberg thinks it doesn't. We can be responsible for others' temporal well being and ill being, and for strengthening and deepening their theistic belief where it already exists, without being responsible for that belief's formation. Since these responsibilities are sufficient for significant freedom, responsibility for other people's theistic belief isn't a great enough good to offset the corresponding evil – the pervasive blindness to God's reality and goodness caused by freedom's misuse. (S 191–9)

It isn't clear to me that this is right. Our freedom's significance is a function of our ability to benefit or harm ourselves and others. Since responsibility for others' temporal welfare, or for their deeper understanding of God, has neither the seriousness nor importance that a responsiblity for their recognition of God's reality and goodness has, an inability to act in such a way that others are blinded to that reality and goodness diminishes our freedom's significance. So if significant freedom really is a great good, it isn't clear that responsibility for others' belief isn't a great enough good to justify its costs.

Furthermore, "*exchange*" is a great good as Charles Williams points out.[23] That is, that each receives his or her good from another, and then bestows that good on a third, is itself a great good. But the *greatest* good we can either give or receive is faith. Hence, our (partial) dependence on others for it is also a great good.

Nevertheless, the good of responsiblity for others' beliefs might not be great enough if the cost was that some people are *never* in a position to freely respond to God's goodness. It does seem, for example, that God's love of my children would prevent Him from permitting me to act in such a way that they were eternally precluded from freely responding to Him.[24] Our responsibility for others' belief, however, does not entail that this is a real possibility. God can provide opportunites to freely respond to Him in the next life. He can also provide opportunities in this life *without interfering with our ability to deprive others of theistic belief.* We will see how God can accomplish this in the next section.

VII

Calvin, Edwards (and arguably Paul) claim that human beings have sufficient awareness of God to condemn them for their failure to love and trust Him. This light isn't sufficient for salvation, however. The illumination of the Holy Spirit is needed for the discernment of God's goodness in Christ without which salvation is a real possibility for no one. This illumination is freely bestowed on only some. Others fail to receive it and are therefore excluded from eternal life. In this view, God deprives some of the good of communion with Him.

This section explores a related but very different position, namely, that even where the good of theistic belief doesn't exist, God has provided sufficient light to make salvation a real possibility for everyone. If He has, then it can be true *both* that nonbelief is a product of (our own or others') sin *and* that God deprives no one of the good of communion with Him.[25]

On the face of it, this view seems false. As Schellenberg says, "a personal relationship with God" appears to entail "belief in Divine existence.... For I cannot love God, be grateful to God, or contemplate God's goodness unless I believe that there *is* a God." (S 30) Many, however, nonculpably fail to believe that God exists. A personal relationship with God (and hence salvation) thus isn't a real possibility *for them.*

But Schellenberg is mistaken. If I don't believe that God exists, I can't respond to God *under that description.* It doesn't follow that I can't respond *to God.* In the *Symposium*, Plato argues that our response to goods is (or can be) a response to *the* Good. According to traditional Christianity, however, *God* is the Good. When the nonbeliever responds to the good she sees, she may therefore be responding to God Himself. And perhaps one can go further.

Robert Holyer contends that it is reasonable to attribute an unconscious belief that p to A if A "displays some of the dispositions constitutive of a belief p [acting in terms of it, experiencing emotions appropriate to it, drawing inferences from it or holding beliefs from which it can be inferred] without giving assent to it."[26] An avowed atheist's response to the Good, or a non-theist's response to the Eternal, may (loosely) satisfy these tests. Acting in accordance with the Good is more or less extensionally equivalent to acting on theistic belief. (The conduct and intentions are similar.) Furthermore, since God is the Good, emotions appropriate to the latter are appropriate to the former. And, arguably, theism can be inferred from the existence of the Good and/or the moral law. It follows that if everyone has a glimpse of the Good, no one is precluded from the possibility of establishing an appropriate God-relationship – a relationship which, with time, may blossom into explicit belief in God, love of God, and trust in Him. While it may be doubted that everyone *does* have a glimpse of the Good, that they do so at some time or other is not clearly false.[27]

This view does imply, however, that the nature and quality of one's awareness of God (and hence the nature and quality of the relation with Him which this awareness makes possible) will differ sharply from person to person and from one group to another. Isn't this unfair? I have two comments.

The first is that, sin apart, we should expect spiritual capacities to differ. Given their cultural and historical circumstances, the San lacked the capacity to develop the calculus or nuclear physics. Nor could they have been expected to exhibit the moral sophistication of an educated and morally sensitive member of modern Western or east Asian society. (There is progress in ethical insight as well as in science – witness ancient and modern attitudes toward slavery and women.) And what is true of science and morality also seems true of religion. The post-axial religions are spiritually more sophisticated or advanced than those they displaced. (For one thing, the emphasis shifted from a concern for this world's goods for oneself and one's community to "Reality-centredness," a new life charactered by "love/compassion [agape/karuna]."[28])

None of this implies that the San were less intelligent, less moral, or even less spiritual than modern Christians, or Muslims, or Hindus. It *does* imply that they were less likely to possess many valuable religious truths. And this is significant since religious truth and its attainment are what concern us in this essay. Can these differences in capacity be explained by sin? I doubt it. The San weren't, as a group, more sinful than modern Christians or Muslims or Hindus. They were only less lucky.

But that a conscientious San and a conscientious Hindu or Christian are equally concerned to live according to the best of their ethical or spiritual lights doesn't imply that the *quality* of the moral or spiritual life of the latter isn't superior to that of the former. Would a loving God permit these inequalities?

It isn't clear that He wouldn't. (And this is my second remark.) There are differences in rank in both Dante's and Jonathan Edwards' heaven because there are inequalities of holiness and happiness.[29] The greater holiness and happiness of some, however, won't "be a damp" to the lesser holiness and happiness of others. In the first place, all are "acted by pure reason." As a result, the less holy ardently love the more holy "in proportion to the perfection and amiableness of the object loved," and so "delight . . . [to] see their happiness proportionable to their amiableness and so to their [own] love to them." In the second, all will "have as much love as they can bear," and as much happiness as they are "capable of enjoying or desiring, like a vessel thrown into a sea of happiness." Finally, those who exceed in holiness also exceed in humility and in their love to the less holy." Thus, in spite of inequalities, the ranks of heaven are joined together by an "inconceivably vehement mutual love." (Misc 5)[30]

Are these inequalities inconsistent either with God's fairness or His love of the saints (the truly benevolent)? If they aren't, then, *provided that God makes sufficient light for salvation available to everyone*, it isn't clear that He injures anyone by withholding the good of explicit theistic belief from some in this life. He doesn't injure those who fail to respond to the light they have, for this failure is their own fault. Nor does He injure those who do respond. For if the inequalities in holiness that exist in heaven are consistent with God's fairness and love, then so too, presumably, are those existing on earth.

VIII

Schellenberg argues that the occurrence of reasonable nonbelief disconfirms theism, and so disconfirms Christian or Jewish or Hindu theism. Schellenberg's argument is formally reminiscent of other evidential arguments from evil such as William Rowe's. Rowe argues that the existence of apparently pointless evils such as the slow and painful death of a fawn disconfirms theism and, hence, the Christian theism which entails it. As Robert Adams has pointed out,[31] however, Christians have a counter to this argument. In their opinion, the evidence *as a whole* (including evil) confirms Christian theism. Since Christian theism entails theism, the evidence as a whole also confirms theism.

My argument is similar. Jonathan Edwards presents a version of Christian theism that explains nonbelief. If the evidence as a whole (including the saints' experience of true beauty) confirms his Calvinian story, then the hiddenness of God does not disconfirm theism. Whether the evidence does confirm his Calvinian story is controversial although, in my opinion, the chief sticking point is not nonbelief's pervasiveness but God's decision to bestow saving grace on some and not others. In the concluding sections I have suggested ways in which Edwards' picture might be modified to address this worry. In either its unmodified, or modified form, however, the Edwardian picture is consistent with God's hiddenness.

Notes

1. J. L. Schellenberg, *Divine Hiddenness and Human Reason* (Ithaca: Cornell University Press, 1993), p. 2f. Henceforth, S.

2. Though Edwards' acceptance of the first premise is qualified. God *antecedently* wills that a reciprocal relationship always obtains between Himself and beings capable of it. But He doesn't *consequently* will this. (For, given that God's will is necessarily efficacious these reciprocal relationships would always obtain if He consequently willed that they obtain – and they don't.)

3. *A History of the Work of Redemption*, ed. John F. Wilson (New Haven: Yale University Press, 1989), 521–2, henceforth HR. Edwards' comments on the issues before us are scattered among a number of works. Particularly relevant are his "Miscellanies" many of which can be found in *The "Miscellanies," a-500*, ed. Thomas A. Schafer (New Haven: Yale University Press, 1994) and *The Philosophy of Jonathan Edwards from His Private Notebooks*, ed. Harvey G. Townsend (Eugene, Ore.: University of Oregon Press, 1955), henceforth Misc. and Misc. T, respectively. Also relevant are *The Nature of True Virtue*, in *Ethical Writings*, ed. Paul Ramsey (New Haven: Yale University Press, 1989), henceforth TV; *An Humble Attempt to Promote Explicit Agreement and Visible Union of God's People in Extraordinary Prayer*, in *Apocalyptic Writings*, ed. Stephen J. Stein (New Haven: Yale University Press, 1977), henceforth HA; *Original Sin*, ed. Clyde A. Holbrook (New Haven: Yale University Press, 1970), henceforth OS; *Religious Affections*, ed. John E. Smith (New Haven: Yale University Press, 1959), henceforth RA; "The Mind," in *Scientific and Philosophical Writings*, ed. Wallace E. Anderson (New Haven: Yale University Press, 1980), henceforth Mind; and "Treatise on Grace," in *Treatise on Grace and other Posthumous Writings*, ed. Paul Helm (Cambridge: James Clarke & Co., Ltd, 1971), henceforth TG. Other references are to *The Works of President Edwards*, 10 vols., Edward Williams and Edward Parsons, eds. (Edinburgh, 1817, 1847; New York: B. Franklin, 1968), henceforth Works.

4. For a more detailed explication of these themes see my *Reason and the Heart* (Ithaca: Cornell University Press, 1995), chapter 1.

5. But one must be careful. Edwards argues that a love of the love of God (i.e., a desire to love Him) which is based on self-interest (i.e., on the belief that it would be *beneficial* to love Him) has no saving force since it isn't really a love *of God*. But need a love of the love of God be self-interested?

6. Edwards thinks that true benevolence is a *supernatural* principle. Couldn't one argue that while true benevolence is *sufficient* for proper attention and due heed to the natural goods and evils associated with religion (the dreadful consequences of disobedience, for example, or the fittingness of proper gratitude for God's benefits), it isn't *necessary* since appropriate *natural* movements of the mind and heart will do as well? Edwards answer is that while natural principles are *inherently* sufficient to discern the truths of natural religion, they don't function properly when deserted by true benevolence. True benevolence is needed to rectify natural principles as well as supply supernatural ones.

7. John Locke, *An Essay Concerning Human Understanding* (New York: Dover, 1959), vol. 1, bk ii, p. 207, my emphasis.

8. Conscience is a "natural principle." (Misc 626, T 111)

9. It supplies sound first principles, frees the mind from its preoccupation with sense objects, and "gives the end" (salvation) for which learning about eternal things

should be sought, "and the only end that would be sufficient to move men to the pursuit." (Misc 350)

10. Quoted in Kenneth P. Minkema, "The Other Unfinished 'Great Work'," in *Jonathan Edwards' Writings*, ed. Stephen J. Stein (Bloomington: Indiana University Press, 1996), p. 55.

11. If I understand Edwards, then, even before the Fall, *saving* knowledge of God depends on the *supernaturally* bestowed idea of true beauty (or, more accurately, on the supernaturally bestowed disposition to love being in general which underlies the perception of true beauty). After the Fall, saving knowledge continues to depend on the gift of a new spiritual sense but now also depends on knowledge of the atoning work that the Fall made necessary. Natural knowledge of God is acquired with more difficulty after the Fall. But both before and after it, natural knowledge is insufficient to establish a proper God-relationship, since the latter involves a perception of the beauty of divine holiness.

12. The sort of "internal evidence" I have in mind is any experience of God's presence or activity that doesn't essentially include a sense of His true beauty.

13. Wouldn't a wider diffusion of natural knowledge multiply instances of earnest striving after God, and thus raise the probability that He will bestow saving knowledge more widely? Edwards' remarks contain two implicit responses to this question. First, given the corruption of the human heart (its lack of true benevolence and failure to discern holiness's beauty), it isn't clear that more widely diffused natural knowledge *would* multiply instances of sincere and earnest seeking. Second, an increase in instances of sincere and earnest seeking *does* raise the probability that God will diffuse saving knowledge more widely, for His normal mode of procedure is to bestow grace on those who make use of his "ordinances" (that is, who employ the "means of salvation" – prayer, Bible reading, the sacraments, etc.). But the latter aren't *causally efficacious*, and hence aren't "means" (in the proper sense) that God should or must employ to achieve the desired end of saving knowledge of Him. Grace is *freely* bestowed and our actions in no way bind God or constrain Him.

14. Edwards argues that population during the millennium will increase enormously, and that almost all will be pious Christians.

15. Edwards also suggests that the thousand years might be a figurative number. Thus, he says, "*if* we should suppose that glorious day to last no more than (literally) a thousand years." (HA 342, my emphasis) implying that the "thousand" years might last for a much longer period of time. Edwards notes that, if it does, the population figures will be much larger than his "conservative" estimate.

16. Cf Miscellany 105. Although Edwards doesn't explicitly *say* that the saint's knowledge of God approaches infinity as a limit, this interpretation of his remarks comports best with what he says elsewhere of the happiness of the saints in heaven. For example, in the *End for which God Created the World*, Edwards asserts that the happiness of the saints, consisting in the "increasing communication" of God's own knowledge, love, and joy, progressively increases, approaching infinity as its limit. (*End of Creation*, in Paul Ramsey, ed., *Ethical Writings*, op. cit., 443, 459.)

17. Both existentially and intellectually. The vast extent of human and animal misery can unnerve us. It is also easier to believe that we shouldn't expect to understand God's reasons for permitting this or that evil than to believe that we shouldn't expect to have some understanding of His reason for permitting so much evil.

18. From *Select Sermons* (1698), reprinted in C. A. Patrides, ed., *The Cambridge Platonists* (Cambridge: Harvard University Press, 1970), pp. 54–5.

19. For a fuller treatment of these points see my *Reason and the Heart*, op. cit.

20. For a discussion of Edwards' views and its difficulties see my "Original Sin," in Thomas V. Morris, ed., *Philosophy and the Christian Faith* (Notre Dame, Ind.: University of Notre Dame Press, 1988).

21. The term is William James'. For more on this point see my *Reason and the Heart*, op. cit.

22. Robert Adams, "Involuntary Sins," *The Philosophical Review* 94 (1985), pp. 3–31. Schellenberg's critique (S 62–4) relies on Richard Swinburne's (*Responsibility and Atonement* [Oxford: Clarendon Press, 1989]. p. 34). As far as I can see, neither Swinburne nor Schellenberg have an *argument* for the claim that we aren't culpable for "involuntary sins," merely an appeal to intuition.

23. For an excellent introduction to Williams see Mary McDermott Shideler, *The Theology of Romantic Love: A Study in the Writings of Charles Williams* (Grand Rapids, MI: Eerdmans, 1962).

24. Schellenberg thinks a good God would ensure that all nonculpable agents were explicitly aware of Him *at all times*. For an explicit awareness of God is necessary for personal communion with Him, and divine–human communion is both needed for human flourishing and prized by God for its own sake. (S chapter 1) If this is a good argument, then so is the following: A good God would ensure that each nonculpable agent was always as happy as he or she could be since happiness is either part of, or identical with, human flourishing, and God prizes human flourishing and His own bestowal of it. If this argument isn't compelling (and I don't think it is), then neither is Schellenberg's. Note that "A good God would make all His creatures happy (or provide them with worthwhile lives) unless they forfeit this through their own actions" doesn't entail "A good God would make all His creatures happy at all times (or as happy as they can be at all times, or provide them with the best possible lives at all times) unless they forfeit their well-being through their own actions." (I want my daughter to be happy, to have a life that is good on the whole. Does it follow that I want her to be happy, or to have a life that is good as a whole, *at each moment*? And precisely what would this involve? That she experience a balance of pleasure over pain at each moment? Or that, at each moment, she could truly say "My life up to now has been good"? What I think is odd here is distributing predicates which properly apply to a whole [a life, or a significant stretch of it] to its parts.) So even if the first is true, the second may not be.

25. The two views are related because, in both views, God ensures that everyone has some awareness of Him. I examine the notion that a loving God can freely bestow saving grace (and therefore presumably also saving illumination) on some and not others in "Jonathan Edwards and the Doctrine of Hell" (keynote address, Society of Christian Philosophers, Marquette University, March 1999).

26. Robert Holyer, "Unconscious Belief and Natural Theology," *The Heythrop Journal* 25 (1984), p. 428.

27. Schellenberg objects to moves of this kind in responding to Karl Rahner's notion of the "anonymous Christian." God desires "unrestricted personal communion with man" (Rahner), and *unrestricted* communion requires *explicit* belief. (S 41–3) But it isn't obvious to me that God's desire for unrestricted personal communion with us entails more than that (1) all agents will have *some* awareness of God (whether under that description or not), and that (2) all agents who respond appropriately to

the light they have will *at some time or other* become explicitly aware of God. (Cf footnote 24.) Note that Schellenberg himself asserts that, in spite of the fact that a weak belief in God's existence may adversely affect our relationship with Him, a weak belief is sufficient to meet the objection that a loving God would bestow knowledge of Himself upon everyone. (S 33) But if a weak belief in God is sufficient to meet the objection, why aren't awareness of God under another description, or unconscious belief in God, also sufficient? "What the Hiddenness of God Reveals: A Collaborative Discussion" dismisses this possibility on the ground that "implicit belief is an extremely distant second best" since "without it one is not in a position to *feel* God and to experience the greatest intrinsic good there is. Think, for example, of those who once believed but now do not, even though they *want* to. Saying that implicit belief will do in their case . . . is like saying that there is nothing out of the ordinary in a loving parent abandoning her child and providing evidence that causes her child to reasonably think that she might very well have been an imposter, leaving her child to wander the halls of the school where she used to work, let's say – to act *as if* she existed when he could summon the courage, while wondering at night whether she was really there. It is like saying that what a woman whose lover is at war (for all she knows, a casualty in the most recent battle) can experience of him at home – remembering him, thinking of him and wondering whether he is still alive – is as good as having him in her arms again." (Page 52, Schellenberg's italics.) But this won't do. In the first place, one can feel or experience God without recognizing that it is God one feels or experiences. In the second, Schellenberg's analogies caricature many non-theists' relation to the Good (which is in fact God). The Platonic lover of the *Symposium*, or the Kantian man or woman of good will who responds in awe to the moral law, or a Lao Tzu who conforms his life to the Tao aren't at all like the child or the woman in Schellenberg's examples. Implicit belief may be second best but it can be very good indeed.

28. John Hick, *An Interpretation of Religion* (New Haven: Yale University Press, 1989), Part One.
29. Which "are all one in heaven." (Misc 6)
30. Compare *Charity and its Fruits*, in *Ethical Writings*, ed. Paul Ramsey, op. cit., sermon 15, section iv.
31. In response to a presentation by Rowe at a Research Conference in the Philosophy of Religion held at the University of Nebraska, Lincoln, in April 1984.

6

Cognitive Idolatry and Divine Hiding

PAUL K. MOSER

Is there such a thing as Jewish-Christian philosophy? Probably. Or, at least, why not? Species of philosophy are pretty much a dime a dozen these days, and sometimes even that price is too high. Is there, however, a distinctively Jewish-Christian *epistemology*, or theory of knowledge? Now, that's a question whose answer does not come cheap. It concerns how, from a cognitive viewpoint, we properly relate to God, the Original Knower. The implications of this topic, we shall see, are profound indeed.

Questions about knowledge of *God* always hinge on questions about what *kind* of God we have in mind. The kind of God pertinent to a theistic epistemology makes all the difference in the world. Are we talking about the tenuous, domesticated God of deism, philosophical theism, or liberal Christianity? Or are we talking about the convicting, righteously loving God of Abraham, Isaac, Jacob, and Jesus? The latter is the gracious but elusive *personal* God who is a consuming fire against evil. This is also the God whose love for all requires divine suffering for us, even in the cross of God's Son, in order to remake us thoroughly in the divine image of holiness and self-giving love. In shying away from the latter robust conception of God, for the sake of a *mere theism*, philosophers and theologians neglect the distinctive epistemological resources of Jewish-Christian theism. They thereby miss the real point of knowledge of God. The result is an epistemology of theism that fails to challenge knowers in the way most needed: namely, in connection with human idolatry. (The pervasive retreat from a robust conception of God since the time of Descartes and the Enlightenment has contributed much, I suspect, to the demise of Jewish-Christian theism in the academy, but I cannot digress to that topic.)

Our topic becomes the world's oldest and largest profession and hobby: idolatry. We are all leading experts at idolatry. We excel at it, like nothing else, and (sad to say) we often enjoy it. Although ancient and Old Testamentish, like Sodom and Gomorrah, idolatry is nonetheless current and popular. In fact, it is all too popular. Ever before our eyes, idolatry is easily overlooked and conveniently ignored. Let's try to bring it to center stage in an area where it is seldom, if ever, mentioned: epistemology, particularly regarding knowledge of God.

Sooner or later, philosophers face the question whether God exists. In doing so, they join the rest of humanity in considering an issue of first importance. Always beware, however, of philosophers bearing theological gifts, as such gifts often come with a high price. The price influences one's mindset, in particular one's *expectations*, regarding God in ways that may be unexamined or unsustainable. It's important to ask, then: What *are* our expectations regarding God? These expectations largely determine our commitments regarding God, and they may say more about *us*, including our own values, than about *God*. In addition, these expectations may prevent us from having the needed eyes to see and ears to hear genuine revelation from God.

Do we expect certain things of God (if God exists) such that those things evidently fail to obtain, thereby calling God's existence or authority into question? Do we, for instance, expect God to entertain us cognitively, with signs and wonders or with dreams and ecstatic experiences? At any rate, what, if anything, grounds our expectations regarding God? Perhaps our expectations clash with God's own aim to bring us freely to acknowledge and gratefully to trust God (rather than false gods) as the ultimate source of our flourishing. We shall see how the nature of the Jewish-Christian God has special implications for familiar questions about God's existence and hiding and for cognitive idolatry.

1. Rationality and God

For philosophers, among others, the innocent-looking ontological question whether God exists moves quickly to the thorny epistemological question whether it is *rational* for us to believe that God exists. The latter question, although common, demands immediate attention to its slippery terms "rational" and "God."

The term "rational" encompasses such things as *prudential* rationality (concerning what is prudent in belief or action), *moral* rationality (concerning what is morally good, right, or praiseworthy in belief or action), and *epistemic* rationality (concerning the kind of warrant appropriate to *knowledge* that a belief is true). Still other species of rationality compete for our attention, but we shall attend to epistemic rationality, the kind suitable for knowledge.[1] Let's also acknowledge that epistemic rationality does not require the kind of deductively valid proof characteristic of logic and mathematics. Otherwise, there would not be much rationality or knowledge at all in the sciences or in ordinary empirical decision-making.

In many cases, epistemic rationality and thus knowledge depend not on deductive proof but rather on an *inference to a best available explanation* of our whole range of evidence found in experience and reflection. Likewise, epistemically rational belief that God exists may depend on whether the thesis that God exists plays an indispensable role in a best available explanation of our whole range of experience and reflection. Aiming for the cognitively best in inquiry, we often pursue true beliefs contributing to a best available explanation of the world, including the whole range of experience.

The term "God" has been used to signify everyone from the mythical Zeus of Greece to the ravenous Thor of Scandinavia to the wretched Jim Jones of Guyana to the righteously gracious Yahweh of Israel. So the term desperately needs refinement. In keeping with a familiar theistic tradition, let's use the term "God" as a supreme title. It requires of its holder: (a) worthiness of worship and full life commitment and thus (b) moral perfection and (c) an all-loving character. This does not settle the issue whether God actually exists, as the title might be satisfied by no one at all. The term might connote while failing to denote. Because God must be worthy of worship and full trust, God must be altogether morally good, a God of unflagging righteousness. A morally corrupt all-powerful being might merit *fear* from us but would not be worthy of our worship and full trust. So not just any unstoppable bully can satisfy the job description for "God." Even an all-powerful being who is altogether just, or fair, but nonetheless unloving would not fit the bill.

A being worthy of worship and full trust must be all-compassionate; otherwise, a moral failing would interfere. So God must have *all-inclusive* compassion and thus must be willing to suffer for the moral good of all those needing help. This holds true regardless of whether all or even most people will accept God's help.[2] Do we have any evidence of such compassion-in-action, past or present? Scanning world history with due care and openness, we find that a plausible candidate for the job of all-compassionate God is Yahweh, the God of Jewish-Christian theism and the avowed Father of that disturbing Jewish outcast, Jesus of Nazareth. We can acknowledge, nonetheless, that some nominal followers of Yahweh have attributed vicious commands and actions to Yahweh for their own self-serving ends.[3] So we may grant that the history of nominal Judaism and Christianity fails to portray Yahweh uniformly as all-compassionate. Bad counterfeits, however, do not destroy the genuine article.

2.   God, Explanation, and Moral Excellence

Turning to *warrant* for acknowledging the Jewish-Christian God, we should consider that God's existence may play a crucial role in a best available explanation of the world, including our own origin and status in the world. God's existing may remove what Bertrand Russell has called "the inexhaustible mystery of existence" of the world.[4] The first explanation-seeking question is: Why is there a material world *rather than no such world at all*? The next such question is: Why is there the present law-governed material world, hospitable to some extent to the emergence of such moral agents as human persons, *rather than a world markedly different?* There might have been a world of just chaotic events, like defective fireworks, and nothing else. Evidently, the material world need not have been hospitable to the emergence of human persons.

The existence of goal-directed intentions of the Jewish-Christian God can supply plausible answers to relevant explanation-seeking questions, thereby removing Russell's supposedly unexplainable mystery of the world's existence. The existence of God as creator and sustainer of the world can figure crucially in a best available explanation of (a) why there is a material world rather than no such world at all and (b) why there is the present law-governed material world, hospitable to some extent to the emergence of human persons, rather than a significantly different world.[5] As an all-powerful creative agent, God has *goal-directed causal powers* that can figure in the needed explanation and thereby remove Russell's mystery.

Even though God's existence may remove the mystery of the world's existence, it will *not* remove all mystery about existence. Doggedly, mystery chases theism all the way up the tree of explanation. If, for example, we can imagine that God does not exist (and it seems we can), then we are left with the mystery of God's existence, and *God* evidently is too. We can ask why reality is such that God exists rather than being such that God does not exist. If God is not the explanation of this feature of reality, mystery ensues – perhaps even for God. (A principle of sufficient reason may thereby be threatened, but God's omniscience is not, because it does not follow that there are truths not known by God. Furthermore, the question at hand does not presume that God had a beginning.) On this approach, theists exchange the mystery of the world's existence for the mystery of God's existence (not to be confused with an ill-formed issue about the origin of God's existence).

One might plausibly wonder what theists really gain here. Even if theological mystery seems more palatable than cosmological mystery, it is mystery still and it trims the explanatory sails of theism. A similar lesson follows from the familiar view that God exists necessarily. On that view, too, we reach a point where explanation runs out, where ontology outstrips available explanation. Even necessitarians about God must grant that some parts of theistic ontology do not enjoy explanation. Mystery does indeed dog theism. Still, not all explanation is lost.

Some relevant explanation-seeking questions focus on us as morally responsible agents. For example, why are there such self-determining beings as human persons with the remarkable feature of conscious free agency? We often act, for better or worse, on *intentions* to achieve our ends, and thereby distinguish ourselves, decisively, from the unconscious material world.[6] The difference is not just that we can *think*; it also includes our being able to *act* intentionally, with an end in view. We are purposive agents who often act in a goal-directed manner. Witness your undertaking the reading of this essay – no fluke of nature, I hope. Our lives thus manifest self-determining *actions*, and not just *happenings*. This is an astonishing fact about us, a fact that calls for careful explanation.

Why, then, are there such remarkable beings as free, self-determining human agents at all? This question concerns why such beings arrived on the scene *in the first place*, not why they have persisted. In addition, it primarily concerns the psychological rather than biological make-up of such beings. *Perhaps* their arrival on the scene was just an astonishing accident of nature, without any intelligent guidance. Acknowledgment of the Jewish-Christian God, in contrast, enables us to answer this otherwise mysterious question in a way that is at least coherent. According to Jewish-Christian theism, God created, perhaps indirectly, beings in God's own image of conscious free agency to enable those beings to sustain properly loving relationships with God and with each other. Such theism affirms that we are thus under-creators created in the image of the original creator.

Of course, as noted, we *might* be a fluke of blind, uncaring nature, but then again we might be dreaming all of our lives, too. Seeking refuge in random chance, or accident, such nontheists as Russell show their willingness to make a significant faith commitment to the world-making efficacy of chance, thereby avoiding acknowledgment of God. So popular opinion about theism notwithstanding, the leap of faith may actually be on the *other* foot, on the foot of theorists invoking chance as world-making.[7]

The true God, being morally impeccable, would always seek what is morally best for us, thereby giving us an opportunity to achieve, without coercion, God's kind of moral goodness. God, in other words, would be a *redeemer* enabling us, through knowledge of God, to be rescued without coercion from our moral deficiencies and thereby to become morally like God. In this regard, we would be able to share in God's moral nature. This opportunity, being inherently moral, would be *volitional* and not just intellectual. It would enable us to have our *wills* transformed, not just our intellects (that is, our thoughts and beliefs). So the kind of knowledge of God valued by the true God would be volitionally transformative rather than merely intellectual. It would concern a change of will, of volitional orientation, that exceeds belief formation, contemplation, insight, enlightenment, and sensory experience.

Knowledge of God would be important in the relevant moral transformation. It would suitably relate, personally as well as psychologically, those being transformed to their personal transformer. The apostle Paul, accordingly, grounds Christian knowledge of God in new reconciliation with God (see 2 Corinthians 5:16–19). He also contrasts such knowledge with "knowledge after the flesh," knowledge independent of suitable moral transformation.[8]

Moral excellence in relationships among agents requires self-giving compassion and interpersonal trust for the sake of the moral goodness of all involved. So any being worthy of the preeminent title "God" must consistently promote such compassion and trust. The true God, accordingly, must aim to transform such typically self-promoting agents as humans into morally new people, renewed after the unselfish character of God. In keeping with that aim, we humans must become agents of God's purportedly all-inclusive kingdom rather than agents of our own exclusive kingdoms.

As morally impeccable, the true God must work in human history to encourage free human agents to seek God's kind of moral excellence via knowing God and God's goodness. More specifically, the true God must seek an all-inclusive community of people guided by knowing God and God's goodness. Our knowing God (at God's appointed time) is central to God's moral project, because such knowing enables the kind of personal guidance and transformation crucial to our renewal toward God's moral character. In the absence of risky and potentially painful redemptive work, God could still be morally *just* in challenging human agents who have rejected God's goodness. God would not then be gracious, however, owing to the absence of God's merciful and forgiving compassion toward wayward humans.

The history of ancient Israel, particularly its prophetic tradition, exhibits patterns of human behavior and instruction that are morally extraordinary.[9] These patterns are arguably best explained by the Hebraic view (suggested, for example, in Genesis 12:3, 22:15–18, 28:13–14) that a morally serious loving God has indeed chosen a certain group of people in order to transform, morally and spiritually, all the nations of the world. (Here and throughout, I use "morally serious" to connote genuine unselfish caring for the moral good of others.) In ancient Israel we find historical evidence, however fallible, of a redeeming God who seeks to liberate a lowly tribal community from its self-destructive ways and to encourage this community to lead outsiders to turn to God for redemption.[10]

3.   Theism: Thin and Robust

Perhaps Jewish-Christian theism plays a crucial role in a best explanation of the world, including ourselves, and thereby gains epistemic warrant. That view is plausible, and I support it. Even so, that view would yield at most *cognitively thin theism*: the view that it is epistemically rational, at least for some people, to believe *that* God exists. Such theism is thin indeed, as even avowed enemies of God can rationally believe that God exists and even endorse cognitively thin theism. One can believe that God exists but hate God. Even the demons believe and shudder, according to the epistle of James (2:19).

The chief human deficiency regarding God is not in our explanatory or intellectual abilities but is rather in our moral orientation regarding authority, or lordship, over our lives. So, desiring genuine reconciliation, the true God would not settle for thin theism but would promote *cognitively robust theism*:

the view that we epistemically should lovingly *believe in*, or trust, God *as the Lord of our lives*. Cognitively robust theism entails cognitively thin theism but requires a life-commitment to a personal Lord, beyond rational belief that God exists. This Lord is not the conclusion of an argument but is rather the personal enabler of any person offering an argument.

Our knowing God as personal Lord reconciles us to God by requiring us gratefully to trust in God as the supreme moral authority for our lives. In such knowing we acknowledge our moral accountability to God and even *rely* on God as our ultimate moral guide. Such knowing is not a matter of mere warranted assent. It entails knowing God as Lord *in the second-person*, as morally supreme "You," rather than as an undemanding object of human knowledge. Divine lordship entails supreme moral leadership, and moral leadership entails a call to moral accountability and direction. This is a call to moral redirection and transformation in the case of selfish human recipients. Knowing God as Lord requires our sincerely committing *ourselves* to God as follows: "Not my will be done, but Your will be done," "Not my kingdom come, but Your kingdom come." Such knowing follows a path through Gethsemane to the cross, as it depends on our volitional sensitivity and submission to the will of God. We come truly to know God not in our own cognitive strength but rather in our thoroughgoing weakness relative to the priority of God's will.[11]

Cognitively robust theism acknowledges that the true God calls us to moral transformation away from our self-centeredness toward the unselfish, loving character of God. Perhaps this call comes through personal conscience, and perhaps it sometimes relies on a message brought by other people. Do we, however, have a *right* to know God? In particular, are we *entitled* to know that God exists without knowing God *as Lord*, as the morally supreme agent over our lives, including our intellectual lives? Some people uncritically assume so, but this is unconvincing.

Who is entitled to decide how one may know God – humans or God? Given our complete inferiority relative to God, can *we* reasonably make demands on God in favor of *our* preferred ways of knowing God? Many people proceed as if we have a right to know God on our preferred terms. This is, however, nothing more than a self-serving assumption. Nothing requires that God supply knowledge of God on our preferred terms. God evidently owes us no such thing at all, despite common expectations to the contrary.

God owes us nothing beyond fidelity to a loving character and to the promises stemming from such a character. On sincere reflection we see that we are in no position to make evidential demands of God beyond such fidelity. Nothing requires that God allow for (i) our *propositional* knowledge that God exists apart from (ii) our *filial* knowledge of God as Lord and Father of our lives. Ideally the two emerge together, although philosophers have a bad habit of neglecting the key role of filial knowledge of God. God can be all-loving in supplying evidence of God's existence in a manner sensitive to human receptivity to filial knowledge of God. We have no right to demand evidence of God's reality that fails to challenge us to undergo volitional transformation toward God's character. So God's hiding from a *casual*, or *indifferent*, inquirer does not count against the reality of God's existence.

God's ways of imparting vital knowledge of God do not meet our natural expectations. This is in keeping with God's surprising offer of redemption by *grace* rather than by *earning*. Divine grace has loomed large in Jewish-Christian accounts of redemption, but it has rarely emerged as significant in treatments of knowledge of God. This needs correction. God's dispensing of vital knowledge of God is truly gracious, a genuine *gift* calling for grateful reception. *How* we may know God depends on what God lovingly wants *for* us and *from* us. Primarily God wants us to become, in relationship with God, humbly loving as God is. As a result, we truly come to know God only if we acknowledge our unworthiness of knowing God. It is thus illuminating to ask about the attitudes of people inquiring about God. What are our *intentions* in having knowledge of God? What do we aim to do with such knowledge? Do we aim to use it for our own honor and self-promotion, treating it as self-credit rather than as an unearned gift? Do we have a bias against cognitively robust theism, in particular against filial knowing of God as a personal Lord who lovingly holds us morally accountable and expects grateful obedience from us? I suspect that we typically do.

The epistemology of Jewish-Christian theism disallows God's being trivialized as an undemanding object of knowledge for our convenient examination or speculation. It calls for filial knowledge of God as the Lord who is the supreme *personal* guide and gift giver for human life.[12] This God is the lovingly commanding agent to whom we are ultimately responsible and the final personal authority over all creation, including over human knowers. In filial knowledge of God, we have knowledge of a supreme *personal* subject, not of a mere object for casual reflection. This is not knowledge of a vague "first cause," "ultimate power," "ground of being," or even a "best explanation." It rather is *convicting* knowledge of a personal, communicating Lord who expects grateful commitment by way of our appropriating God's gracious redemption. Such convicting knowledge includes our being judged and found unworthy by the standard of God's morally supreme love. God's will thereby meets, convicts, and redirects our will. Both sides of this relationship are thus personal.

Filial knowledge of God is *reconciling* personal knowledge whereby we enter into an appropriate *child-parent* relationship with God. Such knowledge is personally transforming, not impersonally abstract or morally impotent. It is communicated by God's *personal* Spirit in a way that demands full life-commitment. Knowledge of a robustly personal God requires *personal* evidence (such as evidence of a will), not mere nonpersonal reasons. So this knowledge is not just a true conclusion endorsed on the basis of warranted inference. Sound argument, however warranted, does not itself offer the kind of personal *power* central to Jewish-Christian theism: namely, God's personal power of self-giving love as our liberator, motivator, and transformer. Filial knowledge of God entails our commitment to participate gratefully in God's purposes with all that we are and have. It is thus purposeful knowledge as loving and obedient discipleship toward a personal agent, not mere intellectual assent. It is inherently person-relational.

The personal Lord who loves, commands, and reconciles is not the silent God of much natural theology. As a result, the Jewish-Christian scriptures are uniformly devoid of what philosophers call "natural theology." A God who is Lord must lead and thus must *call* us in certain directions at the appropriate time. So God must command, and this results in our being convicted and judged at least for our failure to be suitably grateful or otherwise obedient toward God previously.

We cannot have filial knowledge of God if we are seriously dishonest about our *moral* standing relative to God. Genuine reconciliation calls for awareness of the need for reconciliation. So God must begin by trying to convict us of this need by prompting our awareness of falling short of grateful filial relationship with God. For the sake of human good, God as Reconciler must seek to function at the core of our lives, not just at the periphery. So God must seek to be found by us, and to find us, at a level of considerable depth in our lives, rather than at the surface of who we are. The self-reflective honesty and unselfish love sought by God work at the core of a life *or not at all*. We thus can see the inadequacy of "signs and wonders," dreams and ecstatic experiences, and abstract philosophical arguments as the main avenues to God. God must bring us to a level of moral depth, or seriousness, by some means or other, perhaps even through our facing impending death. God leads us to such depth by convicting us of our casual ingratitude, moral dullness, selfish indifference, unwarranted pride, and self-defensive fear. In filial knowledge, God as Reconciler offers to change us by convicting us of the stark contrast between (a) what we are on our own and (b) what we can be as willing participants in God's program of filial reconciliation to God.

Left to our own devices, we are all soon dead and buried, however we may try to obscure this by directing attention elsewhere. (Pascal's *Pensées* identifies many of our typical diversionary tactics on this front.) So our own resources, cognitive and otherwise, bring us finally to nought, leaving us with no genuine hope for our own future. In this respect, time is only on God's side. Our impending death serves as God's firm wake-up call to us. It prompts a focal question: what, at bottom, are we living *for*, and is it worthwhile, even on our own considered values? Given the dismal fate of our own devices, we need a redemptive *word* from God, not just the kind of evidence of God's existence suitable to thin theism. (For Jewish and Christian endorsement of the latter point, see, for instance, Deuteronomy 30:11–14 and Romans 10:6–8.)

As a result, we must be willing to *listen* for the needed word and to obey it when it comes to us.

We naturally resist going to self-reflective moral depth in our lives, because doing so is painful, self-effacing, and humbling. It may also entail exclusion by our peers if the results are socially challenging or awkward. In addition, we typically want to be accountable ultimately only to ourselves and to our own preferred moral and epistemological standards. As Thomas Nagel notes, the existence of God poses a serious "cosmic authority problem" for us (so much so that Nagel hopes that God does not exist).[13] We may say that we *would* be accountable to God *if only* the proper evidence were at hand, but then *we* conveniently set the terms (such as extreme empiricist or rationalist terms) for proper evidence so as to control the outcome. God as Reconciler must therefore play the role of a benevolent reconstructive surgeon, using an uncomfortable procedure of conviction of moral shortcoming to begin a process of filial reconciliation. We must be brought low indeed. God thereby brings us from ungrateful moral shallowness to grateful moral depth, toward personal reconciliation with God.

God must work as an internal, convicting Authority and Assurer who makes people qualitatively new, in a way that makes Cartesian certainty look sterile and weak.[14] God's Spirit must witness with our spirits that we are indeed children of God, that God is indeed our gracious Father. As Reconciler, God must offer a unique kind of personal assurance, as a gift and not as a tool for abusive human control. God, after all, has no need of a cognitive sledgehammer. This fits well with robust theism as well as God's personal character of humble love.

4. Idolatry

Thin theism, focusing on theoretical knowledge that God exists, can obscure the importance of knowing God as the personal Lord who calls us to a change of lordship, mindset, and moral direction. Oversimplifications of God (for example, as merely sentimental, friendly, harsh, or distant) can be similarly obscuring, in a way that enables us to make a self-controllable idol of "God" (where "God" is not the true God). So even devout theism can be idolatrous. For our own good, we cannot master God as just another undemanding object of human knowledge, as a manipulable possession, or as a meritorious reward. As we should expect, God is not ours to control; similarly for proper knowledge and evidence of God. God as known reveals God's knowledge *of us* and thereby seeks to transform us in love, with respect for our freedom. Our knowledge *about* God and our quest for it threaten to become idols if divorced from reconciling, filial knowledge of God as Lord. Robust theism offers a safeguard against this threat.

Idolatry, at bottom, is our not letting the true God be Lord in our lives. It is commitment to something other than the true God as our ultimate authority and source of flourishing. It is inherently a rejection of God's authority and a quest for self-definition, self-importance, and self-fulfillment *on our own terms*. Idolatry flouts the serious challenge we have from the true God to be free of self-defensive fear, self-exaltation, and self-centeredness in general. It exchanges the supremacy of God over one's life for the supremacy of something inferior to God.[15]

Idolaters deny, in deed if not in word, their status as *dependent* knowers and creatures of the true God. They seek independence of God. In doing so, they opt for infidelity toward God and deny God's supremacy over us. Idolaters are not satisfied with being secondary, dependent creators who honor God as the only independent creator. They thus aim to reassign God's authority to something else. Typically idolaters reassign God's authority to *themselves*; they thus seek to be ultimately *self*-governing and *self*-defining. This involves a kind of self-assertion that disregards the supremacy of God. Such self-assertion is as tenuous and ephemeral as the human self behind the assertion. It will soon perish along with that self while the true God endures. The ways of human self-assertion are short-lived indeed. They also obscure our available evidence of God's reality and supremacy.

Cognitive idolatry denies God's supremacy in recommending ways of knowing God. Just as God is properly supreme in the area of recommending ways of human *action*, so also God merits supremacy in prescribing ways of *knowing*. This is particularly true regarding ways of knowing God. Cognitive idolatry relies on a standard for knowledge that excludes the primacy of the morally self-transforming knowledge of God central to knowing God as Lord. It rests on an epistemological standard, whether empiricist, rationalist, or some hybrid, that does not let God be Lord. Such idolatry aims to protect one's lifestyle from serious challenge by the God who calls, convicts, and reconciles. It disallows knowledge of God as personal subject and Lord to whom we are morally and cognitively responsible. It allows at most for knowledge of God as an undemanding object of human knowledge. Cognitive idolatry exploits epistemological standards to refuse to let God be supreme in one's life. A cosmic authority problem lies behind much cognitive idolatry and, for that matter, idolatry in general.

A prominent kind of cognitive idolatry may be called *the idolatry of neutral proof*. Such idolatry includes our demanding decisive evidence of God's existence regardless of the direction of our own will relative to God's will. We thereby place ourselves in the position of judge over God's reality without requiring ourselves to commit sincerely to God as Lord of our lives. This kind of idolatry is opposed vigorously in Isaiah 58, where Yahweh complains as follows about his people of Israel: ". . . they seek me daily, and delight to know my ways, as if they were a nation that did righteousness and did not forsake the ordinance of their God." Note the common desire for knowing God's ways without submission to God's will. Jewish-Christian theism thus calls for an epistemology of faithful obedience as an antidote to the common idolatry of neutral proof. The evidence of the true God's reality comes with a personal call to trust and to obey this God. This is, after all, a *personal* God who calls people to repentance, fidelity, and obedience. This is a God who insists that people, for their own good, be humbly loving as God is.

Questions about our ultimate cognitive authority concern what we ultimately trust as our source of knowledge. Jewish-Christian theism identifies a central human choice between idolatry and respectful, grateful trust in God. Trust in God as our personal Lord, which extends in content beyond the present to our futures, is never fully *determined* by past or present evidence, even when adequately *grounded* in past and present evidence. It respects the openness of God to call people in ways going beyond historical precedent. (Witness the novel call to Jesus as Messiah to die on a criminal's Roman cross.) Such trust also esteems God as the only ultimate source of power to break our bondage to self-destructive idols, whatever they happen to be. Whether cognitive or noncognitive, our idols encroach on God's rightful authority over us. God's idol-breaking power, according to Jewish-Christian theism, stems from God's self-giving, sustaining compassion toward us that frees us from our selfish and self-destructive fears.

We typically favor idols over the true God given our penchant for maintaining authority, or lordship, over our lives. Our typical attitude is thus: I will live my life *my* way, to get *what* I want, *when* I want it. We thereby exalt ourselves over the true God, and then lose our self-control to control by idols, from which we seek success, happiness, honor, and self-approval. We exchange God's supreme reality for a false substitute. Accordingly, we naturally give primary, if not exclusive, value to *controllable* knowledge rather than to filial knowledge dependent on the gracious offer of an *uncontrollable* God. Indeed, the human obsession with self-control over one's circumstances runs afoul of God's calling us to moral transformation through gratefully trusting *God* as Lord of our lives. We tend to trivialize what we can control or what is conveniently available to us. Our controlling available evidence for God would be, in effect, to control God. For our own good, however, God will not be controlled or trivialized; nor are we in control of evidence for God. So we cannot preclude God's hiding from us at times. Indeed, such hiding should be expected, given our self-destructive tendencies and resulting need of God's corrective love.

5. Divine Hiding

We can now begin to ask about suitable evidence for the reality of God's call. Ideally, evidence and assurance regarding God's call come firsthand, from God's direct communication rather than from just our own reasoning.

Accordingly, God gives testimony to God's presence and thus existence in an inherently personal manner. Such testimony is not transferable or reproducible in a decisive way or manipulable by us for selfish, self-crediting ends. As God's call is not coercive but is respectful of human freedom, recipients of God's call need to be sincerely open to God's transforming love. Bringing the Hebrew prophetic tradition to its unique climax, Jesus remarked that the pure in heart will see God. He also suggested, in keeping with the Hebrew scriptures, that God "hides" his ways from ungrateful holdouts and reveals himself to those humbly open to God's program of morally serious loving community (see Luke 10:21–22/Matthew 11:25–27).[16]

How can an all-loving God fail to be manifested so as to remove all serious doubt about God's existence? The Hebrew scriptures and the New Testament present us with an all-loving God who sometimes hides from people, a God whose reality is sometimes less than transparent to people. Many people assume that an all-loving God's existence, if real, would be *obvious* to all normal adult humans. God's existence is not, however, obvious to all normal adult humans. So, according to many people, we may reasonably deny that God exists. Some normal humans, of course, do not believe that God exists. They claim not to have adequate evidence (for reasonable belief) that God exists. Would an all-loving God permit such doubt about God's existence?

One important issue is whether the people in question are readily *able* to acquire evidence indicative of God. If they are thus able, divine hiding is not a basis for agnosticism or atheism.[17] If the God who on occasion hides has left adequate *available* evidence of God's existence, including signals of such evidence, for all people, then theism will be epistemically unscathed by divine hiding. Because people often look in the wrong places for such evidence, we shall take up the latter topic below. The important point now is that God's hiding from some people, at least on occasion, does not automatically recommend agnosticism or atheism. At a minimum, the available evidence in favor of God's existence merits equal consideration. God's hiding from some people, in any case, does not entail either God's hiding from *all* people always or *everybody's* lacking adequate evidence for God's existence or even anybody's lacking *available* evidence for God's existence.

Conceivably, God hides on occasion from some people for various reasons, including (a) to teach people to yearn for, and thus eventually to value, personal relationship with God, (b) to strengthen grateful trust in God even when times look altogether bleak, (c) to remove human complacency toward God and God's purposes, and (d) to shatter prideful human self-reliance. A particularly troubling instance of God's hiding underlies the distressing plea of Jesus on the cross: "My God, my God, why have you forsaken me?" (Mark 15:34; Matthew 27:46). Evidently, God hid from Jesus at the height of his excruciating suffering from Roman crucifixion. As a result of his suffering and God's hiding, Jesus perhaps learned deeper trust in his often unpredictable but nonetheless redeeming Father. Not all of God's hiding, at any rate, aims to judge human rebellion.

God's hiding on occasion from people can be constructively challenging from a moral viewpoint. One's taking the presence of God for granted, as if it were ever at one's personal disposal, entails a kind of presumed self-reliance incompatible with sincerely entrusting oneself to God. God's presence is not servile, or always at our beck and call. Similarly, God's love, unlike so-called romantic love, is not obsequious, doting, or fawning, but is morally transforming for human good, even if much of the transformation is gradual and subtle. In taking God for granted, people neglect the supreme value of filial, reconciling knowledge of God. As a result, God sometimes hides in ways that allow people to have doubts about God, even at times when they apparently need God's presence (see, for example, Psalm 30:7). Part of God's redemptive plan is to remove, without coercion, human moral indifference toward God, which often stems from a presumption of self-reliance. God's hiding for this purpose should not be confused with total abandonment. Temporary hiding can instill in humans proper recognition of the moral gravity of indifference toward God. God's temporary hiding can also build humility and faithful patience in humans, yielding skill in fulfilling the recurring biblical injunction, "Wait for the Lord!" (Psalm 27:14; Isaiah 30:18). God's love, as noted, is morally transforming, not servile, and God seeks humble servants, not self-confident elitists.

In addition, God's hiding at times prevents human profaning of what is holy and sacred, namely, the presence of God. Such hiding may agree with the blunt command of Jesus, in the Sermon on the Mount, not to throw pearls before swine (Matthew 7:6). Still, God's restraint in manifestation of power does leave room for people freely to mock and to reject God. God's redemptive love, in other words, allows people the freedom to make mistakes, even horribly cruel mistakes. (Witness the horrifying Roman crucifixion of Jesus.) Sometimes, nonetheless, God's hiding is often a serious judgment against rebellion (see Deuteronomy 31:16–19, 32:19–20; Isaiah 59:2), a judgment often designed to prompt repentance. Even so, it is sometimes a judgment that does not succeed in prompting repentance. Such lack of success can result from recalcitrant exercise of human free will.

We should avoid some influential approaches to divine hiding, including the following Freedom Response and Proper-Motivation responses.

Freedom Response

Proponents of the Freedom Response contend that God hides in order to enable people *freely* to love, trust, and obey God. In the interest of forming truly loving relationships with people, God does not coerce people to respond in a certain way. In fact, the coercion of love seems impossible; love that cannot be rejected is evidently not genuine love. So God, as loving, hides in order to avoid coercion.[18]

The Freedom Response invites a simple question: could not God supply clear, or at least less obscure, self-revelation without abolishing our freedom in responding to that revelation? God could, it seems, be significantly less hidden while keeping our freedom intact, even our freedom to deny that God exists. *Some* revelations of God's power would indeed overwhelm us in a way that stifles our freedom, but the removal of divine hiddenness seems not to require any such revelation. So we should question the exclusive disjunction: Either God is hidden or human freedom in responding to God is lost. Proponents of the Freedom Response owe us a convincing case for that disjunction. Otherwise, the Freedom Response does not offer an adequate account of divine hiddenness.

Proper-Motivation Response

Supporters of the Proper-Motivation Response hold that God hides in order to discourage a human response based on improper motives. For instance, God does not want people to respond to divine self-revelation out of selfish fear or arrogance. God wants people to develop a relationship with Him out of sound motives. God's self-revelation without hiding, however, would prompt us to selfish fear or arrogance in our response. In the interest of discouraging such fear and arrogance, God hides.[19]

The Proper-Motivation Response is troubled by this issue: could not God supply a less obscure self-revelation without eliciting improper motives, such as selfish fear and arrogance, in our response to that revelation? It seems that God could be noticeably less hidden while not increasing the danger of our responding out of bad motives. *Some* revelations of God's power would perhaps prompt many people to respond out of selfish fear rather than love, but the removal of divine hiddenness seems not to require any such revelation. So we should refrain from endorsing this exclusive disjunction: Either God is hidden or humans will be (more) likely to respond to God out of improper motives. Supporters of the Proper-Motivation Response owe us a reasonable case for that disjunction. Otherwise, their response will not adequately explain divine hiddenness.

Perhaps the Proper-Motivation Response fares better if we consider some positive motivational virtues cultivated by divine hiddenness. For instance, one might propose that God hides in order to prompt sincerity in us about the wretchedness of life on our own, in the absence of God. Such sincerity may lead us to search for God contritely, humbly, and even passionately. If God's self-revelation were very clear, however, then both (a) our sense of our wretchedness without God and (b) our sense of the genuine risk required for a truly passionate faith would be objectionably reduced. God hides, then, to elicit positive motivational virtues of the kind noted.

Trouble persists for the Proper-Motivation Response. Consider a world where God is less obscure. Must that world be less susceptible to human pursuit of God that is contrite, humble, and passionate? It seems not. The mere fact of less obscurity in God's self-revelation does not seem to challenge contrite, humble, and passionate seeking after God. God could readily promote such seeking, with no added difficulty, in an environment of less obscure divine revelation. At least, supporters of the Proper-Motivation Response must explain why this is not so, if they are to account adequately for divine hiddenness.

Divine Purposes Reply

A sound approach to the problem of divine hiding includes the *Divine Purposes Reply*: God restrains divine manifestations, at least for a time, to at least some humans to enhance satisfaction of God's own diverse morally serious and loving purposes regarding humans. The Divine Purposes Reply allows that the amount and kind of God's revelation can vary among people, even if there is a common minimal revelation available to all people. The variation is determined by God's purposes, or intentions. If these purposes are morally righteous and loving, then God can be morally righteous and loving in giving varied revelation. God hides for *various* purposes, not just one purpose, just as God apparently allows evil for various purposes. Still, the exact details of God's purposes are sometimes unclear to us, as we should expect given God's transcendent superiority. When we are unclear on such details, we may nonetheless know and trust the One who hides for a time, for this One has lovingly intervened elsewhere in our common human predicament. Our having evidence of God's existence does not require our being able to explain all of God's intentions and actions, including God's hiding. The Divine Purposes Reply acknowledges that God hides on occasion for reasons other than to judge human rebellion. Throughout, God aims to motivate us, via love rather than via extraneous factors, to become loving as God is loving.

Some of God's hiddenness may result from our own blindness, our own failure to be properly receptive to God. Consider this transliterated non-English linguistic token: *Tov vayashar adonai; tov layisrael elohim; tov vayashar hadavar.* Perhaps most readers do not apprehend the semantic significance of this token. In fact, most readers may not even be confident that this token actually has such significance, while some readers may have a vague and tentative glimpse of some of its significance. The problem, however, lies not in the linguistic token itself. It lies rather in the overall perspective of beliefs and other attitudes a person brings to this token. Call this perspective a *receptive attitude*. The problem of perceiving meaning lies in one's lack of appropriate exposure and sensitivity to ancient Hebrew, particularly to the Sephardic rendition of ancient Hebrew. So the reception of significant evidence sometimes depends on the receptive attitude of people. Failure to receive some evidence comes from psychological and volitional facts about the intended *recipients*, rather than from flaws in the available evidence.

An analogy emerges: people whose receptive attitude is closed to God's program of all-inclusive renewal by grace may be blinded from available evidence for the reality of God. The evidence may be available, just as our transliterated Hebrew token is semantically significant. We need, however, appropriate, God-sensitive "ears to hear and eyes to see" the available evidence. We need a change of receptive attitude to apprehend the available transforming evidence in the right way. Such a change involves the direction of our lives, including our life-priorities, not just our intellectual assent. We must thereby attune ourselves to available evidence of God's self-revelation.

The needed change includes acknowledgment that on our own we have failed dismally at exemplifying God's all-loving character. This failure occurs in the presence of serious challenges to our existence (namely, death), to our well-being (for example, physical and mental decline), and to our moral standing (for example, our tendency to self-centeredness). We have no self-made or self-discovered solution to this universal human predicament. This humbling acknowledgment is significant relative to our knowing God. It requires that we change how we think of ourselves and of our relation to God. It also recommends a change in our intentions regarding our conduct, and such change is volitional, a matter of the will. One result is that we are displaced from the prideful center of moral importance in our supposed universe. We then become able to appreciate the explanatory profundity of Jewish-Christian theism regarding the human condition, in a way that would not otherwise be apprehended. So volitional transformation can contribute to our appreciation of explanatory and thus epistemic value, in giving us a new, epistemically improved perspective on our human predicament. Our appreciation of some evidence is thus sensitive to our volitional stance.

Lacking volitional transformation, we may be blinded from evidence of God's reality by our own counterfeit "intelligence" and "wisdom." (This theme recurs throughout the Jewish and Christian scriptures.) We may then lack the kind of sincere openness, humility, gratitude, and filial obedience appropriate to relating, cognitively and otherwise, to the God of the universe. We will then have assigned the authority of God to ourselves or to some other part of creation. In that case, we would be guilty of self-destructive *idolatry*, perhaps even a kind of cognitive idolatry where we demand a certain sort of knowledge or evidence of God inappropriate to a filial relationship with God. To the extent that we violate God's program of human volitional transformation, we are slaves to selfishness and we need to be set free.

The secular wisdom of philosophers, however sophisticated, does not offer the freedom humans need. It lacks the needed power to set us free from self-defensive fear, to transform us from the inside out toward God's character of all-inclusive love. Only the freeing power of God's transforming and sustaining love toward us by example and revelation can serve this purpose. Only it can prompt the kind of gratitude and freedom from fear central to redemptive transformation. We must sincerely apprehend our genuine need of God's sustaining love to appreciate God properly, that is to say, gratefully, humbly, and obediently.

Cognitive idolatry as characterized above can block us from the needed transformation toward freedom and unselfish love. It often rests on a principle of this form: Unless God (if God exists) supplies evidence of kind *K*, God's existence is too hidden to warrant reasonable acknowledgment.

The problem is not with a principle of this form but is rather with the specification of kind *K*. If we specify *K* in a way that disregards the personal character and redemptive intentions of the Jewish-Christian God, thereby isolating ourselves from the divine challenge of transformation, we exhibit cognitive idolatry. We then embrace a cognitive commitment designed to exclude God as Lord in our lives. This is the basis of cognitive idolatry. It stems from the human desire to be, or at least to appoint, the ultimate authority for our lives, as if we were entitled to this. We thereby isolate ourselves from important *available evidence* of God, blinding ourselves from the supreme reality and authority over us as dependent cognitive creatures. We thereby suppress the truth about God's reality.

The extent to which we know God depends on the extent to which we are gratefully willing to acknowledge God's authority and, as a result, to participate in God's program of all-inclusive redemption. So it becomes clear why humans have difficulty in knowing God. The difficulty originates in our resisting transformation toward God's morally perfect all-loving character. It is altogether presumptuous, then, for us humans to approach the question whether God exists as if we were automatically in an appropriate moral and epistemic position to handle it reliably. Careful reflection on the character and purposes inherent to an all-compassionate God recommends an approach less cavalier than that typical of humans, including philosophers. We are, after all, inquiring about a very special kind of personal agent with distinctive purposes, and not just an ordinary household object or laboratory specimen. We humans cannot easily abide a gracious Being who evades our sophisticated self-approving cognitive nets.

As all-compassionate Reconciler, God is not after mere justified true belief that God exists. God cares about *how* we handle evidence of God's existence, in particular, whether we become more grateful and loving in handling it. Contrary to a typical philosophical attitude, then, knowledge of God is not a spectator sport. It is rather part of a process of God's thorough makeover of a person. It is, from our side of the process, akin to an active commitment to a morally transforming *personal relationship* rather than to a mere subjective state. We come to know God only as God becomes *our God*, the Lord of our lives, rather than just an object of our contemplation or self-indulgence. God refuses, for our own good, to become a mere idol of our cognition, speculation, or entertainment. We exhibit self-destructive arrogance in assuming that we can have proper knowledge of God without undergoing deep, even painful, moral transformation.

Proper knowledge of the Jewish-Christian God is inherently ethical and practical rather than simply reflective. Sad to say, mere spectators complaining from remote regions may in fact remain out in those regions by their own self-isolating choice. Properly knowing God requires one's apprehending a call – a real personal call – to come in from the remote regions and gratefully join God's all-inclusive plan of gracious redemption. This plan is no mere intellectual puzzle for philosophers. God is more serious than our mental gymnastics, for our own good. We do, after all, have *lives* to form and to live, not just thoughts to think or intellectual puzzles to solve.

In the Gospel of John (7:3–4), Jesus faces a version of the problem of hiding raised by his own brothers (who, according to verse 5, did not believe in him). His brothers tell him that nobody works in hiding while seeking to be known openly. Their challenge is straightforward: "Manifest (φανέρωσον) yourself to the world" (John 7:4; cf. John 10:24). Part of Jesus' reply is that the world hates him because he testifies that its works are evil. He thus suggests that the world has the wrong moral attitude toward him. John then portrays Jesus as teaching in the temple that if anyone *wills* (θέλῃ) to do the will of God, that person will know (γνώσεται) whether Jesus's teaching is from God (7:17). Note the importance of one's willing to do the will of God, in John's epistemology.

One of Jesus's disciples asks why he will not manifest (ἐμφανίζειν) himself to the world (7:22). The disciple's thinking is familiar: why hide from the world if you have miraculous powers? Jesus offers, as before, a reply that highlights the importance of human moral attitude. "If a person loves me, that person will keep my word, and my Father will love him, and we will come to him and make our home with him" (7:23; cf. Jn 14:21). The reply assumes that the world does not love the things of God and that therefore God's manifestation would not have a result desired by God. In another context, Jesus remarks that "an evil and adulterous generation seeks a sign" (Matthew 12:39). The key assumption is that God desires not mere acknowledgment or intellectual assent, but an attitude of gratitude, trust, and love.

The Jewish-Christian God is anything but epistemically "safe," or controllable. We cannot control either God or God's hiding on occasion. So we cannot remove God's hiding with our self-made recipes. The Jewish-Christian God leaves us empty-handed when we insist on seeking with our self-made recipes, including familiar recipelike religious practices. We therefore cannot "solve" the problem of divine hiding if a solution requires a self-made recipe to remove such hiding or even an adequate, comprehensive explanation of God's intentions in hiding. We are, after all, neither God nor God's advisers; at best, we are God's obedient children. So we should not be surprised at all that we lack our own means to banish, or even to explain adequately, God's occasional hiding. Even so, this lack does not preclude our having good evidence of God's reality, including the reality of God's self-giving love for us. Our having such evidence does not require our having a theodicy (or, for that matter, any kind of adequate explanation) for divine hiddenness, just as it does not require our having a theodicy for natural and moral evil. In general, one's having evidence of the reality of a person, *S*, does not require one's having a comprehensive explanation of the intentions of *S*.

God's ways need not line up with our preferred ways of approaching God, epistemically, morally, or otherwise. This is one central message of the biblical writings, and it fits with God's distinctive role in the human predicament, including our epistemological predicament. God is the supreme Gift-Giver who seeks us prior to our seeking God. This is what Hebraic covenant love (*chesed*) and Christian grace (*charis*) are all about. If we love God, it is because God first loved us and offered God's love to us.[20] The order here is crucial, epistemologically and morally. For our own good, God calls for our grateful surrender to the compassionate Gift-Giver, not for our anxiously casting about with our own self-crediting recipes for finding God. So the Jewish-Christian God is not the God of our own schemes, however well-intentioned they may be.

God reveals God on God's gracious terms, as a gift, rather than on our self-crediting terms. Some widely favored epistemological conditions for God involve displays of miracle, power, and sophisticated wisdom. Such conditions amount to a triumphalist epistemology that readily promotes self-exaltation instead of God's humble love. Rather than settle for grateful acceptance of God's gift of (a) personal, filial knowledge of God and (b) God's personal assurance of God's presence, we often prefer to *earn* our knowledge of God, on our own terms. We prefer to have epistemological control here as elsewhere in our lives. The Jewish-Christian God, in contrast, favors an epistemology of humble, self-giving compassion, where God serves as the eager but humble epistemological Gift-Giver and we serve as grateful recipients. It is only out of our acknowledged weakness – our recognized need – that we have true gratitude toward God. We should let God be God, that is, be disarmingly and transformingly gracious, even in epistemology. Otherwise, frustration awaits us.

The Jewish-Christian God values knowing as unselfish loving, rather than knowing as merely contemplating or theorizing properly. Such knowing as loving is altogether fitting for members of God's family, and it has obvious moral consequences. We grow in knowing God by sharing in God's compassionate nature and thereby becoming genuinely compassionate. In other words, God's children are conformed, willingly and gladly, to the character of the parent and thereby increase in knowledge of the parent. The relevant compassion is not a self-made or independent precondition for knowing God. Rather, it results, as God's gift, from sincere openness to conformity to God. God's transforming love is poured out in our hearts in a way that is epistemically as well as morally crucial for knowing the God of unmatched love. In the absence of such love, we are ever prey to a kind of self-defensive fear incompatible with genuine love and thus with properly knowing God.

Our habitual refusal to love as God loves blinds us from seeing the things of God. Our recurring attitude of ingratitude is particularly self-blinding with regard to God. Indeed, ingratitude is the poisonous root of resistance to God; it is a corrosive attitude that drives God into hiding. Via gratitude for gifts received, in contrast, we come to trust and even to love God, thereby growing in knowledge of God.[21] We must welcome the gift of God's presence for it to benefit us by transforming us. Proper seeking of God entails inviting and welcoming God with gratitude. Merely drawing inferences, however sound, will not fill this bill.

6.   Evidence, Signs, and Love

Corresponding to thin and robust theism, we have noted two kinds of knowledge of God: (i) *propositional* knowledge that God exists, and (ii) *reconciling, filial* knowledge as one's humbly, faithfully, and lovingly standing in a relationship to the Jewish-Christian God as righteously gracious Father. Filial knowledge of God requires propositional knowledge that God exists, but it obviously exceeds propositional knowledge. One can know that God exists but fail altogether to love God. Filial knowledge of God, in contrast, includes our being reconciled to God (at least to some degree) through a loving filial relationship with God. It requires our entrusting ourselves as obedient children to God in grateful love, thereby being transformed in *who we are* and in *how we exist*, not just in what we believe.

As compassionate, God is not satisfied by our merely knowing that God exists. Such mere propositional knowledge falls far short of what God values by way of redemption: namely, that all people freely choose to be transformed by God from self-serving to self-giving, loving servants of the God of morally serious love. (For Jewish and Christian suggestions of this ideal, see, for example, Deuteronomy 6:5, 10:12–13; Leviticus 19:18; Mark 12:28–30). As all-loving, God aims that all people freely come to be morally perfect as God is morally perfect. Given this aim, God has no reason to offer *undeniable*, or *insuppressible*, evidence that would produce *mere* propositional knowledge that God exists, even if God has offered adequate *available* evidence for our coming to know that God exists. Love of God cannot be coerced but must be freely given. In respecting human freedom, God has offered evidence of God that allows for deniability of God's existence. God does not value knowledge that God exists apart from filial knowledge of God, given God's redemptive aim. God desires that we know God *as God*, specifically, as *our gracious Father*. God is *epistemically sovereign* and *morally demanding* in that God, rather than humans, sets the conditions for personally knowing God, and these conditions are sensitive to our receptive attitude toward God. We are, as suggested previously, in no position to demand that the God of the universe meet our favored evidential strictures.

The Jewish-Christian approach to filial knowledge of God gives primacy to *revelation from God*. It thus offers a top-down rather than a bottom-up approach to the source of filial knowledge of God. This explains the absence of esoteric philosophical reasoning about God in the Jewish and Christian scriptures. Even if filial knowledge of God is available to all honest seekers, its realization comes via – and not in advance of – an attitude of sincere openness to our loving God with the kind of love characteristic of God. This fits with the Christian message that God *is* love, that is, inherently loving (see 1 John 4:8,16; cf. 2 Corinthians 13:11). In light of this message, our resisting God's characteristic kind of love, in practice as well as in mindset, is to reject God.

Given God's redemptive aim to transform all persons morally via knowledge of God, each person must individually seek filial knowledge of God. You cannot give me your filial knowledge of God; nor can anyone else. In fact, only God can show you God in a way that constitutes reconciling, morally transforming knowledge of God. Other people cannot accomplish this on their own for you. Others can only help with some of the preconditions for knowing God. The needed turning away from selfishness, ingratitude, and self-righteousness – the core of resisting God – demands a kind of repentance, or turning of mindset, that is necessarily personal. It cannot be done by proxy. Personal repentance is not, however, evidentially arbitrary, as all mature human persons have evidence from moral conscience that their self-righteousness and selfishness toward others lack adequate support from the quality of their actual moral character. Our frequently presumed status of superior moral importance is but presumption and presumptuousness, and we can readily know this on due reflection. Our recurring moral pride is indeed a thin veneer.

Critics will object that God's presence is too ambiguous, at best, to merit reasonable acknowledgment. Surely, so the objection goes, God owes us more miraculous signs and wonders, whatever God's redemptive aims. Why does not

God entertain us, once and for all, with some decisive manifestations of God's awesome power? After all, it would not cost God anything, and it may vanquish nagging doubts about God's existence. Surely, a truly loving God would use miraculous powers to free us from our doubts. God's redemptive purposes, many will therefore object, do not exonerate God from the charge of excess restraint in manifestation. N. R. Hanson, for example, rejects theism given the absence of striking observable happenings that establish God's existence.[22] If God exists, God is blameworthy for inadequate self-revelation.

Many people have misguided expectations about what exactly miraculous signs will accomplish in a person. Miracles, like ordinary events, are interpretively flexible. They logically admit of various coherent (not to be confused with *correct*) interpretations, including naturalistic, nonmiraculous interpretations. Miraculous events do not impose their interpretations on us. For better or worse, we interpreters must decide on our interpretations of events, and various background beliefs and motives typically influence our interpretive decisions. We thus should not regard miraculous signs as *proofs for all inquirers*. A miraculous sign can prompt and build trust toward God in people genuinely open to God's intervention, but not in all people.

The best explanation of a striking event may be that it is miraculous, but if your background assumptions were thoroughly materialistic, such an explanation would not prevail for you, by your standards. You would then find an alternative treatment of the striking event, perhaps even withholding judgment on its interpretation. Even the best explanation of events can be freely and consistently rejected, given certain alterations in a system of beliefs. Accordingly, the conclusion of the New Testament story of the rich man and Lazarus is: "If [people] do not listen to Moses and the prophets, neither will they be convinced even if someone rises from the dead" (Luke 16:31). The Gospel of John concurs regarding the ineffectiveness of miraculous signs in producing faith: "After Jesus had said this, he departed and hid from them. Although he had performed so many signs in their presence, they did not believe in him" (John 12:36–37).

What about people open to God's intervention but not yet believing in God? Would not they benefit from miraculous signs by coming to believe in God? Perhaps. Let's distinguish between people *passively* open to belief in God and people *actively* open to belief in God. People passively open to such belief do not put any serious effort into examining whether God has intervened, for example, in the life, death, and resurrection of Jesus Christ. Such people are "open" to God with striking indifference. This indifference manifests itself in failure to act in ways that take seriously the availability of evidence for God. Passive openness is, accordingly, mere lip service to taking an interest in the availability of evidence for God. We do not appropriately value evidence for God if we do not take a morally serious interest in the availability of such evidence. Passive openness is thus an improper, insufficiently serious attitude toward available evidence for God. It trivializes a matter of the utmost importance.

People actively open to belief in God take a *morally serious* interest in the availability of evidence for God. Such an interest has potential morally transforming effects. These people are not morally indifferent about whether God has intervened, for example, in the life, death, and resurrection of Jesus Christ. They take a morally serious interest in available evidence for God's intervention.[23] The aforementioned Jewish-Christian conception of filial knowledge of God implies that people suitable for such knowledge must be *actively willing* to be morally transformed toward the character of God. An important question regarding such people is whether their coming to believe in God – at least for some of them – requires their being directly presented with a miraculous sign from God. Are there, in other words, morally serious seekers who would believe in God if and only if they had firsthand a miraculous sign from God? Perhaps, but the question is perplexing owing to vagueness in the phrase "a miraculous sign from God."

Let's distinguish *morally impotent* and *morally transforming* miraculous signs. Morally impotent miraculous signs can entertain people but cannot transform their moral character. Morally transforming signs, in contrast, change one's moral character toward the moral character of God. People often seek mere entertainment from visible phenomena, whereas God seeks our moral transformation, from the inside out. As noted previously, Isaiah 58:2 portrays the Hebraic God as complaining about the Israelites that "day after day they seek me and delight to know my ways, as if they were a nation that practiced righteousness and did not forsake the ordinance of their God." The New Testament likewise discourages our seeking after morally impotent signs from God. It nonetheless promises a morally transforming sign to genuine seekers after God, seekers actively open to moral transformation toward God's moral character. Because this sign is a definitive sign from the God of morally serious love, we should expect it to manifest the character of God: God's morally serious love. The New Testament confirms this expectation repeatedly. Paul, for example, states: "Hope in God does not disappoint, because God's love has been poured out in our hearts via the Holy Spirit given to us" (Romans 5:5; cf. 2 Corinthians 5:16–17; 1 John 4:12–13,16,19. On the role of the Spirit in Paul's epistemology, see 1 Corinthians 2:4–16.)

The presence of God's morally transforming love is the central *epistemic*, or *evidential*, foundation for filial knowledge of God. Such love is a foundational source of knowledge of God (cf. Colossians 2:2; 1 Corinthians 8:2–3.) It is real evidence of God's reality and presence. This love is a matter of personal intervention by God and the basis of a personal relationship with God. It is the distinctive presence of a personal God. So the filial knowledge in question rests on morally transforming divine love that produces a loving character in genuine children of God, even if at times such people obstruct God's transformation. This transformation *happens to one*, in part, and thus is neither purely self-made nor simply the byproduct of a self-help strategy. (I say "in part" owing to the role of human freedom in seeking and responding to God.) This widely neglected supernatural sign is available (at God's appointed time) to anyone who turns to God with moral seriousness. It transforms one's will (a) to have gratitude, trust, and love toward God and (b) to love others unselfishly. Accordingly, we *know* that we have passed from death to life because we love one another . . . Whoever does not love does not know God, for God is love" (1 John 3:14, 4:8, NRSV). We need to learn, then, how to apprehend, and to be apprehended by, God's love for all people. Such divine love is neither a proposition nor an argument.

God's self-revelation of transforming love will take us beyond mere historical and scientific probabilities to a firm foundation of *personal acquaintance* with God. As Paul remarks, in our sincerely crying out "Abba, Father" to God (note the Jesus-inspired filial content of this cry), God's Spirit confirms to our spirit that we are indeed children of God (Romans 8:16). We thereby receive God's personal assurance of our filial relationship with God. This assurance is more robust than any kind of theoretical certainty offered by philosophers or theologians. It liberates a person from dependence merely on the quagmire of speculation, hypothesis-formation, probabilistic inference, or guesswork about God. Such assurance yields a distinctive kind of grounded firm confidence in God unavailable elsewhere. God thus merits credit even for proper human confidence in God (cf. Ephesians 2:8).

The evidence of God's presence offered by character transformation in God's genuine (not just nominal) children deserves serious consideration. It goes much deeper than the comparatively superficial evidence found in entertaining signs, wonders, visions, ecstatic experiences, and philosophical arguments. We could consistently dismiss any such sign, wonder, vision, ecstatic experience, or argument as illusory or indecisive, given certain alterations in our beliefs. In contrast, genuine character transformation toward the Jewish-Christian God's ideal of all-inclusive love does not admit of easy dismissal. It bears directly on *who one really is*, the kind of person one actually is. Such transformation cuts too deeply against our natural tendencies toward selfishness to qualify as a self-help gimmick. It thus offers a kind of firm evidence that resists quick dismissal.

God takes us too seriously to have us settle for entertaining signs and wonders rather than character transformation toward all-inclusive love. If ultimate value lies in filial knowledge of God, rather than in mere propositional knowledge that God exists, manifestational pyrotechnics will be optional and not mandatory for God. They are not suitably morally transforming in the way required by filial knowledge of God. In this regard, they are markedly inferior to the supernatural sign just identified: the transforming presence of God's morally serious love. An all-loving God would, by nature, make God's presence *available* to humans at God's appointed time. God's presence, however, need not exceed the presence of God's morally serious love or be available apart from morally serious inquiry and seeking. In particular, God's presence need not include miracles irrelevant to moral transformation toward a character of morally serious love (although God could use such miracles to attract the attention of some humans). An all-loving God can properly make confident knowledge of God's existence arise simultaneously with filial knowledge of God. Accordingly, God is exonerated from the charge of irresponsibly refraining from entertaining signs, so long as God reveals God's presence to anyone suitably receptive. N. R. Hanson's demand for striking entertaining signs from God trivializes God's central aim: to bring unloving people to love God and others, even enemies. No aim is more difficult or more important.

As all-loving Reconciler, God does try (at God's appointed time) to draw all people into the kingdom of God, through (for example) human conscience and the explanation-seeking why-questions noted previously. God, however, does not extinguish our free choice. Neither God nor anyone else can coerce genuine gratitude, trust, or love. Free choice is a prerequisite for loving relationships, and in keeping with full moral goodness, God seeks such personal relationships above all else. In general, God seeks the freely chosen grateful union of our wills with God's morally serious loving will; only then is genuine all-inclusive community possible. Given the signs of personal excellence left by God in ourselves and the rest of creation, we *should* seek after God and thereby come to know God. It does not follow, however, that all of us will accept the responsibility of seeking after God. The demands of discipleship are simply too inconvenient for many of us, given our chosen priorities. We thus refuse to be displaced from the center of our universe. Still, a gracious God challenges our self-destructive blinders that aim to shut out God's program of all-inclusive redemption. We cannot plausibly blame God, then, for the blinders we sometimes stubbornly choose to wear.

7. Hiding, Seeking, and Theodicy

The Divine Purposes Reply to the problem of God's hiding enables Jewish-Christian theism to assume the burden of support for its commitment to a God of morally serious love. It also enables us to acknowledge that Jewish-Christian theism not only is testable now in a morally serious manner, but also *should* be tested now by every person. Each person must test for himself or herself by seeking God with due humility and moral seriousness, as pride and frivolity will automatically blind one from seeing God and our genuine need of God. The appropriate test cannot be accomplished by "neutral" examination of evidence, whatever that might be; it requires one's willingness to forsake all diversions for the required moral transformation. Filial knowledge of God is by grace, not by earning, but the grace is available (at God's appointed time) to all who call on God with sincere humility and due moral seriousness.

My position implies that we can "reconcile" divine hiddenness and a perfectly loving God at a personal *evidential* level but not at a comprehensive *explanatory* level. It rests on the following biblical promise: "When you search for me, you will find me; if you seek me with all your heart, I will let you find me, says the Lord." (Jeremiah 29:13–14; cf. Matthew 7:7–8). In addition, my position maintains a sharp distinction between: (a) When you search for God aright, you will find God, and (b) When you search for God aright, you will find an adequate, comprehensive explanation of why God hides at times. Promise (a) does not rely on promise (b) and thus does not underwrite a theodicy or any comprehensive explanation for divine hiddenness. Promise (a) is limited to the issue of one's acquiring evidence of God's reality.

Even though a theodicy for divine hiddenness is unavailable to us, promise (a) can hold good and be valuable to humans. Human seeking can contribute to a valuable learned appreciation of God's revelation involving volitional conformity to God's character. In demanding human seeking, God upholds the value of divine revelation, thereby saving it from becoming "cheap and easy" to humans. God's aim is to have humans appreciate, treasure, and be transformed by, divine love, not just to think about it.

Human seeking, even when followed by one's finding God, does not produce a theodicy for divine hiddenness, because it does not yield an adequate, comprehensive explanation of God's hiddenness. The Jewish-Christian God not only is *hidden* at times but also actively *hides* at times (as is assumed by Jesus's cry of dereliction on the cross). If God does indeed actively hide from people at times, then an adequate explanation of God's hiddenness will have to appeal to God's *intentions* in hiding, beyond any human cognitive restrictions owing to sin. Even when human seeking delivers evidence of God, one can be ignorant of the specific intentions motivating God's hiding at times. In fact, we often are ignorant in that regard. This should be no surprise given the differences between God and humans. (This is one of the main lessons of the book of Job.) The important point, however, is that our lacking an adequate explanation of divine hiding does not challenge anyone's having good evidence of God's reality and love. Having such evidence is one thing; explaining God's intentions in hiding is quite another.

It would be question begging to portray divine hiddenness as falsifying widespread religious experience of God's reality. Divine hiddenness facing some people at some times, or even some people at all past and present times, does not underwrite divine hiddenness relative to all people at all times. So there is no clear defensible way to generalize on actual cases of divine hiddenness to encompass all people. A generalized argument for atheism or agnosticism, then, seems not to emerge from divine hiddenness. Any such argument would require specific premises independent of divine hiddenness. It is unclear, however, what such premises would be. Their absence suggests a special problem of hiddenness facing a generalized case for atheism or agnosticism from divine hiddenness.

The "proof" of God is, finally, in morally serious testing. Seek aright, then, and you will find incomparable knowledge and new life as well. What's more, the joyous firstfruits of the eventual redemption (where God will wipe away every tear and death and suffering shall be no more) are already apparent in our sadly broken world – if only we have eyes to see and ears to hear. When our diagnosing God gives way to our thanking and even praising God, we shall know for sure that we have been made new. The Jewish-Christian God is, in the end, hidden only in God's unique superhuman love for all.[24]

Notes

1. On epistemic rationality, see Paul Moser, *Knowledge and Evidence* (New York: Cambridge University Press, 1989), chap. 5, and Moser, *Philosophy after Objectivity* (New York: Oxford University Press, 1993), chap. 4.
2. On the theme of God's suffering and its relation to divine love, see Paul Fiddes, *The Creative Suffering of God* (Oxford: Clarendon Press, 1988), and Terence Fretheim, *The Suffering of God* (Philadelphia: Fortress Press, 1984), chap. 9.
3. For ample evidence, see Paul Hanson, *The People Called: The Growth of Community in the Bible* (San Francisco: Harper and Row, 1986).
4. See Russell, "A Free Man's Worship," in Russell, *Mysticism and Logic* (Garden City, NY: Doubleday, 1957), pp. 44–54.
5. For discussion of the theistic relevance of (b), see Peter Forrest, *God without the Supernatural: A Defense of Scientific Theism* (Ithaca: Cornell University Press, 1996), chap. 2. Cf. Kenneth Miller, *Finding Darwin's God* (New York: HarperCollins, 1999), chaps. 7–8.
6. On the constituents of intentional action, see Alfred Mele and Paul Moser, "Intentional Action," *Noûs* 28 (1994), 39–68, reprinted in Alfred Mele, ed., *The Philosophy of Action* (New York: Oxford University Press, 1997), pp. 223–55.
7. For an overview of some relevant empirical evidence and pertinent references, see Gerald Schroeder, *The Science of God* (New York: Free Press, 1997), chap. 2.
8. On the New Testament theme of reconciliation with God, see Ralph Martin, *Reconciliation* (Atlanta: John Knox Press, 1981), Peter Stuhlmacher, *Reconciliation, Law, and Righteousness* (Philadelphia: Fortress Press, 1986), and H. H. Farmer, *Reconciliation and Religion*, ed. C. H. Partridge (Lewiston, NY: Edwin Mellen, 1998).
9. On the prophetic tradition, see Abraham Heschel, *The Prophets* (New York: Harper and Row, 1962), and Gerhard von Rad, *Old Testament Theology, Vol. 2: The Theology of Israel's Prophetic Traditions* (New York: Harper and Row, 1965).
10. On this theme, see Will Herberg, *Judaism and Modern Man* (Philadelphia: Jewish Publication Society, 1951), chaps. 17–19, and Hanson, *The People Called*.

11. On the important theme of volitional weakness in Jewish-Christian theism, see Timothy Savage, *Power Through Weakness* (Cambridge: Cambridge University Press, 1996), and D. J. Dales, *Living Through Dying* (Cambridge: Lutterworth Press, 1994).

12. On the important cognitive and moral implications of God as personal, see H. H. Farmer, *The World and God* (London: Nisbet Press, 1935), Farmer, *Towards Belief in God* (London: SCM, 1942), and John Oman, *Grace and Personality* (Cambridge: Cambridge University Press, 1917).

13. See Nagel, *The Last Word* (New York: Oxford University Press, 1997), p. 131.

14. On the role of God as convicting authority and assurer, see P. T. Forsyth, *The Principle of Authority* (London: Hodder and Stoughton, 1913), and F. W. Camfield, *Revelation and the Holy Spirit* (New York: Scribner, 1934).

15. On idolatry, see Luke Johnson, *Faith's Freedom* (Minneapolis: Fortress Press, 1990), chap. 4; cf. John Mackay, *Christian Reality and Appearance* (Richmond, VA.: John Knox Press, 1969), and Moshe Halbertal and Avishai Margalit, *Idolatry*, trans. Naomi Goldblum (Cambridge, MA: Harvard University Press, 1992).

16. On the recurring theme of divine hiding in the Hebrew scriptures, see Samuel Balentine, *The Hidden God* (Oxford: Clarendon Press, 1983), and Samuel Terrien, *The Elusive Presence* (San Francisco: Harper and Row, 1978).

17. This point receives inadequate attention in J. L. Schellenberg, *Divine Hiddenness and Human Reason* (Ithaca: Cornell University Press, 1993).

18. For relevant discussion, see M. J. Murray, "Coercion and the Hiddenness of God," *American Philosophical Quarterly* 30 (1993), pp. 27–38.

19. For relevant discussion, see Pascal's *Pensées*, trans. A. Krailsheimer (London: Penguin, 1966), Richard Swinburne, *Faith and Reason* (Oxford: Clarendon Press, 1981), p. 156, and Swinburne, *Revelation* (Oxford: Clarendon Press, 1992), p. 95.

20. This is rightly emphasized by Anders Nygren, *Agape and Eros*, trans. P. S. Watson (New York: Harper and Row, 1953), Pt. II, chap. 6, and Leon Morris, *Testaments of Love: A Study of Love in the Bible* (Grand Rapids: Eerdmans, 1981), chap. 7.

21. On the central role of gratitude toward God in the Jewish and Christian scriptures, see Harvey Guthrie, *Theology as Thanksgiving* (New York: Seabury Press, 1981), and Daniel Hardy and David Ford, *Praising and Knowing God* (Philadelphia: Westminster Press, 1985).

22. See N. R. Hanson, *What I Do Not Believe and Other Essays* (Dordrecht: Reidel, 1971), p. 322.

23. For some elaboration on the relation between God and moral seriousness, see Helmut Thielicke, "What Has God to Do with the Meaning of Life?," in Thielicke, *How to Believe Again*, trans. H. G. Anderson (Philadelphia: Fortress Press, 1972), pp. 104–13.

24. I gladly thank Peter Bergeron, Tom Carson, Paul Copan, Stephen T. Davis, Garry DeWeese, Doug Geivett, Linda Mainey, Tim O'Connor, Alan Padgett, and Jonathan Westphal for helpful comments on ancestors of parts of this essay. I presented earlier versions at Biola University, Wheaton College, North Park University, Loyola University of Chicago, Hope College, George Fox University, and the 2000 Annual Meeting of the Evangelical Philosophical Society. I thank the audiences on those occasions for helpful discussions and Daniel Howard-Snyder for arranging an excellent conference on divine hiddenness at George Fox University in Oregon.

7

Divine Hiddenness:
What Is the Problem?

JONATHAN L. KVANVIG

The problem of evil centers on the claim that some evil is so bad that God would not allow it. If evil has such a character, it might be claimed that evil constitutes evidence against the existence of God. Even more, it might be held that evil constitutes an epistemic problem for theism, that the presence of evil has the power to alter the epistemic status of theism. For even if there are reasons which in themselves might confirm theism, factoring in the presence of evil might decrease the status of theism from, say, being rational to believe to being counterbalanced. Though not universal, this account of the epistemic implications of evil is widely shared, an account on which evil constitutes evidence with sufficient epistemic force to alter the epistemic status of theism. On this conception, then, evil constitutes an epistemic problem for theism.

This account of the nature of an epistemic problem for a point of view focuses on the concept of change (that some piece of information has the power to *alter* the epistemic status of that point of view), and that isn't quite right. The real issue is whether the new information has the power to make the epistemic status of a point of view different from what it would have been otherwise, different from what it would have been had that information not been present or available. Information can do the latter without ever changing the epistemic status of any point of view. For ease of expression, however, I will continue to speak with the vulgar on this matter by saying that epistemic problems are created by information with the power to change the epistemic status of some point of view.

In addition to this epistemic problem of evil, some have maintained recently that there is an additional epistemic problem regarding the existence of God, the problem of divine hiddenness. The most detailed investigation of this problem is that of J. L. Schellenberg who, in *Divine Hiddenness and Human Reason*, argues that the epistemic hiddenness of God presents a strong argument for atheism; in particular, that it yields an argument with the power to change the epistemic status of theism from counterbalanced to disconfirmed.[1]

I believe there is a mistake underlying any such project, for I do not think that there is an epistemic problem of hiddenness. There are ways in which God is hidden, some of them evidential in character. But there is no epistemic problem of divine hiddenness. Nothing about the hiddenness of God has the power to change the epistemic status of theism.

Before arguing for this claim, I want to take it back, but only a little. For there is an epistemic problem of hiddenness if you agree with me about matters epistemic. Regarding such matters, I am a subjectivist, inclined toward coherentism, save for an articulated account of the possibility of justified inconsistent beliefs.[2] I believe that what a person is justified in believing is not determined by what is true or objectively likely to be true nor by what the evidence actually confirms. Such facts can give way to a person's subjective conception of the world and the evidential connections perceived in that conception. The heroes of my epistemological faith are Keith Lehrer and Richard Foley.[3] On their theories, and on any subjective theory, there clearly can be an epistemic problem of hiddenness. For on such theories, nearly any piece of information can be embedded in a cognitive structure in which that piece of information counts against the existence of God, and the epistemic status of theism could be diminished by coming to learn of that information and seeing its significance. All that is needed on such subjective conceptions, to repeat, is a cognitive structure that ties the two pieces of information together in an appropriate way. So on such conceptions, the existence of a pair of scissors on my desk can pose an epistemic problem for theism.

Just as true, however, is that solutions to such epistemic problems come in a wide variety for subjectivists. For almost any set of beliefs, there is some belief system in which those beliefs would have good subjective epistemic standing. Of course, there are some beliefs for which this may not be true – for example, it is not possible to be justified in believing (in the same way, at the same time) both *p* and *not-p*. But the set {*God exists, God is hidden*} is surely such that there are many ways of embedding it in a system of beliefs that has universally high subjective epistemic status. And the same point holds even for those who have read and fully grasped attempts to argue against the consistency of this set, such as the one Schellenberg develops. There will or might be individuals for whom it is subjectively more reasonable, or rational, or justified, or warranted, to deny the premises of such arguments than to deny either that God loves us or that God is hidden.

Such is a project familiar in recent religious epistemology. To resolve an epistemic dilemma, find a belief system in which it is rational to hold both purportedly inconsistent claims – *God is hidden* and *God is perfectly loving*, or *evil exists* and *God is perfectly good, all-powerful and all-knowing*. In one way, this game is boring because the outcome is sure, at least if you lean toward subjective conceptions of the key epistemic terms. For there is always some belief system adequate to the task of epistemic absolution. The only question is how long it might take to find it.

Some of these belief systems will even be quite familiar. Regarding the problem of hiddenness, for most traditional Christians such as I, the explanation of how God is perfectly loving and yet hidden lies in the doctrine of the Fall. Schellenberg considers, all too briefly, this line of response to the problem he raises. He notes that much of Pascal's approach to the hiddenness of God hinges on Pascal's assumption that "a historical "Fall" actually took place." In response he says, "But in light of the findings of disciplines like evolutionary biology and biblical criticism, it is hard to see how such an assumption could be successfully defended."[4]

There are several things to complain about here. First, I think Schellenberg must be thinking that a historical doctrine of the Fall must treat the Adam and Eve story as literally true. Without this assumption, I don't see how the findings of evolutionary biology and biblical criticism could undermine the view. But that assumption is false. Adopting a literal interpretation of the Adam and Eve story is only one way of understanding the Fall historically. The story of Adam and Eve might be representative of the fall of peoples, or of the fall of each individual person, or of some cosmic catastrophe that needs to be redressed through the process of redemption. Second, it is far from clear that a historical doctrine of the Fall is required to resolve the difficulty Schellenberg presents. The story of Adam and Eve might be a mythic account of a fallenness endemic to the created order, perhaps a fallenness that results from the inclusion of freedom in the created order, the rectification or removal or cleansing or purification of which God has undertaken and is in the process of completing. Whether historical or not, the doctrine of the Fall points to a need, both cognitive and conative, that can be addressed only by the intervention of the divine. We are more used to the phenomenological data of conative fallenness, but there are data on the cognitive side as well. For example, there is a logical and empirical gap between recognized sufficient warrant and actual belief formation very much like the fallenness of humanity displayed in cases of weakness of the will. There are also other aspects of cognitive fallenness: the possibility of self-deception and the Jamesian possibility of such paranoia over the prospect of false belief that one sets the standards for warranted belief too high, for two other examples. A doctrine of the Fall is but a theological interpretation of such fallenness, a doctrine according to which all aspects of fallenness, including both cognitive and moral aspects, are somehow fleeting and regrettable aspects of our earthly existence which God is in the process of removing. The traditional form of such explanation, whether through a literal story about Adam and Eve or some mythic interpretation of this story, ties fallenness in all its aspects to a desire (or purpose) to be Godlike, to a desire for complete autonomy, or self-control, culminating in some desire (or purpose) to be rid of God, perhaps even to spite Him or show Him up. The common element of such explanations is that an account of fallenness is tied directly to a rejection of God, either through wanting to take His place (by being the most important thing there is), or not caring about His existence, perhaps wanting Him to exist in order to defy Him, perhaps even denying His existence altogether.

There are many questions that remain about this account of divine hidden-ness, including questions concerning the competitor explanations that might be proffered for the data of fallenness and questions about the epistemic effects of such a doctrine, including the question of whether such a doctrine defeats any reason we could have for believing it. Recall, however, the context of our discussion here. I am considering how an epistemic subjectivist will look at the possibilities for reconciling any perceived tension between the claims that God is hidden and that God loves us, and have claimed that one such possi-bility is found in the doctrine of the Fall. Schellenberg demurs, but my point has been that the epistemic utility of this doctrine simply can't be undermined by some passing remark about what evolutionary biology and biblical criti-cism shows.

In the present context, there is another aspect of Schellenberg's rejection of an appeal to the doctrine of the Fall that is puzzling, for he claims, not that the doctrine is false, but that it cannot be "successfully defended." For any subjec-tivist about justification, such a remark is completely irrelevant. What is rele-vant are the connections, partly explanatory ones, among the various beliefs a person has. The doctrine of the Fall, whether conceived historically or not, provides an explanation both of fallenness and of the hiddenness of God. We are, according to this doctrine, *damaged goods* both conatively and cognitively, and the damage in question is so intimately linked to the nature and existence of God that there is a strong incentive for self-deception and confusion regard-ing the truth or falsity of theism. Given these explanatory connections, one will be hard-pressed to find subjective grounds that undermine the power these explanatory connections possess to generate warrant for belief. Most important, such power won't be affected in the slightest by the issue of whether the beliefs can be defended successfully. That is a completely different matter, having to do with the capacity of a person to answer criticisms of his or her view. But that is irrelevant to epistemic questions subjectivistically construed.

So the caveat I must make to my initial remarks questioning the existence of an epistemic problem of hiddenness is that we must focus on more objec-tive construals of key epistemic terms in order for the project of finding a trou-bling epistemic problem of hiddenness to get off the ground. I think such a construal is just what Schellenberg needs to make his worries about whether certain claims can be successfully defended to the point. For a complaint that some claim cannot be successfully defended might also mean that the totality of the evidence, objectively conceived, does not support the claim. What I want to defend is that there is no epistemic problem of hiddenness, no factor involved in the hiddenness of God that can change the epistemic standing of theism, when such an objective understanding is assumed.

In order to explore this issue, I first want to begin by looking more carefully at Schellenberg's argument. The value of this approach is that the failures of his argument give us insight into what must hold in order for there to be an epistemic problem of hiddenness. So after looking at a particular attempt to find such a problem, we will be in a position to look at the issue more generally, a perspective from which we will be able to see that there is no such problem to be found.

I. Schellenberg on Divine Hiddenness

Schellenberg begins his work by making several assumptions, one of which he formulates as follows: "I will further assume that the relevant evidence . . . does not clearly favor either the conclusion that God exists or its denial" (pp. 11–12). I think Schellenberg means to assume that the evidence is counterbalanced for and against theism, though the claim does not quite say this. Instead, it notes a lack of clarity on the issue (the evidence doesn't "*clearly* favor" either view, he says), which is not a point about what the evidence supports, but rather one about our understanding, our grasp of what the evidence shows. Throughout the work, however, Schellenberg takes the significance of his project to be that of altering the epistemic status of theism, claiming that "the weakness of evidence for theism . . . is evidence against it" (p. 2). So, in spite of language not quite endorsing this conclusion,[5] I conclude that an initial assumption that Schellenberg makes is that evidence for theism is counterbalanced, favoring neither theism nor atheism.

Schellenberg argues for this assumption by saying that it seems warranted by recent discussion in philosophy of religion which often ends in deadlock, and it is widely granted by those inside and outside the academic study of religion (p. 12). The former claim, that disputes in philosophy of religion end in deadlock, yields a bad argument for the counterbalanced claim. All the point about ending in deadlock shows is that the issues are controversial and consensus is not likely to be achieved soon. Nothing follows about the quality of the evidence for a claim just because people can't agree on what it shows. Positing the counterbalancing of the evidence might be thought to explain the disputes and their irresolvability, but it doesn't; it merely sides with some of the disputants over others. So the only argument left is Schellenberg's claim that the assumption is widely granted, and that is not much of an argument at all. At the very least, it is not a method by which we ought to decide matters philosophical. (I might point out here that the confusion between two assumptions, the first being that the evidence does not favor theism, and the second that it is not obvious that the evidence favors theism, may incline Schellenberg toward this argument, since it is a good argument for the claim that the evidence doesn't obviously favor theism, but not for the assumption that the evidence doesn't favor theism.) So Schellenberg does not have a good argument for the assumption that the evidence is counterbalanced. More important, I want to argue that the assumption can't be granted unless we employ a different conception of evidence and belief from the ones that Schellenberg uses.

After assuming the evidence is counterbalanced, Schellenberg argues that a loving God would put us all in a strong epistemic situation regarding his existence. That is, a loving God would provide evidence adequate to make us believe that He exists. In defending this position, Schellenberg responds to two attacks. One questions whether any evidence at all is needed. Why not just require God to *make* us believe that He exists? The other questions whether adequate evidence is good enough. Perhaps what God should give us is absolutely conclusive evidence that He exists, so that those who examine the evidence won't see it as less than conclusive and thereby fail to believe.

Neither response is adequate, I want to argue, and I'll take up the response to the latter objection first. In response to the objection that God should provide conclusive evidence, Schellenberg licenses inferring belief from taking the probability of the claim to be greater than .5. He says, "Of course, if I consider the evidence to be evenly balanced, I will be uncertain whether G [the claim that God exists] is true. But if I see G's probability as greater than .5, it seems natural to suppose that I believe it to some extent" (p. 37).

One problem with this response is that it implies that no reflective theist will be able to agree with Schellenberg's initial assumption that the evidence is counterbalanced as to whether God exists. For Schellenberg says that if you consider the evidence to be evenly balanced, you will be uncertain whether God exists, "uncertain," in the psychological sense of failing to be convinced one way or the other on the question. He further identifies belief with having at least a weak disposition to feel the claim to be true, a disposition clearly lacked by those who are uncertain in the psychological sense of the existence of God. Hence, believing that the likelihood of theism is no greater than .5 is incompatible with believing that God exists, on Schellenberg's account. So every reflective theist thinks there is adequate evidence for the existence of God, given Schellenberg's conceptions of evidence and belief.

There are, of course, reflective theists who think that the existence of God is not probable at all. Here come to mind Pascal and, even more starkly, Kierkegaard. But such reflective theists don't conceive of the relationship between belief and probability the way Schellenberg does. My point is not that every reflective theist must think that there is good evidence for the existence of God, but rather that this claim follows when we adopt the accounts of evidence and belief that Schellenberg employs.

More important, however, is the perplexity we should experience upon hearing Schellenberg's reply to the objection. The objection, recall, suggested that God ought to give us absolutely conclusive evidence, not merely evidence adequate to show that He exists. Schellenberg's reply attempts to answer this objection by weakening the notion of belief, and tying it to our assessments of the probability of a claim. The idea, I take it, is that if we weaken the notion of belief sufficiently, it will be harder to imagine cases where a person has adequate evidence for a claim but misjudges the quality of evidence. But I don't see how the reply accomplishes that. I don't see how it gives us any reason at all to think that mistakes about quality of evidence are less likely than we might have supposed. Furthermore, even if such mistakes are less likely than we might have thought, they are not impossible, and if they are not, it is hard to see how Schellenberg's reply is to the point at all.

There is nonetheless an adequate reply to the objection, I think. If mistakes about the quality of evidence are possible, I see no reason to think that such mistakes are not possible about even absolutely conclusive evidence as well. No matter how good the evidence is, it still appears possible to mistake its quality, and if so, you can't argue that God should have provided absolutely conclusive evidence so as to eliminate the possibility of people seeing it as less than conclusive and thereby failing to believe.

The other objection has no such simple confusion in it, however. That objection questioned why the discussion is phrased employing the concept of evidence at all. Why, it asked, doesn't God simply force belief on us? To stave off this criticism, Schellenberg endorses a broad understanding of evidence that includes "anything that can serve as a ground of belief" (p. 33), so that if it merely seems strongly to a person that a claim is true, that very experience of it seeming to him or her to be true is evidence for the belief (p. 33). The idea here is that if we broaden the notion of evidence so that more counts as evidence than we thought, and tighten the connection between belief and evidence so that it is more difficult to find cases in which belief and evidence come apart, there will be less opportunity to raise the possibility of belief forced on us without evidence.

There are two problems with this reply. The first is that it commits Schellenberg to a fairly strong and subjective epistemic conservatism principle in conflict with a more objective conception of evidence and rational belief required for the central arguments of the book. In the passage just quoted, Schellenberg only infers the existence of evidence where a proposition seems strongly to a person to be true. Yet, he also claims that anything that can serve as a ground of belief can be evidence for a belief, so there is no reason whatsoever to count only strong seemings as evidence. For moderately strong seemings, and even weak seemings, ground belief as well. It would be appropriate, perhaps, to hold that the evidence these seemings provide is not as good

evidence as that involved in cases of strong seemings, but it would be unprin-
cipled to count only strong seemings when one's understanding of evidence
is supposed to include anything that can serve as a ground of belief. It is a
truism, however, that everything we believe seems to us to be true, so in order
to answer the worry that evidence for belief is not required, Schellenberg
endorses a conception of evidence broad enough to imply that we have evidence for every single one of our beliefs.

Schellenberg is thus committed to a strongly subjective conservatism principle, according to which merely believing a claim constitutes evidence for it.
I do not believe that any such conservatism is adequate,[6] but I will bypass that
point here to focus on the relationship between Schellenberg's conservatism
and important claims made throughout the rest of the book, claims that require
a strongly objective notion of evidence that are in tension with the subjectivity involved in conservatism. I shall look quickly here at only one. Near the
end of Part I of his book, Schellenberg considers Stephen Wykstra's claim that
if God exists, we should expect some goods to be inscrutable, and that the
apparent pointlessness of evil can be rebutted by that fact. Schellenberg wishes
to attack the strategy of applying Wykstra's position to the particular evil of
reasonable nonbelief. He says,

Suppose that it is likely as not . . . that if there is a god, at any rate some evils of human
experience serve inscrutable goods. How can we know, with regard to the occurrence
of reasonable nonbelief, that it is a *member* of this class? Without independent information bearing on the question, we would have to say, 'Well, it might belong to that
group, but then again it might *not*.' Hence the probability that reasonable nonbelief will
be apparently pointless if God exists would seem to be at most *half* that of the proposition that *some* instances of evil will be so. But then, given that we can surely say no
more than that the latter proposition is as probable as not, the probability of the claim
that reasonable nonbelief will be apparently pointless if God exists is clearly too low
for rational acceptance. (pp. 90–1)

There are several mistakes in this passage, but let me focus on two central
ones. First, the probabilistic assessment of reasonable nonbelief serving
inscrutable goods is a complete wash. It endorses the faulty principle that when
you have no idea what the probability of a claim is, you should assign a probability of .5 to it. That's obviously wrong, however. When someone shows you
a deck of cards, revealing it to be a normal deck of cards, one has a basis on
which to consider it a fair bet at 3 : 1 odds that the next card drawn will be a
spade. If all you know is that there is a deck of 52 cards, with no information
whether it is normal, the principle in question would require considering it a
fair bet at even odds that the next card drawn will be a spade, but that is clearly
mistaken. For it confuses uncertainty about the fairness of the deck with a
precise understanding of a particular bias of the deck. The correct attitude in
the latter case would be to hold no opinion whatsoever about which bets would
be fair bets.[7]

The more important point, however, concerns Schellenberg's last claim. He performs his untoward probabilities calculations, and then announces that the results are "too low for rational acceptance." But this conclusion is in tension with his conservatism. Whatever the actual probability, Schellenberg's conservatism principle implies that if I mistakenly judge the probability to be high, then I have evidence that the probability is high. The mere fact that the actual probability is low doesn't imply anything at all about what is rationally acceptable for a person, once Schellenberg's subjective conservatism is accepted, for a person can acquire additional, relevant evidence just by making a probabilistic mistake.

I don't claim, of course, that there is a straightforward inconsistency here, but the tension cannot be dismissed lightly, either. Schellenberg wants to let in just enough subjectivity into his theory of evidence and rationality to avoid certain objections to his view, but you can't do that responsibly without endorsing some subjectivist arguments about how a theory of rationality ought to be constrained by actual probability.

There is a worse problem, however, with Schellenberg's reply to the claim that God should simply force belief on us. To see it, note the seeming irrelevance of Schellenberg's reply to this objection. The objection quarrels with evidence playing any part in the discussion; why doesn't God just build us so we believe that He exists? Schellenberg's response is that there's a lot more evidence for any belief than you might initially have thought. But how is that relevant? The only way I can see to make it relevant is to hold that the question of God making us believe is not logically distinct from the issue of having adequate evidence, so that if God were to make us believe, He could only do so by providing us with adequate evidence. Otherwise, no matter how much evidence exists in virtue of our beliefs seeming to us to be true, the question can be raised again – namely, why this focus on evidence when God could simply have placed the belief in us? In order for Schellenberg's discussion of this question to be to the point, belief and evidence would seem to need to go hand-in-hand to such an extent that mere belief carries its own implication of adequate evidence. Such a viewpoint endorses an irresponsibly strong epistemic conservatism principle, irresponsible because it is inconsistent with the obvious possibility of irrational belief.

What we are left with, then, is that if we travel with Schellenberg we end up construing the problem of hiddenness as a doxastic issue about why God doesn't force belief on us. And if God's merely forcing us to believe that he exists solves a problem of hiddenness, the problem that it solves is not an *epistemic* problem of hiddenness. It is not a problem concerned with the concepts of evidence or rationality at all.

One might think that the solution is simply to abandon Schellenberg by adopting better construals of the key epistemic terms, and an epistemic problem of divine hiddenness will be easily formulable. Let us see if that is so.

II.   Is there an Epistemic Problem of Hiddenness?

To find an epistemic problem of hiddenness, we need to establish some parameters. A first reasonable parameter is something like Schellenberg's assumption that the evidence for theism is counterbalanced, for if there is adequate evidence for the existence of God, there is no epistemic problem of hiddenness. We should also note that there is no such problem, if the evidence is adequate, *regardless of whether anyone believes that there is a God.* There may be some other problem lurking here, but it is not because of God's hiddenness. The problem would rather be one of human density or resistance to what the evidence shows.

Again, Schellenberg holds a contrary position, one that comes to grief fairly quickly and underlies the host of difficulties uncovered in the last section. He holds that a loving God would provide "evidence that is sufficient to produce belief" (p. 33). This requirement involves two aspects: First, the evidence must be adequate, and second, it must be efficacious. The tension between these two elements turned out to be intolerable, as we saw in the last section, for Schellenberg ends up with no good answer as to why there should be any focus at all on evidence once we introduce the question about efficacy. Once that question was introduced, Schellenberg had no good answer to the question of why mere forced belief wouldn't be good enough. Avoiding this problem is simple, however. We need only note that the question about the efficacy of evidence is not a problem concerning the hiddenness of God. If you can't see me standing in front of you in broad daylight, even though your eyes are open and directed at me, the problem is not that I'm somehow mysteriously hidden from you. The problem, instead, is that you just can't see. Now, we might want to investigate the problem of the epistemic defects of human beings if it should turn out that there is adequate evidence for the existence of God and many people do not recognize it as such. We might ask under what circumstances we should expect adequate evidence to fix belief and when we shouldn't. Perhaps we could even do a bit of scientific investigation of the issue, perhaps positing that we should expect belief fixation by evidence when it has survival value and not otherwise. Then Schellenberg's concern for the efficaciousness of evidence would receive the scientific answer that God should have limited the survival and reproductive capacities of nontheists.

But I mock; perhaps I mock a bit too much. Perhaps evolutionary explanations themselves raise problems, so that the problem of the epistemic defects of human beings is not answered by such evolutionary explanations, but only raises the further question of why a good God would have chosen a set of laws for the actual universe that leaves room for such defects. Such is not my topic here, however; suffice for the present to repeat that this issue is not one of divine hiddenness, even if it does raise issues that are important in their own right.

So, in order for there to be an epistemic problem of hiddenness, we must assume that the evidence is counterbalanced between theism and nontheism, or at least not favorable to theism. For the sake of simplicity, I will talk of the needed assumption in terms of a counterbalancing of the evidence, for the same points I will make will apply if we take a bit broader interpretation of the assumption. The implications of this assumption, however, undermine the attempt to find an epistemic problem of hiddenness.

If the evidence is counterbalanced between theism and atheism, one of two accounts of the quality of the evidence must be accepted. On one picture, what is proffered as evidence for or against the existence of God is not really evidence at all. On this picture, the proofs for the existence of God are not even defeasible pieces of evidence; they don't make for the objective rationality of accepting theism even an iota. The same would be said on this picture about other defenses of the rationality of religious belief, defenses that appeal to the nature of religious experience or the grounds which are sometimes claimed to support the proper basicality of certain claims.[8] In no such case is there anything to the claim that there is any positive evidence or grounds in support of theism. But equally true on this picture is that there is no evidence in the other direction, either. The problem of evil is a mere pseudoproblem; the existence of evil counts no more against the existence of God than does the existence of grass, or stars, or trees. There is just no objective epistemic connection at all between the claim that God exists and the claim that evil exists.

It is not hard to see that on this picture, there will be no epistemic problem of divine hiddenness. For the purported problem of hiddenness is just a special case of the general problem of evil. If hiddenness is an epistemic problem, it is because the inscrutability of divine existence is a bad thing that a perfectly loving God would not or could not allow. But that, of course, is simply a special case of the problem of evil, and on the picture above of how the evidence is counterbalanced between theism and atheism, no instances of evil are relevant at all to the truth or falsity of theism.

So we must turn to the other picture of how the evidence is counterbalanced. On this picture, there is good, objective evidence for the existence of God. Of course, none of it is indefeasibly good evidence, for then it could not be counterbalanced by evidence against the existence of God. So the good evidence must be defeasible, capable of being counterbalanced by evidence against the existence of God. The proofs, religious experience, and the grounds which might be cited on behalf of the proper basicality of theistic belief can provide strong evidence for theism, but the evidence must not be conclusive. For its positive impact on the claim that God exists is offset by other information.

This other information is in the form of defeaters. Defeaters come in many forms, but the relevant form here is that of a rebutter. A rebutter of evidence e for p is some evidence r for $\sim p$, such that $e \& r$ leaves p less than justified. As we saw above, there will be no epistemic problem of divine hiddenness if no instance of evil counts against the existence of God, so we must assume here that evil is evidence against theism and for atheism. In order for the total evidence to be counterbalanced, evil must provide sufficient evidence for atheism to offset, to counterbalance the evidence available for theism in the form of arguments for the existence of God, appeals to religious experience, and grounds for the claim that belief in God is properly basic. So the picture we get is one for which the metaphor of the scales of justice is appropriate. Each pan of the scale has something in it, and the two sides balance each other out.

Yet, if this is the picture we adopt of the claim that the evidence is counterbalanced, what room is left for the claim that there is some further evidence provided by the fact that God is hidden, that God's existence is not as obvious as it should be, which will tip the scales on behalf of atheism? We ought to find the suggestion initially quite puzzling, for such a problem can only arise after evaluating the evidence for and against theism, and finding that evidence to be counterbalanced. Yet, it is also obvious that the problem of hiddenness is but a special instance of the problem of evil, the epistemic weight of which has already been factored in. So how could hiddenness be a further problem, a further piece of information to be weighed in the balance?

One might wonder why a defender of the epistemic problem of hiddenness can't reply as follows: "I'm imagining the scales to be balanced when all is taken into account *except for the hiddenness of God*. Once hiddenness is added, the scales tip toward atheism." Such a claim is precisely one that Schellenberg makes. He qualifies his remarks about the counterbalanced nature of evidence for theism by formulating the epistemic indifference point "exclusive of the evidence adduced in this book," the book he writes (pp. 11–12).

But such a reply cannot work. Since the problem of evil is already present in the balance, adding a new kind of evil to the scales will have no more effect on the balance than would adding some new religious experiences to the other side of the scale. The theist can say, "I'll see your hiddenness problem and raise it five religious experiences." That is, if adding new evils to one side counts, certainly adding new proofs, or new grounds, or new religious experiences (I don't mean new *kinds of* religious experiences, but I don't rule that out either) has to be allowed on the other side. So citing a special evil won't have the required effect, if we are assuming that all evil counts against the existence of God.

Moreover, the scales must include all known information relevant to theism, if it is to be an adequate representation of the epistemic question in mind. And the fact that God is hidden is not unknown, not even to theists – they have discussed it for centuries. The most that could be claimed is that there are some implications of the claim that have not been appreciated by theists, and it is these implications that constitute the epistemic problem of divine hiddenness.

That is hardly the case, however. The reason that theists from Butler to Pascal to Kierkegaard have discussed the question of the hiddenness of God is precisely because of a perceived tension between their explicit theology about the nature of God and the facts of unbelief. The question of why God would allow certain states of affairs to obtain generally arises when a threat is perceived to the coherence of a system of beliefs. The question of why God is hidden is a much different question from the question of why there are dogs, or why stars exist. The latter pose no threat to one's conception of God, but the former does, and the reason the question is addressed is because of the obviousness of the threat. So it is simply false that the implications of hiddenness have somehow escaped theists – the fact is they address the issue precisely because they see the problem.

There is another point worth making as well. We are imagining that the epistemic balance is equally weighted for and against the existence of God. We have noted that for this to be so, there must be information on the negative side to counteract the positive evidence for the existence of God on the other side. We have focused on rebutters above, but there is an important presupposition to be noticed here regarding the possibility of such rebutters. In order for there to be rebutters, there must be defeaters present of a different sort. These defeaters must delimit the evidential force of the information on each side of the scales. These defeaters, that is, must operate so as to prevent, on the one side, any information from compellingly establishing the existence of God. In some cases, the evidence itself implicitly reveals this defeating information, such as in the case of probabilistic arguments derived from sampling. In other cases, the presence of such defeaters is signalled by the author of an argument when he or she draws a conclusion preceded by a phrase such as "So it is probable that." Regarding the question of the existence of God, the delimiting defeaters are best identified with the objections to the traditional proofs and arguments against appeals to religious experience and proper basicality. These objections and arguments must be effective enough to prevent the positive evidence from conclusively establishing theism. Equally so, there must be delimiting defeaters to prevent the problem of evil from decisively establishing atheism. Presumably, the standard responses to the problem of evil, whether in terms of necessity for a greater good, soul-making, the importance of freedom, or simply the fact that we do not know what all the good things are, provide this kind of defeater. Most generally, these defeaters must have the power to neutralize sufficiently the evidential force of both sides of the scale so that such force can be rebutted by the information on the other side of the scale to result in counterbalancing. If so, however, it is hard to see what evidential force could be added by the problem of hiddenness. This problem could tip the scales toward atheism if the delimiting defeaters for the problem of evil failed to delimit the implications of hiddenness. In this way, hiddenness would constitute a different *kind* of problem for theism than the general problem of evil. But if it does not constitute a different kind of problem in this way, then all it does is add further examples of a problem already weighed in the scales, and we have already seen the failure of this attempt to argue that hiddenness constitutes an epistemic problem for theism. So all that is left is to argue that it constitutes a different kind of problem than the general problem of evil, and for that to be true, the delimiting defeaters regarding the problem of evil will have to fail to delimit the evidential power of hiddenness. No one has argued such, and it is hard to see how such an argument could be successful. If we consider the plausible candidates for such delimiting defeaters – the value of freedom, necessity for a greater good, the importance of soul-making, cognitive limitations, and the like – there is no particular reason to think that such responses succeed only for the general problem of evil but not for the specific problem of divine hiddenness. If not, however, there simply is nothing for hiddenness to add to the scales that won't be neutralized sufficiently by information already present.

I might encode the view I am defending by saying that the evidential value of hiddenness is merely epiphenomenal. I am not arguing that hiddenness does not constitute evidence against the existence of God; instead, I am merely claiming that this evidence, if it be such, cannot do any epistemic work. It is akin to my testimonial evidence to you that you exist. What I say is evidence that you exist, but it can't do any epistemic work, for whatever the evidential status of your existence for yourself, it won't be changed by such testimony.

I believe that there are other examples of epiphenomenal evidence as well. For example, our awareness of the lack of complete reliability in our sources of information and in our own cognitive abilities is awareness of evidence against most everything we believe. But it is merely epiphenomenal evidence, for in the absence of more specific concerns about reliability or our fallibility regarding a particular subject matter, it doesn't alter the epistemic status of our beliefs: factoring in the information that we are not infallible does not make any of our beliefs less rational than they would have been, had that information been ignored.[9] And when there are more specific concerns present, it is these concerns that are responsible for the epistemic change, not the awareness of general facts about fallibility.

My interest, however, is not to defend or articulate any general theory of such epiphenomenal evidence, but merely to point out the existence of such, and to use that concept to articulate my thesis about the nature of the hiddenness of God. If we grant that such hiddenness is evident against the existence of God, it is merely epiphenomenal evidence: It does no work regarding the overall epistemic status of belief in God.

All this is premised on our initial assumption that key epistemic notions are to be understood objectively, and my point has been that there is an epistemic problem of hiddenness only when subjectivity intrudes in a strong way into our understanding of these terms. Once we restrict our discussion to objective construals, there is no good reason for thinking that there is any epistemic problem at all regarding the hiddenness of God. Because of its epiphenomenal character, it is not a piece of information that affects the epistemic scales regarding theism at all.

Notes

1. J. L. Schellenberg, *Divine Hiddenness and Human Reason*, (Ithaca: Cornell University Press, 1993). Page references in the text are to this work.
2. For more on the relationship between coherentism and inconsistency, see Richard Foley, *The Theory of Epistemic Rationality*, (Cambridge, MA: Harvard University Press, 1986).
3. Keith Lehrer, *Knowledge*, (Oxford: Clarendon Press, 1977); Richard Foley, *The Theory of Epistemic Rationality*, (Cambridge MA: Harvard University Press, 1986).
4. Schellenberg, p. 146.
5. I must note, however, that I am engaging in charitable interpretation of remarks that recur throughout the work. As another example, Schellenberg asks in the Conclusion of the work, "Consider . . . the situation in which *S* takes the relevant (independent) evidence to strongly *favor* the claim that there is a God . . . Must *S*, to be rational, deny or come to doubt the existence of God because of the undefeated argument [from hiddenness]?" (p. 209) If we construe the epistemic notions here objectively, the supposition preceding the question is irrelevant, for what makes for rationality is not what a person *takes* the evidence to favor, but what in fact it favors. I interpret the actual language as unfortunate. What Schellenberg meant to ask, I believe, was what his purportedly undefeated argument would imply epistemically, on the supposition that the evidence strongly favors theism.
6. See my "Conservatism and its Virtues," *Synthese* 79 (1989), pp. 143–163.
7. For further discussion on the failure of this principle, see, e.g., Bruce Reichenbach, "The Inductive Argument from Evil," *American Philosophical Quarterly* 17 (1980), pp. 221–227.
8. Claimed most famously by Alvin Plantinga. See his "Reason and Belief in God," in *Faith and Rationality: Reason and Belief in God*, Alvin Plantinga and Nicholas Wolterstorff, eds., (Notre Dame, IN: University of Notre Dame Press, 1983), pp. 16–93.
9. To prevent a possible misunderstanding here, I note that failing to factor in the information that one is fallible is not to be identified with factoring in the claim that one is infallible. The middle ground is that of making neither assumption.

8

A Kierkegaardian View of
Divine Hiddenness

M. JAMIE FERREIRA

> All this heaven-storming you want to do. If God wanted His tracks
> discovered, wouldn't He have made them plainer? Why tuck them into
> odd bits of astronomy and nuclear physics? Why be so *coy*, if You're the
> Deity?
>
> Roger's Version, John Updike

In one of his Hasidic portraits, Elie Wiesel tells the story of a rebbe whose
student complained to him about God's hiddenness. The rebbe replied, "True,
God may be hiding, but you know it. That ought to be sufficient."[1] For some
people the idea of God's hiddenness is not a problem as long as we 'know' or
at least reasonably believe that 'God' is hidden/hiding. In *Divine Hiddenness
and Human Reason*, J. L. Schellenberg examines the implications of divine
hiddenness for theism, and distinguishes three possible versions: the "obscuring of God's existence," (2) the "incomprehensibility of God's nature," and
(3) "our inability to detect the exact pattern of God's activity in the world."[2]
"All I seek to show," he insists, "is that we might expect God's *existence* to
be more obvious. I am happy to allow that the same claim made in respect of
the depths of God's nature or the exact pattern of his activity would have much
less to recommend it." Schellenberg's contribution to this volume also maintains this emphasis on "existence."[3] His argument is as follows: Divine hiddenness is constituted by the lack of evidence "sufficient" or "adequate" to put
belief in God's existence "beyond reasonable doubt,"[4] thus, divine hiddenness
implies the possibility of reasonable (nonculpable) nonbelief; nonculpable
nonbelief occurs;[5] nonbelief (on religious terms) has negative consequences;
there is no overriding benefit derived from divine hiddenness which compen-
sates for its potential negative effects; thus, there is no reason for "a morally
perfect being – good, just" and "perfectly loving"[6] to allow a world in which
nonbelief could be reasonable (nonculpable). Further, the reasonableness of
nonbelief provides good grounds for atheism (more provocatively, weak evidence is evidence against).

Schellenberg offers an extended critique of historical arguments put forth
by believers in which divine hiddenness is said to serve a purpose which justifies God's allowing the possibility of reasonable nonbelief. In one of these

accounts, the Johannes Climacus writings of Søren Kierkegaard, Schellenberg sees the justification for God's hiddenness defended in terms of the value of subjective, passionately inward, development. That is, divine hiddenness either serves the positive function of generating subjective passion (which requires objective uncertainty about God's existence) or it serves the negative function of preventing certain states that would "inhibit" such subjectivity. He concludes that this Climacan strategy fails to show a reason for, or overriding benefit from, divine hiddenness. While there is some textual warrant for seeing Climacus's rationale in the way Schellenberg does, I want to revisit the Climacus writings to explore another, more fundamental, response to be found there. I will argue that some of Climacus's deepest commitments highlight and challenge the probabilistic model underlying Schellenberg's whole critique, and that Climacus's best case does not lie in any psychological-empirical claims about the relation between uncertainty and passion or risk, but rather in a challenge to Schellenberg's understanding of the grammar of divinity and divine hiddenness. In what follows, I will begin with the question of the distinction between God's existence and God's nature; but my focus in this chapter will be on Climacus's polemic against the relevance of probability to decisively religious categories.

1.   Existence Versus Nature

Taken at face value Schellenberg's formulation of his concern – namely, "God's existence," as contrasted with "God's nature" – raises an initial exegetical question. What counts as "God's existence" for Schellenberg? This simple question has far-reaching implications because Schellenberg insists that he is arguing on "traditional" theology's own terms. Schellenberg argues that although some post-Enlightenment theologians (e.g., Barth) might disagree about the obviousness of God's existence, "the majority of patristic, medieval, and reformation theologians affirmed [the Pauline view] that God's existence could be 'clearly seen, being understood through the things that have been made' (Roman. 1:20), while maintaining that 'such knowledge or demonstration could not comprehend God as he was in himself'."[7] This means, for Schellenberg, that traditional theologians have not always insisted on the hiddenness of "God's existence."

It is important to note Schellenberg's claim that "We may therefore conclude that the traditional emphasis of theology on the hiddenness of God does not imply that the evidence for God's existence must be weak, and hence does not sanction a dismissal of our inquiry, as it might otherwise be thought to do."[8] In other words, he admits that if his challenge is not on "traditional" theology's own terms, it is (or might be thought to be) irrelevant. Although I think he later depends on a more generous reading in which he challenges traditional theology's terms, he initially sets up his project on what he sees as theology's own terms, and defends it as therefore not automatically ruled out by theology's own assumptions. But Schellenberg lets himself off the hook a little prematurely. First, he has assumed that "clearly seen" implies that "non-belief" would be "irrational" (which is what he contrasts with reasonable nonbelief);[9] he ignores the fact that an argument which renders G probable and hence makes it reasonable to believe G need not, thereby, make it unreasonable to believe not-G. Second, he has assumed that what could be "clearly seen" refers to precisely what he means by the term "perfectly loving and just God." I will now argue that his conclusion illegitimately conflates the "existence of God" which on traditional theology's terms is available to reason with the belief of traditional theology that God is perfectly loving and just. That is, Schellenberg trades on the ambiguity found in the phrase "existence of God" when he claims that "traditional" theology does not require the "existence of God" to be hidden and then argues for the availability of evidence strong enough to make nonbelief in the existence of a good, loving, and just God unreasonable.

Let's look at two poles of the Christian tradition with which I am familiar in order to assess his conclusion.[10] One unproblematically "traditional" account which appears to support Schellenberg is found in Aquinas's writings. Presumably, Aquinas's claim in the *Summa Contra Gentiles*, that "if we do not demonstrate that God exists, all consideration of divine things is necessarily suppressed," would be taken as a perfect example of how the traditional task of natural theology is the establishment of some minimal base of divine 'existence,' to be perfected by a revelation of the divine nature.[11] Aquinas's further reference here to the demonstration of the "existence" of God "as the necessary foundation of the whole work" might seem to suggest that Aquinas is not committed to what Schellenberg describes as the first form of divine hiddenness (the hiddenness of God's existence). But Aquinas's "preamble" to "faith" does not consist in the conclusion of a morally good, a loving and just God, such as Schellenberg's argument depends on. If we look closely at the conclusions of the five ways and the explications of God's perfection and goodness which immediately follow the five ways, as well as every other of Aquinas's formulations of what we can know in this life by natural reason, we will see that "what everyone understands by God," what can be "clearly seen," is a category which refers to something religiously neutral. There is nothing decisively religious about the notion of goodness that reason attributes to God since it is merely the goodness which is identified with being actual and desirable[12] and does not include the religiously relevant notion of "loving" or wanting to be in relationship with us. So what Aquinas means by God's existence and what Schellenberg means by God's existence are not the same.[13] For

Aquinas, God's religiously uncharacterizable existence, God with religiously-unspecifiable nature, is *not hidden*; God-with-any-religious-content-at-all (loving, just) is *hidden*.[14]

Turn now to the non-Catholic account which Schellenberg explicitly addresses – namely, Kierkegaard, or more precisely, his pseudonymous author, Johannes Climacus. What does Climacus think about whether God's "existence" is hidden? Climacus thinks "the existence of God" is perfectly evident; this is because for him "the existence of God" is the way of characterizing the logical space (the qualitatively different) which the understanding reaches in its Kantian striving, its passionate and irresistible seeking to know; here I take him to be in agreement with Aquinas. Consider Climacus's discussion of the paradoxical passion of the understanding which is "to want to discover something that thought itself cannot think." He continues: "But what is this unknown against which the understanding in its paradoxical passion collides, and which even disturbs man and his self-knowledge? It is the unknown. But it is not a human being, insofar as he knows man, or anything else that he knows. Therefore, let us call this unknown the god. It is only a name we give to it."[15] In other words, we reach "the unknown" and we call it "the god." This is Socratic religiousness (which Climacus later calls religiousness A), comparable to Aristotle's and Aquinas's first cause, *causa sui*, or unmoved mover, "what everyone understands by God." The God that is not hidden, for Climacus, is the "unknown," the "concept" whose "*essentia involvit existentiam*."[16]

Climacus's equation of "the unknown" with "god," and his distinction between religiousness A and religiousness B (Christian paradoxical God – a God whom we believe to be a God of Love[17]), both suggest that there is nothing with any religious relevance which he thinks we can determine to exist, prior to determining that it is also loving and just. Hiddenness, for Climacus, applies to a God whose religiously relevant existence cannot be determined apart from his nature. Moreover, Climacus explicitly refers to the intellectual difficulties of any teleological argument – the circularity of arguing from "God's works" to the character of (a religiously relevant) God. We know "the existence of God," for both Aquinas and Climacus, but what we know when we know *only* the existence of God is what Climacus calls Socratic (not decisive) religiousness.

In other words, I am suggesting that both Climacus and Aquinas believe that the existence of God is necessarily subject to reasonable nonbelief as long as it refers to a providentially loving God.[18] Schellenberg's assumption that "unsurpassably great" implies perfectly loving[19] goes beyond that found in such accounts. While Climacus and Aquinas both affirm that God is perfectly loving, they do not allow that such a loving God is beyond reasonable nonbelief – rather, God's providential love for us, God's concern to be in a loving relationship with us, is subject to the same "incomprehensibility," the same openness to reasonable nonbelief, as 'the rest' of God's nature. Why should it be exempt? Aquinas insists that *even revelation* "joins us to him [God] as to an unknown."[20] In others words, for most traditional theology human reason cannot get to God's providential love; because such providential love must be revealed, it cannot be put beyond reasonable doubt (i.e., nonbelief in a loving God cannot be irrational).

Let me approach this now in a different way. We need to distinguish two propositional attitudes: (1) belief that there exists something [which is in fact a perfectly loving God], and (2) belief that there exists a perfectly loving God. Given the intensionality of belief (or the referential opacity of propositional attitudes), evidence for the first conclusion does not in itself serve as evidence for the second conclusion. Even if X = GL, from the fact that someone believes that X exists one cannot infer that the person believes that GL exists.[21] If Schellenberg is arguing that it should be possible to put beyond doubt the belief in the existence of something [which happens to be perfectly loving], then he is too late; he ignores the fact that Aquinas and Climacus already believe that such an existence is beyond reasonable doubt. If he is arguing that it should be possible to put beyond doubt the belief that a perfectly loving God exists on the basis of the claim that belief in something [which happens to be a perfectly loving God] is not required by the tradition to be hidden, his argument is illegitimate (precisely because of the intensionality of propositional attitudes). In other words, the traditional theology to which he alludes already concedes (1), but only (2) is religiously relevant; no argument for (1) provides an argument for (2).

In sum, any discussion of the hiddenness of the "existence of God" needs to attend carefully to how much is packed into the notion of God when God's existence is said to be able to be put "beyond reasonable doubt" and how much is packed into it when God's existence is said to be hidden. Schellenberg recognizes the religious irrelevance of such a denuded concept of God's existence, so he builds into the concept of God's existence a minimal characterization of God's nature as perfectly loving and wanting to be in relationship with us. He argues that it is precisely the religiously relevant notion of the existence of a perfectly loving God who wants to be in intimate relation with us which should not be open to reasonable nonbelief; belief that such a God exists should be sufficiently supported as to be "beyond reasonable doubt" (39), if we humans are not to be deprived of the benefits that go with such belief. In suggesting that such a belief should be guaranteed as a condition for the possibility of the relationship with God which a perfectly loving God desires, Schellenberg does not represent but rather challenges traditional theology. Let me turn now to a Kierkegaardian response to Schellenberg's challenge.

2. Degrees of Hiddenness – The Probabilistic Model

On Schellenberg's reading of Climacus, God's elusiveness is intentional; God could reveal himself more clearly but chooses not to. Divine hiddenness fulfills a positive function – faith intensifies subjectivity. Risk, passion, subjective inwardness: All of these are goods which presuppose objective uncertainty about God's existence. Without such uncertainty we would be led to avoid the strenuousness of passionate striving.[22] At bottom, Schellenberg's critique of Climacus's rationale for divine hiddenness is that it is psychologically unfounded. First, according to Schellenberg, Climacus cannot make the case for a necessary connection between passion and objective uncertainty, between lack of striving and lack of risk. Some people might be more passionate or strive more in response to God's making his presence unambiguously known to them. Moreover, even if the connection were necessary, even if passionate inwardness were inversely related to risk, why do we need the maximum, why such intense inwardness? Why that much uncertainty – wouldn't *some* be enough? Uncertainty about God's nature would allow sufficient passion – there would always be enough of that to be passionate about. Why would God not at least reveal God's existence? Knowing God's existence wouldn't preclude a very passionate engagement with God.[23]

Schellenberg's plea for moderation endorses Robert M. Adams's criticism that the *extreme* subjectivity advocated by Climacus is not really a good after all. In this rather common criticism of Kierkegaardian religiousness, Adams writes: "[T]he doctrine that it is desirable to increase without limit, or to the highest possible degree (if there is one) the cost and risk of a religious life is less plausible (to say the least) than the view that *some degree of cost and risk* may add to the value of a religious life. The former doctrine would set the religious interest at enmity with all other interests, or at least with the best of them."[24] Adams's assumption of "degrees" of religiosity is evident. Following Adams, Schellenberg concludes that Climacus "seems to have an 'all-or-nothing' view, " and "surely this view is mistaken."[25]

Climacus certainly emphasizes passionately striving inwardness, but I submit that Schellenberg's examination of Climacus's rebuttal is one-sided, and does not address what lies at the heart of Climacus's account of hiddenness. Schellenberg reads Climacus as making divine hiddenness a psychological requirement for the exercise of passion; even the Climacan idea that, as Schellenberg puts it, faith "logically implies Divine Hiddenness,"[26] is read by Schellenberg as if it were simply an empirical psychological one (i.e., passionate response requires the presence of objective uncertainty) rather than a logical one. I suggest, on the contrary, that Climacus is speaking not about a psychological all-or-nothing, but rather about a *grammatical* requirement – namely, that divine hiddenness is logically implied in the notion of God's absoluteness. I will argue that Climacus's rationale for divine hiddenness does not (as Schellenberg implies) lie simply in an appeal to empirical psychological claims about the relation between passion and hiddenness (claims which are falsifiable). Rather, Climacus's rationale depends far more deeply on his commitments to the *absolute* nature of divinity, the *qualitative difference* between human reality and divine reality. In this section, I will explore this other dimension of Climacus's response – namely, his commitment to absoluteness and qualitative difference – in terms of his rejection of the "probabilifying case" which Schellenberg seeks. I will focus on Climacus's polemic against the confusion of coupling the notion of "probability" with *decisively religious* categories.[27]

Do the Climacan texts point to such a reading? I suggest that the polemic against "a certain degree," which is used repeatedly by Climacus (and Kierkegaard in other writings), is a crucial underpinning to any Climacan (or Kierkegaardian) understanding of the hiddenness of a loving God. This phrase, "to a certain degree," is used by Climacus to ridicule a *quantitative* understanding of religious categories. He inveighs against what he calls the "perpetual prattle about 'to a certain degree' " precisely because it assumes that something can be a "paradox to a certain degree," or that one can be "an existing person to a certain degree," or that there can be a "decision to a certain degree."[28] It assumes that Christianity can be "true to a certain degree," or, more generally, that what a person says "is true to a certain degree."[29] As a group these are not claims about psychological intensity – rather, they seem to make a philosophical point about conceptual confusion. There are not, for Climacus, degrees of truth any more than there are degrees of paradox – P is not partly true or partly paradoxical (though we may, of course, decide that part of P is entirely true or entirely paradoxical). (Here Climacus is in the company of someone as theologically and philosophically different from himself as the Victorian Catholic John Henry Newman, for whom it does not make sense to speak of "degrees of truth."[30]) Climacus is pointing to the notion of what I will call an "absolute concept" – one in which the modifier "perfectly" (or, if you like, "unsurpassably") is understood. 'True' and 'paradoxical' are judgements of qualitative perfection to which all-or-nothing applies.

Was Kierkegaard sophisticated enough to be making such a claim? In his nonpseudonymous *Book on Adler*, Kierkegaard charged the pastor, A. P. Adler, with being confused about the grammar of Christian faith, confused about the way in which Christian categories like revelation and authority are normatively used. Kierkegaard concluded that Adler's "confusion" was due to not having a "mastery of Christian conceptual language."[31] I think the repeated Climacan jibe – "to a certain degree" – points to a similar charge of conceptual or grammatical confusion.

Climacus calls attention to the god's attempt to reveal godself; he provokes us with the claim – "Look, there he stands – the god. Where? There, can you not see him?"[32] He insists that what we *can* see does not take away any genuine hiddenness – the possibility of offense is always there. It is indeed all or nothing. He allows that the god's aim is not to "mock human beings" so that we necessarily miss him, but he also concedes that any "accommodation for the sake of comprehensibility . . . may just as well alienate the learner as draw him closer."[33] Anti-Climacus, Kierkegaard's idealized Christian, explicitly raises the question whether we can show (i.e., render nonbelief an irrational response) that Jesus Christ was God, and his answer is a decisive 'no!' Moreover, Anti-Climacus connects this peculiar unrecognizability and "offense sensu strictissimo" with the rejection of an "indefinite quantifying" and the requirement of a "qualitative" definition which "insists upon *worship*" – precisely because, he says, it is a question of "absoluteness."[34] Climacus's account of the hiddenness within revelation similarly claims that the God must give us some signs, but the qualitative nature of the revelation in those signs simply hammers the point home again – we do not see some of God's divinity, we do not see "a certain degree" of divinity. If we distinguish between content (of proposition) and mode (of holding proposition), we can say that we either see the whole (content/object) in a particular way (mode, e.g., dimly), or we do not see it (content/object) at all – Climacus's message is that in the case of seeing God, we never see some extent of the whole.[35] We do not see the "existence" of a religiously relevant (loving) God without seeing religiously characterized divinity, and that requires a qualitative, not a quantitative, shift in perception.

Climacus appeals to the plausibility of the all-or-nothing character of a qualitative change. Loving divinity's qualitative difference from nondivinity means that our perception is in some sense always all or nothing. Climacus's polemic against degrees of either truth or paradoxicality underlines his view of the qualitativeness of the shift in perception which occurs when one recognizes or affirms divinity.[36] There is no distinction to be made for Climacus between recognizing the existence of a loving God and recognizing the loving nature of God – it is a question of "absoluteness." Any notion of the hiddenness of divinity as susceptible to degrees or "depths" is religiously confused.

Suppose we agree for the moment with Climacus when he highlights the absolute content of what is believed – i.e., agree that the character of what we address ourselves to is absolute. Is he, nevertheless, confused about what follows from such a commitment? Does the absoluteness of the content imply the absoluteness of the mode? Can we not hold more or less strongly that X is absolute; can we not have degrees of revelation that X is absolute? This is perhaps the crux of Schellenberg's case against Climacus. Schellenberg's contention seems to be that the all-or-nothing character of the content does not require an all-or-nothing hiddenness – i.e., that we can have, as he says, "probabilifying evidence"[37] for the *existence of a perfectly loving God* and as a result have a correlative degree of passion.

Climacus does seem to treat the mode as all-or-nothing, and he does this in two respects: first, the mode considered as the way in which we hold a belief (weak or strong adherence), and second, the mode considered as the way in which evidence can make something available to us (weak or strong argument/evidential probability). Let me try to make the case that Climacus is not simply confusing the need for an absolute content with the need for an absolute mode (i.e., the perfection of passion and/or the rejection of probabilities).

Mode of Holding a Belief

It is interesting to note that Climacus's examples of all-or-nothing concepts range quite freely over a variety of kinds; we have seen that some, like truth or paradox, plausibly refer to content, but he goes on to speak of others, like enthusiasm or love, as equally all-or-nothing. The latter, which are varieties of passion, are relevant to the *mode* of believing; here the doctrine of degrees is, for him, a failure to appreciate the Biblical pronouncement that "the person who is neither cold nor hot is an abomination."[38] Now perhaps Climacus mistakenly assumes that because content is absolute, the mode of adherence must automatically be so as well. Perhaps – but perhaps he is suggesting, instead, that there is something peculiar about the attitudes one can hold toward an absolute which render them not subject to degrees.

There are concepts in which a qualitative shift is designated and to which degrees don't apply – e.g., "boil" and "explode." Water gets hotter and hotter but it doesn't boil little by little, by degrees (we say 'it is not boiling yet'); an explosive doesn't explode by degrees ('it didn't explode yet'). Moreover, with regard to at least some qualitative shifts we assume that degrees are not relevant once the critical threshold has been reached: we don't speak of further increases in boiling; the higher temperatures the water can reach do not seem decisive once the boiling occurs. Perhaps Climacus is arguing by analogy that love or passion is not a question of degree because what matters is the qualitative shift involved in having the attitude – (a) the attitude does not count *at all* as passion, love, or enthusiasm until it has a certain quality and (b) that quality is decisive in the sense that there is no sense in speaking of "more" of it. Is being a little passionate (somewhat in love, slightly enthusiastic, moderately religious) like being a little pregnant or a little schizophrenic?

I mentioned J. H. Newman earlier – let me now briefly explore how his position in his *Grammar of Assent* can support Climacus's view. Newman's account of "assent" implies that belief is a *threshold* concept; there is a point at which the belief crystallizes, and at that point it is constituted by whatever is necessary to its integrity. He writes: "At the utmost we say that we are inclined to believe this proposition or that, that we are not sure it is not true, that much may be said for it, that we have been much struck by it; but we never say that we give it a degree of assent. We might as well talk of degrees of truth as of degrees of assent."[39] Moreover, he distinguishes between the propositional object of our belief and the integrity of the mode of assenting to it: "A half-assent is not a kind of assent any more than a half-truth is a kind of truth. As the object is indivisible, so is the act."[40] Finally, he distinguishes between the mode of adherence and the *concomitants* of (or circumstances surrounding) the adherence. He admits that it is natural to speak of "'strong' and 'feeble' faith," and to contrast "the faith which would move mountains" with "ordinary faith." But, he suggests, what looks like an "increase or decrease of strength does not lie in the assent itself, but in its circumstances and concomitants; for instance, in the emotions, in the ratiocinative faculty, or in the imagination. . . . Such strength is adventitious and accidental; it may come, it may go; . . . it does not interfere with the genuineness and perfection of the act of assent."[41]

In other words, it might be argued that there are modes in which it is plausible to see the idea of "more" as simply idling. For example, this is what I think Wittgenstein meant when he intriguingly commented: "'I never believed in God before' – that I understand. But not: 'I never really believed in Him before'."[42] His suggestion is that belief in God is an all-or-nothing sort of belief; there is not some minimum to which "really" can add an optional 'extra' bit. Believing in God just is "really believing" – not "really believing" in God is not believing at all. Without the "really," there is not yet belief in God at all.

If these suggestions about the irrelevance of degrees to certain modes of holding beliefs do not render the idea plausible, I'm afraid there may be no other way to do so. Climacus, however, has another proposal in mind which deserves to be examined, but before turning to that I want to comment on Schellenberg's and Adams's construal of the Climacan claim that passion is all or nothing. They take this to imply an impossible or undesirable extreme goal of subjective inwardness – i.e., the goal of a constant and total psychological state of intensity which would, as Adams says, be "at enmity with all other interests, or at least with the best of them." Even if you believe that adherence to beliefs is subject to degrees, it is important to be fair to Kierkegaard's emphasis on passionate inwardness. Schellenberg's and Adams's construal ignores important explications which are available to Kierkegaard. Anti-Climacus, the most idealized Christian in Kierkegaard's corpus, offers a description which belies the inevitability of extremism when he writes: "[W]hat it means in the strictest sense to be a Christian, is to confess honestly before God where he is so that he might still worthily accept the grace that is offered to every imperfect person – that is, to everyone. And then, nothing further – then, as for the rest, let him do his work and rejoice in it, love his wife and rejoice in her, joyfully bring up his children, love his fellow beings, rejoice in life." Indeed, Climacus may well have gotten it wrong, since he admits he is not a Christian – but the emphasis on passionate inwardness need not imply such a monomania as Adams suggests. What is normatively urged is not a matter of extreme psychological engagement to the exclusion of other concerns. The requirements of "ideality" should "be heard again and again in their entire infinitude,"[43] but they command a deepening of our joy in life, rather than a compartmentalization or alternation of moments of subjectivity or faith with moments of ordinary daily life.

Mode of Appropriating Evidence

Let us leave the question of the mode of adherence to belief, and turn to Climacus's second proposal concerning the rejection of degrees. Climacus may have been proposing a connection between the absolute content of religious belief and the ways (the mode) in which evidence is relevant to religious belief. The doctrine of degrees, he says, "smuggle[s] in probability."[44] That is, the polemic against degrees applies as well to the way evidence is appropriated – it is all-or-nothing. Climacus's general insistence on the decisiveness of qualitative rather than quantitative transitions and his correlative rejection of probabilistic models of religious argumentation are perhaps the most striking and pervasive themes in his writings. Schellenberg's view of evidence is probabilistic in just the sense Climacus rejects in his polemic against "degrees." Schellenberg argues that what should be available to truth-seekers is "probabilifying evidence." Of course, he admits, it need not be theoretical argument; it can be experiential evidence. His probabilistic view of the matter of evidence is clear when he claims that "the evidence actually available to individuals who inculpably fail to believe does go *some way* toward showing that there is a God." There are, e.g., "such phenomena as the order manifested in the universe and religious experience as confirming *to some degree* the proposition that there is a God. And surely no one could reasonably deny that such phenomena do render the existence of God at least *somewhat more likely* than it would otherwise be" (emphasis mine).[45]

I want to claim that when Climacus ridicules the idea of "probabilifying evidence" for decisive religiousness, he has not conflated the absoluteness of the content of the proposition (or object of belief) with an absolute mode of appropriating evidence for it. Rather, I suggest that he wants to point to a peculiarity in speaking of "evidence" for an absolute concept in the religious case – namely, in the religious case there cannot be a gradual build-up, because there is nothing comparable in such a case to the way in which ordinary separate pieces of evidence can accumulate to make a case. Just as there is no question of an accumulation of evidence for the conclusion of Aquinas's five ways, so Climacus presumably sees a parallel with his claim for the decisive further qualitative shift which constitutes religiousness B.

Degrees are irrelevant to some concepts – like perfectly loving or divine – in the sense that one cannot recognize or affirm such concepts partially or by degrees.[46] Any genuine evidence for the conclusion is evidence for it in its totality, all or nothing. (Here the examples of boiling and exploding are relevant again.) One formulation of Climacus's point is as follows: there is a characteristic required of any element which would in principle go into making a probabilistic religious case; if any one of those elements in such a putative case is not taken in an absolutely qualitative way as having *religious* import, it will not contribute at all to the religious case. In other words, to see the whole of nature as God-given, or gift in the strict sense, is not possible without seeing any single flower in the same way. Conversely, to see a single thing as God-given is to buy the whole of nature as such. It is not that several cases of God-givenness could be identified independently and could make a case for the God-givenness of the whole.

Why is there not a cumulative case for the recognition of a perfectly loving God, of the sort where different items of evidence can build to the irrationality of not drawing such a conclusion? Consider what must be true if we have a successful cumulative case. For any given items not to be redundant, they have to add to the likelihood of the conclusion. If they do not add, they are expendable; if they do *add* to the probability of the conclusion it must be that any one of them could not by itself be a sufficient determinant. But that means that different elements could be distinguished, each of which could add to the whole, to the probability of the conclusion. Consider the example of our increasing recognition of Paris as the fog slowly lifts. Here we recognize successively various elements which suggest that the city before us is Paris – some examples of row houses of a distinctive architecture, a waterway in front of the houses. Our evidence can accumulate, making the case more and more probable, and recognizing an Eiffel tower-looking structure is certainly an important additional element which leads to the (highly probabilistic) conclusion that we are in Paris, as opposed to, say, Copenhagen where the houses on one side of Lake Poeblinger are actually quite Parisian-looking. But in the case of divinity, there are no aspects that could be recognized independently and so make for a more likely conclusion. There are no degrees of divinity or aspects of divinity such that we can know some independently of others. Climacus is arguing, therefore, that there are not bits and pieces of unambiguously religious evidence which add up to a probable religious case; rather it is ambiguous whether *anything* is a (neutral) given or a (divine) gift – and only the latter view of it would allow it to count as evidence for the religious inference. Similarly, "perfectly loving" is not a quantitative notion; in any case for judging that a perfectly loving God exists, we would have to count any of the items of which we could compose a case as already an example of perfect love.

For Climacus the decisive religious transition is a matter of *absolute* risk. Climacus's claim – the more risk, the more faith – applies to the general notion of subjectivity, but it does not apply once the critical threshold of religiousness is reached.[47] Why does Climacus see it that way? Is there any thing one can't risk if one has some evidence in hand for it, if one has minimized the risk by making the belief more probable? Can one risk *everything* for something about which there is some evidence? As always in Climacus, there is a distinction between the 'how' and the 'what' – in this case it contrasts the mode and the content of risk. There is an ambiguity about the possibility of risking *everything* – one could risk everything, up to and including one's life (total What) on something that was slightly probable, but one could not *totally* risk everything (total How) in another sense. If there were any evidence it would not be an "absolute risk." Degrees of risk correlate with degrees of probability; absolute risk is qualitative – all or nothing.[48]

3. Concluding Applications

The two aspects I have considered – the question of the content of existence claims (section 1) and the question of degrees (section 2) – are related in the following way. To ask for an unambiguous revelation of "the existence of a perfectly loving God" is already to ask for a putatively 'minimal' description which is subject to the same problems attending any inquiry into god's nature.[49] The heart of the matter for Schellenberg seems to be the following question: What reason could a perfectly loving God have for not revealing himself adequately to preclude reasonable (nonculpable) nonbelief. I will draw two conclusions concerning his argument. First, I find his sense of what a "probable"evidence can accomplish to be an unduly strong one; as I noted earlier he assumes that if there were adequate or sufficient reason for belief in God, it would be "irrational" of someone not to believe, whereas I suggest that someone can be in a situation that recognizes "epistemic parity" and would allow the reasonableness of either belief or nonbelief. Second, he locates Climacus's rationale in the psychological realm, rather than in the grammatical understanding of absoluteness which underlies it all. Schellenberg implies that the only plausible rationale for divine hiddenness that needs to be rebutted is a claim about some ulterior motive God could have for not allowing His existence to be sufficiently evident: as if God hides because we are naturally lazy and need to be motivated; as if there were something God thought we needed to learn from His hiddenness. He attributes to Climacus the idea that a revelation of God might deceive us into thinking that God could be understood in terms of objective categories. But for Climacus, it is not that an objective revelation of God by God would be misleading – the problem is that it would not be God revealing *Godself*. What would it be like for the absolutely different to reveal itself as such? What would count as "a loving and just God" making His presence known in such a way that it would be unreasonable not to believe it? Schellenberg, after all, requires the kind of evidence it would be irrational not to see as adequate. Schellenberg assumes a particular grammar which treats God as qualitatively similar to other things which could reveal themselves, or let themselves be revealed. He suggests that there could be an "experience as of God presenting Himself to [people]"[50] – but what would this be like? What kind of evidence, even experiential, could be nonambiguous, so as to make nonbelief irrational? More precisely, what would nonambiguous evidence be evidence for?

I have been arguing that the grammar of absoluteness is the rubric in which to locate the heart of the Climacan understanding of divine hiddenness. The empirical psychological claims are too easy a target, and they are irrelevant if there is any sense to be made of the notion of a *grammar of absoluteness as usable* by a religious believer. Earlier in his book, Schellenberg addresses the religious claim that God's transcendence implies hiddenness.[51] His conclusion there is that it would be a Pyrrhic victory for a religious believer to use such a defense, since it would mean that nothing meaningful could be said about God. My reading of Climacus can be seen as a kind of appeal to transcendence, so it is important to ask whether Schellenberg is right that no appeal to transcendence could work, since either it would be limited, by allowing the possibility of analogical predication, and so let his argument go through, or it would be absolute and deny the possibility of analogical predication, and so be unusable by a believer. The real question, it seems to me, is: What is the relation between analogical predication and a grammar about what is qualitatively different?

The issue of transcendence is brought up again indirectly at the end of the dialogue in Schellenberg's contribution to this volume, where the problematical character of what "unsurpassable greatness" implies is brought up by C.[52] S's reservation seems to be little more than that philosophers want "clarity" and that he has a "sense" that the linking between "unsurpassable greatness and love" is analytical. S's last word, however, seems to represent an openness to the idea that no evidence for the existence of a loving God can be totally unambiguous.

I have tried throughout this essay to make comparisons between Climacus and Aquinas on this score because Aquinas might provide an example of a theology that affirms analogical predication alongside a radically hidden God. For example, Aquinas's claim that our language about God is "accurate" even though it is not adequate does not imply a neutral God whom we can then decide is perfectly loving. *Even revelation*, he says, "joins us to him [God] as to an unknown."[53] In fact, Aquinas's description of three kinds of knowledge of God involves very sophisticated claims concerning the distinction between 'how' and 'what' (as applied to how and what we know in this life, and how and what we see in heaven) which seem very Climacan.[54] To explore this would require an in-depth study of Aquinas's views on the knowledge of God and religious language, but it seems to me a fruitful place to look.

Notes

1. *Somewhere a Master: Further Hasidic Portraits and Legends*, Elie Wiesel, trans. Marion Wiesel (New York: Summit Books, 1982), p. 21.
2. Schellenberg, (Ithaca: Cornell University Press, 1993), p. 4.
3. See "What the Hiddenness of God Reveals: A Collaborative Discussion," in this volume.
4. Pp. 33–5. Although he begins with the notion of "sufficient" evidence, he goes on to say that the psychological sense – i.e., "sufficient to produce belief" (p. 35) is not enough; rather one needs to have "adequate" support for the belief (p. 34) and it must render the belief "beyond reasonable doubt" (p. 33) identify these formulations.
5. His argument for a rejection of the Calvinist position in which there is no non-culpable nonbelief is found on pp. 58–82.
6. Schellenberg, p. 1, p. 83.
7. Schellenberg, p. 5; even my limited familiarity with Luther's account of divine hiddenness, encompassing both God's hiddenness in himself and His hiddenness in his Revelation, suggests that Schellenberg's appeal to Luther is misleadingly oversimplified.
8. Schellenberg, p. 5.
9. This is an important part of Schellenberg's argument; he seems to assume that if there were adequate reason for belief in God, it would be unreasonable ("irrational") of someone not to believe – that is, he assumes that what will assure the rationality of belief will thereby guarantee the irrationality of not believing (p. 36 note, p. 38). This is a strong sense of what a "probable" argument can effect; I suggest that "epistemic parity" would allow the reasonableness of either G or not-G (p. 65).
10. Since he has ruled out the Calvinist position, I am going to ignore it here; others can argue for it.
11. *Summa Contra Gentiles, Book One: God*, Chap. 9: 5. Note also the claim in *Summa Theologiae*, Ia, 2, 2.3: "God's effects, therefore, can serve to demonstrate that God exists, even though they cannot help us to know him comprehensively."
12. The goodness of God which reason can establish amounts to "complete actuality" and the possession of "every kind of perfection by nature"; God is called good "as being the first source of every perfection things desire"; "inasmuch as they exist, all things are good" (*Summa Theologiae*, 1a, 5.1, 5.3, 6.2).
13. The discussion which follows on intensionality will support this claim.
14. I am here of course referring to the epistemological sense of hidden – i.e., as Aquinas notes, what is evident in itself can be nonevident to us.
15. *Philosophical Fragments*, Kierkegaard's Writings VII, eds. Hong and Hong (Princeton University Press, 1985), pp. 37, 39.

16. *Fragments*, p. 41; Wittgenstein reads such a claim as a grammatical one, when he writes: "God's essence is supposed to guarantee his existence – what this really means is that what is here at issue is not the existence of something" (*Culture and Value*, trans. Peter Winch (Oxford: Basil Blackwell, 1980), p. 82e, 1949.

17. *Concluding Unscientific Postscript to the Philosophical Fragments*, Kierkegaard's Writings XII.1, eds. Hong and Hong, Princeton, 1992, pp. 570–9.

18. This is not to deny that there may be other important differences between them.

19. Schellenberg, pp. 10–11.

20. *Summa Theologiae*, Ia, 12, 13.

21. Aquinas himself makes this point when he writes: "man is by nature aware of what by nature he desires, and he desires by nature a happiness which is to be found only in God. But this is not, simply speaking, awareness that there is a God, any more than to be aware of someone approaching is to be aware of Peter, even should it be Peter approaching" (*Summa Theologiae*, Ia, 2, 1).

22. Schellenberg, pp. 154–65.

23. Schellenberg, p. 162–3.

24. Adams, "Kierkegaard's Arguments Against Reasoning, " p. 227, cited by Schellenberg, pp. 162–3, emphasis added.

25. Schellenberg, p. 163.

26. Schellenberg, p. 158.

27. For Climacus, as for Aquinas, the notion of the god is qualitatively different from the effects which it is used to account for, but there is also a further qualitative difference between this god (religiousness A) and a loving God (religiousness B). My further references to divinity will therefore be shorthand for religiously-relevant divinity.

28. *Postscript*, pp. 219–33; in particular, pp. 219, 226; p. 219; p. 221.

29. *Postscript*, pp. 228–9. I am aware that for some philosophers this locution does make sense, but I would argue that truth and belief are all-or-nothing threshold concepts. P cannot be partially true, though a part of it may be (entirely) true; P cannot be probably true, though that P is probable may be (entirely) true. One can't properly believe that P is "to a certain degree true," though one can believe that P (namely, X is .5 probable) is true. Holding P to be true is an act which we can perform or withhold, but which we cannot do in part. See note 40.

30. *An Essay in Aid of a Grammar of Assent* [1870], ed. I. T. Ker (Oxford: Clarendon Press, 1985), p. 174.

31. *The Book on Adler*, Kierkegaard's Writings XXIV, eds. Hong and Hong, Princeton, 1998, p. 123; he says also that Adler "is not adequately familiar with basic Christian conceptual language" (p. 115), lacks "education in Christian concepts" (116) and does not know the "use of the concept of revelation," e.g. (p. 117).

32. *Fragments*, p. 32.

33. *Fragments*, p. 56.

34. *Practice in Christianity*, Kierkegaard's Writings XX, eds. Hong and Hong (Princeton, 1991), pp. 23–36; p. 87. He suggests that the so-called "sensible person in the situation of contemporaneity [who] censoriously says of Christ, *He is literally nothing*," is correct – "quite so, for he is the absolute" (63).

35. I take this to be what Aquinas means when he says that "the word totally applies to the object" (*Summa Theologia*, Ia, 12, 8.3).

36. See note 35.

37. Schellenberg, p. 35.

38. CUP, 219, 221–33.

180	M. JAMIE FERREIRA

39. Newman, p. 174.
40. Newman, p. 175; "When I assent to a doubtfulness, or to a probability, my assent, as such, is as complete as if I assented to a truth; it is not a certain degree of assent"; the reason is that we speak of "not variations of assent to an inference, but assents to a variation in inferences" (p. 174).
41. Newman, pp. 184–5. See Gilbert Harman for a similar rejection of the notion of "degrees of belief," *Change in View: Principles of Reasoning* (Cambridge, MA: MIT Press, 1989), pp. 21–7 (which contrasts with Schellenberg's proposal of "degrees of belief" [p. 31], "some degree of belief that G is true" [p. 45], and belief as a "graded concept" [p. 31].
42. *Culture and Value*, p. 53e (1946).
43. *Practice in Christianity*, p. 67. It may be that the author Climacus did not appreciate the possibility which Anti-Climacus did, but it is at any rate an understanding which can be used in Kierkegaard's defense.
44. *Postscript*, p. 233.
45. Schellenberg, p. 46.
46. Something cannot be partially perfectly flat; someone cannot be partially perfectly loving or partially divine; at most one could speak of "almost" perfectly flat, but then one sees the ludicrousness of believing in something "almost" perfectly loving, "almost" divine.
47. Climacus argues that it is senseless to talk about degrees of a leap, to say that it is great or small, so long as it is more than we can manage; this seems to hold true of risk as well.
48. Contrast Climacus's use of the category of "absurd" with "improbable."
49. When Schellenberg argues that a perfectly loving God would reveal at least His existence, perhaps he is thinking that a perfectly loving God could reveal the existence of something [which was in fact perfectly loving], but Schellenberg is talking about probable arguments for belief being perceived by people (i.e., intensional belief).
50. Schellenberg, p. 48.
51. Schellenberg, p. 46.
52. See "What the Hiddenness of God Reveals," in this volume.
53. The paradox is apparent: "Although in this life revelation does not tell us what God is, and thus joins us to him as to an unknown, nevertheless it helps us to know him better" (*Summa Theologiae*, Ia, 12, 13).
54. See Aquinas's views on our threefold knowledge of God (*Summa Theologiae*, Ia, 12, art. 1–13), and his views on religious language (Ia, 13, art. 1–12).

9

The Hiddenness of God – A Puzzle or a Real Problem?

JACOB JOSHUA ROSS

In philosophical circles such as ours, we have become accustomed to express-ing our religious ideas, and offering our analyses and arguments regarding these ideas, in terms that are associated with what we call "theism." I take this usage to be a convenient abbreviation.[1] Perhaps we should better characterize the terms that we like to use and the concepts with which we operate as belong-ing to "monotheistic" discourse, rather than as simply being "theistic." More-over it should be noted that our discussions almost invariably relate to monotheism of a very specific type, such as the type that has become foun-dational in all the current religious traditions which are the successors of the Hebrew scriptures, namely, Christianity, Islam, and Judaism. Because this is so, there are two things that we shall do well to take into consideration. First of all, we must note that the theological discussions within these three great historical traditions have sometimes been more inclusive and of wider range than what is just contained in these simple monotheistic terms, no matter how foundational these terms may be. Each of the traditions has included philo-sophical currents and mystical movements that have modified, in different ways, the basic concepts behind the skeletal monotheistic terms with which they have operated. Of this we shall speak more later on. Second, we must recognize that when, in the course of our philosophic discussions, we do for-mulate our ideas in the simple monotheistic terms, as these are understood by the ordinary believers within those religious traditions, we do so at a cost. That cost is the puzzlement and frustration attendant upon the realization that this shared concept of the monotheistic personal God is irredeemably anthropo-morphic, since our model of God is based upon the primacy of human agency and human personality.[2] This model is also largely anthropocentric as well, because our interest in God's activity comes to explain all sorts of things that concern us as human beings. Moreover, the measure of the good and evil that we attribute to the world that we believe to have been created by God is *our* measure, the measure of human beings. The puzzlement of which I talk reflects the fact that we can easily come to recognize that we want to say so much more about the divine than this model can possibly bear. We may want to move beyond the most simple and direct religious messages that this concept of God, as presented in the holy scriptures, comes to emphasize. We may wish to work out a clear unified doctrine, or a set of consistent beliefs that might be taken to represent the underpinnings of biblical monotheism. But the moment we attempt to do this we are frustrated by the fact that we find lacunae, inconsistencies, paradoxes and theological impasses, which are answered by such would-be answers as "So God wills," or "So God's inscrutable wisdom demands." Ultimately our "whys" – such as "Why did God create the world?" "Why did he create it when he did?" "Why did he create in this way, rather than in any other way?" – are left unanswered.[3] They continue, as it were, to hang in the air, and become delegitimized.

So I am not in the least surprised to learn from reading J. L. Schellenberg's very interesting book,[4] that the hiddenness of God can form the basis of an argument for God's nonexistence. In a nutshell, what is there argued is that a perfectly loving God, if such a God existed, would not have withheld from his potential and would-be believers the strong evidence of his existence that would have guaranteed the belief in him so necessary for their proper religious behavior. Indeed, in most versions of Christianity, such an express belief in God is absolutely necessary for one's very *salvation*. Because no such strong evidence is available (as may be seen from the existence, nowadays, of so many doubters, agnostics, and outright atheists) we may therefore conclude, according to Schellenberg's argument, that God does not exist.

If I may start with a preliminary criticism, which may be tangential, but is by no means lacking in importance, my Jewish background makes me hesitate to follow the notion that God is "perfectly loving" in the sense described by Schellenberg. Jewish tradition is firmly convinced that God loves His people Israel, and that there is an imperative necessity for the Children of Israel, both corporately and individually, to love God. These are indeed the basic principles of the book of Deuteronomy. But that God loves every individual person equally and indiscriminately is not an explicit teaching of the Hebrew scriptures or a central theme of rabbinic teaching. It is perhaps for this reason that George Schlesinger suggested,[5] as Schellenberg notes,[6] that the hiddenness argument should be reformulated in terms of a perfectly just God who, so it might be claimed, would distribute evidence of His existence evenly in order to ensure that everyone might acquire belief and its benefits. Schellenberg will have none of this suggestion. I think we can follow the reason for his insistence that only God's *love*,[7] rather than his justice, would enable what he regards as the stronger form of the argument for God's nonexistence, because such love would lead God to pursue a personal relationship with each of us which seems incompatible with His hiding from us. But this might easily turn Schellenberg's argument into a special criticism of Christianity rather than an argument against monotheism in general. And that would be a pity, for the question Schellenberg raises really does point to a *prima facie* difficulty which all monotheists of the biblical type must address: How can a just, and *a fortiori* a loving God (in the Christian sense), have withheld from us strong evidence of His presence? It may be true that justice can be served in other ways, such as by rewarding, with special compensatory points or by divine grace, those seekers of the truth whose insistence on a rigorous standard of belief ethics ("Don't believe what you can't prove!" or "Believe only what is strongly evident!") prevents them from assenting to a belief that God exists. Even so the puzzle remains so long as there is some practical advantage or desirability, at least in the eyes of God, for human seekers to have actual and explicit belief that God exists.

Of course, as Schellenberg rightly points out, this sort of argument from the divine hiddenness really assumes a modern postemancipatory attitude of doubt or agnosticism that has the status of a live possibility within our culture. For persons of the medieval period, and for citizens of the ancient world as well, the existence of God (and of other divine beings) was not subject to the initial skepticism which has become customary in modern times as part of our cultural heritage. The notion that one can, and that one needs, to *prove* God's existence struck the medievals as worthwhile, and served as a topic to which leading theologians paid much attention, only because it seemed to the premedieval thinkers of the later Hellenistic age, during which Christianity and present-day Judaism were formed, that the "First Cause" or "Unmoved Mover" of what came to be the basis for medieval science, based on Aristotle, just like the "One" of neo-Platonic philosophy, which also became absorbed into some leading versions of medieval science, and for both of which there existed arguments in the respective philosophies, could so easily be identified with the one God of the biblical tradition. For this reason these philosophical arguments, and others of a similar nature, figured readily as purported proofs of the existence of God. For many (perhaps most) religious believers in medieval times, the existence of such proofs may have been comforting, but was certainly not the basis for their religious belief, which was largely the result of education, tradition and culture. These served as the framework for any personal and direct religious experiences, which, if and when they existed, strengthened or deepened the faith of the individuals concerned. This probably remains true for most religious believers in the modern post-Enlightenment period as well, particularly since many have accepted the view, supported by Immanuel Kant, that the traditional proofs for the existence of God can no longer be regarded as compelling. Most of these believers also regard the purported proofs for the nonexistence of God as mere sophistries that are inconclusive. However in modern times, at any rate, as we see all around us, a rejection of the belief that God exists is certainly a live option.

For this reason, in an age, such as ours, in which religion has lost its hold, at any rate in what is called Western civilization – which is, roughly, the civilization of those countries in which Christianity became the dominant religion – it becomes philosophically relevant to assess the arguments for and against religious belief with what is presumed to be an open mind. So I want to enter into the spirit of the game and essay a first answer to the argument Schellenberg formulated, before I turn to a second and, I trust, a more definitive assessment of the situation in which such arguments figure.

My first answer to the hiddenness argument will be a version of what Schellenberg calls the Moral Freedom Argument[8] and of which Schellenberg takes John Hick and Richard Swinburne to be the prime contemporary exponents among philosophers. To this I will add a twist that belongs to the "Importance of Inwardness" Argument, particularly the "Stimulus Argument" inspired by Pascal, but with a non-Kierkegaardian overtone. I will present this, if I may, as a sort of rabbinic *Midrash* on the verse in Psalms 145:18 "The Lord is nigh unto all of them that call upon Him truly." To what may this be likened? To a royal father who built a palace and installed his infant son in it, to be attended by nurses and servants, while he himself took off for foreign parts to watch affairs keenly, but from afar. He had a great love for his son, but his plan was that his son should develop independently, enjoy the benefits of the exotic garden surrounding the palace and make good use of the estates in the periphery. He wanted his son to appreciate all that had been done for him, and the unique opportunity that he had been given. His hope was that such an appreciation would encourage his son to follow the few written instructions with which he had been left, and then seek the father out to thank him and express his love. If the son would do so, the father planned to give the son more gifts and rewards. However, as he grew up, the son became totally absorbed in the daily tasks of running the estates and enjoying the fruits of the garden. He forgot about his father altogether, and neglected even to observe the few written instructions with which he had been entrusted. The father watched from the distance in growing dismay. In a manner similar to this, the Heavenly Father and Creator of the Universe and of us all, does not "wish" or "permit" (Schellenberg's expressions) the fact of His existence to remain obscure. We may suppose that his goodness, justice and love for us render him simply bursting with expectancy and the desire for our acknowledgment of His royal presence (for, as Schellenberg writes, love requires and feeds on reciprocity) to enable him to return and be providentially near to us. However the original plan was, and remains, that this acknowledgment must come from us, his children, that is, from mankind. And we human beings have forgotten, over the generations, His creation of the world, and take for granted the munificent gifts and bounties He has provided for us in nature. Having become absorbed in our daily secular existence, we find it progressively more difficult to even sense His watchful presence in any way. So we have to struggle to feel our way into God's presence once more, and develop anew our conceptual awareness of his role as the Creator of the Universe, who is the father of us all. Nonetheless (so says this approach and so is implied in the verse from the

Psalms as well), the initiative *must* be ours. Without our seeking Him out, God remains far from us. Only when we call upon Him truly does He become nigh and a close presence for us.

This parable (which I have here invented, but which echoes many themes in existing *Midrashic* literature) speaks as if from within. It takes us, as it were, behind the scenes, so that we can appreciate the purported motives of the Heavenly Father. We are dealing then – so the parable implies – with a sort of test or trial where success will bring its special reward. (As someone said, correctly, a whole theology is required in order to discuss God's hiddenness!) In this account, we human beings are expected to come to acknowledge God's presence, thereby autonomously recognizing the religious significance of the world in which we live. If we come to accept the prescribed way of life (the 7 Noahide laws for the whole of humanity and the 613 commandments for the Children of Israel) of the Torah, which, according to tradition, is the revealed set of divine instructions for comporting our lives, we will achieve and maintain a personal link with God. Then, and only then, will we all be eternally blessed. For the whole purpose of the creation will thereby have been achieved. As John Hick writes, "The reason why God reveals Himself indirectly – meeting us in and through the world as mediating a significance which requires an appropriate response on our part . . . is that only thus can the conditions exist for a *personal* relationship between God and man."[9] The bit that I have added here about the additional rewards has been adapted from a common traditional account as worked out by a leading Jewish thinker, Saadya Gaon (tenth century), who develops the idea of man's centrality as the aim of all creation. The achievement of perfection and true happiness is the end of man, and man's performance of God's commandments is the means whereby man is guided to achieve this end. To the question "Why does God not grant man his perfection and his true happiness naturally, by Grace, without our need to observe God's commandments?" Saadya offers the answer that this is because reason enjoins that the observance of something that a person is commanded to do is more meritorious than something done naturally, and deserving of a double portion of the good that he would receive by virtue of God's loving-kindness alone.[10] Saadya's theory can thus be regarded as a form of the Moral Freedom Argument into which I have incorporated something of what Schellenberg calls the Stimulus Argument as this is presented by Pascal. It should be noted that a later and more famous Jewish thinker, Maimonides (twelfth century) – in common with lesser-known earlier, contemporary and later Jewish thinkers – rejects this whole anthropocentric position as incoherent.[11] For Maimonides, then, the notion of human existence as a trial or test is unacceptable. The concept of a supernatural reward for seeking out God in order to observe His commandments will be no more than a simplistic version of a more profound concept. This is the idea that man achieves his perfection and his soul its immortality by devoting himself to the love of God, which is the crowning experiential stage of the upward path of intellectual growth.[12] It appears clear then that this version of the Moral Freedom Argument will not be one that Maimonides will be disposed to use.

Let us note the similarities and dissimilarities between Saadya and Pascal. We may say that for both thinkers God's hiddenness is required because it prompts human beings to recognize their true condition. In Pascal this true condition is one of depravity, whereas in Saadya it is one of ingratitude. For both of them God's hiddenness thus helps to bring about the necessary inwardness, clearing the way for a revelation and a restored relationship with God.[13] But whereas for Pascal (and especially for Kierkegaard) the divine hiddenness of God is meant to elicit a leap of faith, such a leap, for Saadya, is totally unnecessary, since, like most medieval thinkers, he regards God's existence as manifest to all who think properly and something that can even be proven by logical argument. God's hiddenness is thus simply a distressing fact of life, for human beings are often blind to what simply stares them in the face. Moreover none of us can fully appreciate the workings of cosmic justice, which, as in the case of the biblical story of Job, often tempts human beings to deny divine Providence and perhaps even the divine existence altogether.

I found Schellenberg's treatment of this answer (the Moral Freedom Argument) as given by Hick to be somewhat over-hasty. Hick's version of the traditional story, of course, no longer retains all its medieval components. No longer is it assumed that God's presence is manifest and easily discoverable by human reason. Hick treats the religious interpretation of the world (that is, a world with God) as opposed to the naturalistic interpretation of the world (that is, a world without God) as both equally possible. As he puts it, our world is a "religiously ambiguous" world. No doubt this ambivalence expresses the predicament of human beings in a post-Enlightenment and secular world. But what is being maintained is some truth about the human condition in general. So according to Hick's position, as also for Pascal, Kierkegaard and many moderns since then, our placement in a religiously ambiguous world was really the position of men in the medieval period as well, even though, since they lived in an age dominated by religion, they supposed otherwise. Man's "cognitive freedom," as well as his "moral freedom" to do the right thing rather than follow evil temptations, was always something to be tested, as something necessary for the achievement of God's loving purposes. Schellenberg rightly rejects the misinterpretation of Hick that takes him to be primarily concerned with freely believing that God exists.[14] As he says, Hick is primarily concerned not with the belief *that* there is a God, but with the belief *in* God, that is, with religious commitment or trust. Nevertheless, Schellenberg finds some confusion with regard to what the "act of interpretation" (religious versus naturalistic) might amount to. I do not myself find Hick's view to be as confused as

Schellenberg suggests. While Hick does indeed speak of this interpretive activity as a "recognition" that the religious person *finds* himself justified in adopting, he explains that the "cognitive freedom" rests on different stages of one's interpretation of the religious experience. As he writes: "[B]ehind all conscious experience there lies a phase of unconscious interpretive activity . . . it is here that . . . the free response to ambiguity occurs. In the conscious experience the ambiguity has been resolved in a distinctively religious way."[15] In view of Hick's declared "critical realism" in the book from which this last quotation is taken, I interpret this "ambiguity" as a sort of under-determination belonging to the experience as such, which requires to be consciously interpreted in one way or another, yielding either its religious reading or its naturalist reading. This would make it something like the duck/rabbit drawing, an example of the type of perceptual situations of which Gestalt psychology made so much. In these both "seeings" or "readings" are equally well-based and present right *there* in the text. There is no problem here which would involve the false assumption that belief is something voluntaristic, and that anyone can believe whatever he likes (which is the criticism of Hick that Schellenberg seeks to raise). The interpretation of what one is seeing (duck or rabbit) or believing about the world (religious interpretation or naturalist interpretation) does not depend on the perceiver's or the believer's arbitrary will at all, but rather on the perceiver's or the believer's frame of reference or point of view. Schellenberg's more important criticisms of Hick's view are (1) that it is not true that openness to God is *sufficient* for religious experiences, since some who earnestly seek them do not have such religious experiences and (2) even if they have such religious experiences, some people may remain in doubt as to the existence of God. Finally (3) even if belief is the product of religious experience which is available as soon as a capacity for personal relationship exists, it is not clear why individuals who came to believe should not be free to *resist* the belief. Where motives of self-deception or sheer cussedness exist, one who has had the religious experience may nonetheless refuse to acknowledge what seems, to religious people, to be entailed by the experience. Thus Schellenberg concludes that "If, as Hick suggests, it is only in the direct presence of God that we should be morally unfree, and if, as he also states, we can never be in the direct presence of God in this life, it follows we could never be morally unfree in this life, no matter what form our experience of God might take."[16] Thus religious experiences strong enough to remove the possibility of *reasonable* nonbelief need not be so overwhelming as to "crush our autonomy." Why then should God hide Himself instead of providing such reasonable evidence? So argues Schellenberg. I think that Hick's answer could be that God does indeed provide such minimal reasonable evidence in the form of religious experience; His hiddenness lies simply in His refusal to make such experience so explicit as to make other interpretations impossible.

But I regard this answer that I have offered to the problem raised by divine hiddenness, either in the form of my *Midrashic* parable, or in Hick's version of the Cognitive/Moral Argument, to be insufficient. From a purely naturalist point of view it seems no more plausible to accept the theological account which attributes to God such profound and devious motives ("testing and rewarding" or "developing the capacity for pure interpersonal love") than for believing God not to exist at all. Once the skeptical doubt regarding God's existence has found its legitimacy in our culture and any particular individual has given the doubt sufficient anchor in his heart, then such considerations as are raised by arguments like those of Schellenberg are not to be brushed aside so easily. So I think Schellenberg's argument regarding the possible implications of God's hiddenness may well be acceptable. There is no obvious fallacy in his reasoning as such. What is at fault – and here we come to what I earlier announced as "the more judicious consideration of this sort of philosophic treatment of theological claims as a whole" – lies in one of Schellenberg's assumptions. He assumes throughout that in the theological talk of God's "love of man" we are using this expression precisely as in we do in our everyday talk regarding man's love of man. If there is to be any difference between the two loves, so it is assumed, it can only be that since God is so much greater than man ("infinitely greater"), His love for man will be correspondingly so much greater ("infinite love"). And the same could be said of any parallel argument that based itself on God's justice, where we probably would be assuming that God's justice is the same as man's justice, only, if anything, much more so. There is a certain literal-mindedness about such assumptions which the more profound thinkers in Christianity, Islam and Judaism have long had occasion to suspect. A large part of so-called "natural theology," as this was practiced since the seventeenth century and even as this has been revived in parts of the philosophical discussions of religion in the twentieth century, has been overliteral in its understanding of religious language. And the antitheology (or atheology) that has developed since David Hume has therefore had too easy a victory. The victory has, however, been over a certain concept of religion that Hume correctly diagnosed as "popular religion."[17]

Let me explain. At the beginning of his book,[18] Schellenberg writes that because traditional theology has always insisted on the hiddenness of God in some sense or other, his attempt to derive from this a proof regarding the nonexistence of God may be dismissed *a priori* as displaying theological naïveté. Schellenberg wishes to remove this charge by a more precise definition of the hiddenness-of-God thesis. His attempt seems to me to be competent and admirable. But the first premise of Schellenberg's more precise attempt to define this thesis is that "God exists and has intentionally withheld (or has permitted to be obscured) strong evidence of his existence." We need go no further than this in order to realize that the whole problem has been packed into this premise and that to swallow this seemingly innocuous premise without further comment would be to do something which is seriously amiss. In the traditional discussions, God's hiddenness was firstly connected with his deliberate intention, because of their sins, to withhold his intervention to protect and safeguard the righteous and the innocent from harm. This is the dominant form of the notion in the Hebrew scriptures.[19] Secondly it concerned the idea of the *deus absconditus*, which was a theological notion that intended to stress the gap between our limited understanding of the divine and God's own nature. The concept too was based on the biblical sources themselves,[20] but was much magnified in postbiblical times to develop the view that God's nature was for us something totally mysterious and beyond our comprehension. Neither of these traditional senses is the one intended by Schellenberg. His interest is rather one that concerns the claim regarding the existence of God and our evidence for such a claim. Schellenberg is aware of these three different senses of the hiddenness-of-God thesis and makes it clear that he will be concerned with this third sense only. But he seems to regard this sense as primary and the other two senses as somehow dependent on it. It would seem that for him the express claim that God exists and the evidence that would support that claim are more important, in this post-Emancipation age, than the question of the *extent* of our knowledge of God's nature, or the withholding by God of his providential protection from sinners. However, this opinion regarding the primacy of the claim that God exists and the question of the evidence for this claim may well seem highly problematic to anyone who knows something of the subtlety and sophistication of some of the great thinkers of the past in the three monotheistic faiths. It treats God as one more object in the inventory of those objects that exist and that may be known (thus allowing us to raise the question of our evidence for our knowledge of their existence). But a profound religious intuition, which many of the great sophisticated religious thinkers seem to share,[21] leads one to realize that, in a sense, God's existence may be conceived as being in a class of its own. If God exists and his glory fills the universe where is there room for anything else to exist? Alternatively, if other things may be said to exist, in the ordinary everyday sense, surely God's existence must be regarded as something belonging to an entirely different order. For this reason some of the great theologians referred to God's sort of existence as "infinite" or "necessary" existence (as opposed to the everyday "finite" or "contingent" existence). A few leading mystics, reflecting this line of thought, referred to God as the great Nothing – the *Ayin*[22] (which in the Hebrew can serve as an abbreviation of His being the Infinite or *Eyn-Sof*). To put what may be learnt from this religious intuition more prosaically, it may said that the distinction between the epistemic question regarding God's existence or nonexistence cannot be kept separate and treated apart from the question of God's nature. We must have some inkling of what "God" means in our religious parlance before we can say whether or not something could possibly answer to that description, or whether it could be listed among the things we can be said to know.

The history of the notion of God that forms the background to the tradition upon which the Hebrew scriptures is based, is simple and well known. Traditional Jews recite each year as part of the ritual of the seder (the communal meal held on Passover commemorating the Israelite exodus from Egypt) the declaration: "In the beginning our forefathers were idol-worshippers ... but now the Lord has drawn us into His service." There is here implicit recognition of the historical memory that the ancient concept of the polytheistic gods to be worshipped was a forerunner, out of which the monotheistic conception of father Abraham developed by opposition. The ancient polytheistic gods were something like animated beings or humanlike spirits somehow represented by idols of different sorts. In the fight against idolatry that is so characteristic of the Hebrew scriptures, the insistence on the one true God who revealed Himself to our forefathers Abraham, Isaac, and Jacob, involved not only a rejection of the idols, but also of the claim to divinity of the various powers, spirits and local deities which these idols represented. The one true God of the forefathers whose great prophet was Moses, the redeemer of the Children of Israel from the bondage to Egypt, is described as invisible and incapable of being represented in material form, the creator of heaven and earth and all that these contained. He was hidden to all but the prophets, who heard His voice. The Children of Israel of the period of the First Temple are reported to have been constantly sliding back into the worship of the local deities and idols alongside their worship of the one God. Hence the wrath of the great prophets and preachers of the time, who predicted the destruction of the First Temple and their exile in Babylon. But after their return to the Land of Israel and through the influence of Ezra and Nehemiah and the last prophets, idol worship gradually disappeared. The people worshipped solely the one invisible God whose works alone were visible in history and whose word (the Torah) became the constant and unique embodiment of all that was holy. Since the time of the Book of Psalms, at the very latest, God's invisibility and inaccessibility to all except to the bearers of His word, was the shared belief of all the true monotheists in this tradition. It is this belief that inspires the returnees to Judea who rebuild the Temple in Jerusalem. But the growth of institutional prayer in houses of prayer worship, alongside the reestablished sacrificial cult of this Second Temple, seems to be a new feature characterizing the religious life from early on in the period. In the latter part of the period of the Second Temple, with the conquest of the whole of the Middle East by the Greeks, followed by the Romans from the middle of the second century B.C.E., some ideas of Greek philosophy and science were combined with Jewish biblical themes. In the last century before the destruction of the Second Temple, many of these ideas and speculations led to a more philosophic approach to monotheism, which began to cause dissension among rival religious Jewish groups. The ideas of the Pharisees won out, and their followers among the Jews during the first to the sixth centuries of the Current Era laid the foundations of what we now call rabbinic Judaism. Some neo-Platonic as well as some Stoic ideas had already long influenced many in Jewish circles, especially those outside the Land of Israel. In the period after the eighth or ninth centuries, these philosophic influences brought about an attempt to cleanse Islam and Judaism from all vestiges of the attribution of material attributes to the idea of God. When Maimonides attempted to add to and to complete this purification of Jewish ideas in the twelfth century, he found himself faced with the task of reconciling rabbinic Judaism with Greek science which was represented to him by the version of Platonised Aristotelianism, which he found in the works of Avicenna and Alfarabi.

We may follow the contribution of Maimonides to the purification of the idea of God by examining how he interpreted the notion of "nearness to God" in the verse from the Psalms (as well as similar verses elsewhere) that served as the point of departure for the *Midrash*-like version of the Moral Freedom Argument we suggested above. In one of the chapters in the section of his philosophical masterpiece *The Guide of the Perplexed*[23], where he discusses the equivocal terms used in the scriptures, he deals with expressions such as "approaching," "touching," and "coming near" and explains that sometimes they signify relations in space while elsewhere they signify the union of cognition with what is cognized, which is, as it were, similar to the proximity of one body to another. In this connection he goes on to say:

Every mention of approaching and coming near that you find in the books of prophecy referring to a relation between God and a created being has this last meaning. For God is not a body, as shall be demonstrated to you in this treatise. And accordingly He does not draw near or approach a thing, nor does anything draw near or approach Him, inasmuch as the abolition of corporeality entails that space be abolished; so that there is no nearness and proximity and no remoteness, no union and no separation, no contact and no succession. I do not think you shall grow doubtful or perplexed because scripture says "the Lord is nigh unto all them that call upon Him.". . . for in all these verses nearness through cognition, I mean cognitive apprehension, is intended, not nearness in space.[24]

The nearness to God is here interpreted as a form of cognition, i.e. a form of "union of cognition with what is cognized." This is in terms of the notion of cognition characteristic of Greek and medieval thought, which is very different from the more modern conception according to which the model for this relationship is copy and original, rather than union of any sort. The type of cognition here hinted at by Maimonides is the Platonic ladder in which the knower rises step by step to a contemplative confrontation or "union" with the ineffable "One" which is the top rung of this ladder. This confrontation or "union" is elsewhere in Maimonides called the true "love of God,"[25] that is conceived as a mystical experience that fills the soul with joy and satisfaction. However this "love of God" is not merely a passive experience, but also serves as the inspiration for a whole way of life in which the individual who seeks this true knowledge devotes himself to the preparatory achievement of moral perfection and spiritual growth. Such spiritual growth is what enables the select individual to cleave more and more to the "One" through the intermediacy of a close union with the "Active Intellect." However this constitutes an ideal that is obviously elitist in character, and unattainable by the ordinary simple Jew who continues, therefore, to retain a more emotional understanding of God's nearness as representing a close personal relationship. For Maimonides the personalist attributes predicated of God retain something of their physical and material associations and must therefore be regarded merely as homonyms that serve to get the Jewish masses to live a moral and spiritual life in imitating God's actions. The philosophical truths that this personalist residue attributed to God comes to popularize are summed up in the details connected with the oblique reference to the Aristotelian "First Cause," which is also identified, following Avicenna, with the Platonic "One," which is above words and description. So God's existence, for Maimonides, is by no means simply reducible to the existence of a spiritual personage with humanlike characteristics, as in the view of "popular religion."

This is not the suitable occasion to refer to subsequent Jewish thought since Maimonides, or to do more than mention the ideas of the mystical/kabbalistic school, which became progressively more influential in Jewish thought and practice since the thirteenth century. Modern Jewish thought of the traditional sort has been profoundly affected by the Safed school of mysticism of the sixteenth century. In eastern European Jewry (which had become during this period the largest and leading Jewish community in the world) the two leading social movements of the eighteenth century were Hassidism and Mitnagdism (the opponents of the Hassidic movement). Both of these movements based themselves on different interpretations of the doctrine of Tsimtsum,[26] one of the central ideas in the later mysticism. This doctrine constituted the most radical transformation of the simple monotheist ideas since, sharing the profound religious intuition of God's omnipresence referred to above, it spoke of the creation of the universe in a manner that almost completely lost sight of any personalist conception of the creator. Starting from the premise that God filled the whole of metaphysical space, it argued that the metaphysical space for the physical world was created by God contracting himself, as it were, so that a world could come into being. But this empty space was never completely empty, and in any case, the allegorical interpretation of the doctrine that became prevalent insisted that the whole contraction involved was something that could be said to have existed only from the point of view of ourselves in the created universe alone.[27] From God's own point of view, as it were, the contraction had never really taken place at all. God continued to fill metaphysical space as before, whereas the created world of appearance struggled to regain the identity with godhead that its own separate existence, in its own eyes, belied. Such mind-boggling concepts, though complementary to the simple monotheistic terms that continued and continue to be foundational, have nonetheless so changed the latter that it is difficult to recognize in them anything like the simple conception of a personal God with which "natural philosophy" and the simple believer operate.

I have used the situation in Judaism as my illustration, but I have no doubt that similar remarks apply to many forms of Christianity and Islam. I have reason to think that Schellenberg has broadened his terms of reference since writing his book, and has more tolerance for this sort of mystery and the mysterious.[28] In each of the great religions this element makes the attitude of the believer far richer than can be summed up reductively by the claim that he must first give a simple Yes/No answer to the question "Do you believe that a personal God exists?" (Personal to what extent? What sort of a person? And what do we mean here by "existing"?) Religious language, it has been said, must be taken *seriously*, but not necessarily *literally*.[29] Monotheism of the simplistic sort is but one conception of God; it does not exhaust the religious consciousness of the great religious traditions. Many leading contemporary Jewish traditionalists whose ideas have been enriched by the study of Jewish thought include mystics (such as Rabbi A. I. Kook) who have allowed themselves to say of this simplistic monotheism that it is a primitive and unsatisfactory religious conception.[30] Some of them (Rabbi A. I. Kook too) have said the same of the philosophic conception of God (such as that of Maimonides), which had its heyday in medieval times. Rabbi Kook regarded the kabbalistic sephirotic grid as developed in the later Jewish mysticism as closer to the truth and the most satisfactory conception available. With great respect I prefer to approach these matters somewhat more conservatively, and to regard each of these conceptions as containing partial truths. Elsewhere I have suggested that they be regarded as nets (i.e. webs of ideas) each of which captures some part of the riches in the sea of our religious experience.[31] Each of them has virtues, but all of them have their limitations. I do believe, therefore, that even a more careful and exact attempt to delineate biblical monotheism in philosophic terms, that is, to form the foundational monotheistic net, will be found to contain all sorts of inconsistencies and distortions. Hence I am perfectly happy to thank Schellenberg for demonstrating this once more, this time in the case of the notion of God's hiddenness. There is indeed a puzzle here, given the imperfections of the simplistic monotheistic net; but it is not the sort of problem that will render that net, not to speak of the alternative and more sophisticated nets, totally inefficacious. No net is perfect. But there are more fish in that particular sea than can be captured by any of these particular nets or by all of them together.

Notes

1. This is the term used throughout Schellenberg's book, see note 4.
2. It has been argued by Stewart Guthrie, *Faces in the Clouds* (Oxford University Press, 1993), that all religion is simply anthropomorphism. I agree that anthropomorphism is a very natural first move in most religions, a first move that has indeed been made in the monotheism of which we are speaking. However I disagree, first, that this move is so necessary as to constitute the very basis of religion, and, second, that it precludes the possibility of a modification in which the terms used can be interpreted in such a way as to allow for different and nonanthropomorphic conceptions.
3. For these questions and such answers see Moses Maimonides, *Guide of the Perplexed*, translated with an introduction by S. Pines, Chicago University Press, Part II, chapter 25. It is worth noting, however, that Maimonides does not regard these answers as simply leaving the questions hanging in the air and delegitimized. For him the combination of God's will and wisdom constitutes a philosophical doctrine that combines internal teleology within a contingent framework. But this doctrine is difficult to interpret and no consensus has yet been reached among the scholars regarding its precise meaning.
4. J. L. Schellenberg, *Divine Hiddenness and Human Reason*, which will be referred to hereafter simply as "Schellenberg". The present essay was written before the philosophical dialogue "What the Hiddenness of God Reveals: A Collaborative Discussion," authored by Schellenberg and included in this volume (to be referred to hereafter as "Collaborative Discussion"). An earlier version of that dialogue was presented by Schellenberg at the conference at which an earlier version of this present paper was presented. I already noted then, with satisfaction, that the dialogue seemed to anticipate some of the points I was concerned to make. I shall interpret at least one section in "Collaborative Discussion" as a reaction to my remarks and comment. See note 28 below.
5. G. Schlesinger, "The Availability of Evidence in Support of Religious Belief," *Faith and Philosophy* 5 (1988) pp. 424–5.
6. Schellenberg, pp. 3–4.
7. ad loc.
8. This and all the other terms delineating positions with regard to the hiddenness problem are here used in the sense in which they appear in Schellenberg.
9. Schellenberg, p. 105, quoting from J. Hick, *Faith and Knowledge* (Oxford: Clarendon Press 1981), p. 140.
10. A convenient translation, with notes, by Alexander Altmann of selected passages from Saadya's philosophical work "Book of Doctrines and Beliefs" is found in the relevant section of *Three Jewish Philosophers – Philo, Saadya Gaon, Jehuda Halevi* (New York: Atheneum, 1972). The sections upon which my brief summary is based are chapter III, pp. 93–4 and chapter IV, pp. 115–16.
11. See Altmann's note 5, loc. cit., p. 116.
12. For Maimonides views see *Guide iii*, chapter 13; see also his introduction to Perek Helek of the *Commentary to the Mishnah* in Isadore Twersky, *A Maimonides Reader* (New York: Behrman 1900), pp. 403–6.

13. Schellenberg p. 139.
14. Schellenberg pp. 98ff.
15. Schellenberg p. 101, quoting from J. Hick, *An Interpretation of Religion* (London: Macmillan) p. 153.
16. Schellenberg p. 115.
17. See Hume, David, *Natural History of Religion*, in Oxford: World Classics edition with an introduction by J. C. A. Gaskin, p. 176.
18. Schellenberg p. 4.
19. The standard expression for this in the Hebrew scriptures (from which I presume Schellenberg's usage ultimately is derived) relates to God "hiding his face." There are three such verses in Deuteronomy (31:17, 31:18, 32:20), ten verses in Psalms, four in Isaiah (notably 59:2 "Your sins hid [God's] face from you"), one in Jeremiah, two in Ezekiel, one in Micah, two in Job. As the translated verse from Isaiah indicates, this is invariably connected with man's sin. The hiddenness in these cases seems to consist in a lack of providential protection.
20. The two verses in the context of the book of Job would presumably indicate this.
21. See, for example, the *Confessions* of St. Augustine, trans. Vernon J. Burke (Washington, D.C. Catholic University of America, 1953) chapter 3.
22. See Gershom Scholem, *Major Trends in Jewish Mysticism* (New York: Schocken, 1941), p. 5, 25, and 217–18.
23. See Maimonides, *Guide of the Perplexed*, Part I chapter 18.
24. pp. 43–4.
25. See Twersky, op. cit., pp. 45–6.
26. See Scholem, op. cit., pp. 260–4.
27. See Tamar Ross, "Two Interpretations of the Doctrine of Tsimtsum; R. Shneur Zalman Miladi and R. Hayim of Volozhin," (*Mehkarei Yerushalayim Bemahshevet Yisrael*), vol 2 1981, pp. 153–69 (Hebrew).
28. The interesting discussion of agnosticism and religious agnosticism toward the end of "Collaborative Discussion," leading up to the suggestion that "maybe even common agnosticism is sometimes more purely religious than belief," comes very close to the line of argument I have been pursuing in this paper. Schellenberg's (partial?) rejection of this line of thought, on the ground that the desire for clarity that belongs to the analytic tradition in philosophy should bring us to seek out certain propositions about God that are clearly true (and perhaps what he means is that we must have propositions that are univocally and literally true) seems to me somewhat disappointing. Analytic clarity surely also includes a recognition that in some parts of the woods we must make do with what we have, and not seek to impose an order and regimentation that are inappropriate.
29. This surely is the minimum that can be learnt from the Maimonidean tradition. Maimonides' distinction between the popular religion of the ordinary simple believer, which is a very primitive version, having mostly pragmatic value, of a much more profound religious truth, can and has served, as the foundation of many philosophically sophisticated religious viewpoints in the history of Judaism. His Platonized Aristotelianism may no longer be acceptable, but his negative theology allows for development in many directions. My own predeliction is for a view based on Vaihinger's neo-Kantian theory of als-ob fictions, which I combine with a neo-Wittgensteinian view that reads the theistic personal model of God essentially as an attempt to represent the religious experience of teleological, meaningful order in the cosmos. This joins forces with the model theory of Ian Ramsey, Ian Barbour, Frederick Ferre, and others. This is not the place to do so, but it would

be enlightening to work out the implications of such a view for the interpretation of God's "nearness" and his "presence" in a way that avoids the exaggerated personalism of religious existentialist thought (Buber and Rosenzweig) and the sort of literalism that we find in some conservatively minded practitioners of contemporary natural theology.

30. See A. I. Kook, *Oroth Hakodesh*, vol 2 pp. 399–401 (Hebrew) and *Igroth Rayah* vol 1 p. 48. (Hebrew)
31. See my article "The Primacy of the Personalist Concept of God in Jewish Thought," *The Journal of Jewish Thought and Philosophy*, vol 8, no. 2, 1999, Harwood Academic Publishers, pp. 171–199.

10

Seeking but not Believing: Confessions of a Practicing Agnostic

PAUL DRAPER

For some, belief in God – that is, belief in a perfect supernatural person – is very naturally produced or sustained by religious experiences. If, however, there is a God, then I suspect his plan for me is more subtle. For though I occasionally have experiences at least analogous to those Rudolf Otto calls "numinous," they are vague and fleeting – they don't come close to producing belief. And while I do feel strongly inclined to form beliefs about God when I read theistic scriptures, the beliefs are of the sort, "Surely *this* wasn't inspired by God"; so what Calvin calls "the secret testimony of the Spirit" is clearly a secret kept from me. In general, then, I simply do not have vivid experiences of the sort that directly cause people to believe in God. Seeing is believing, but if God is real then I suffer from religious blindness or at least blurred religious vision.

Of course, the visually impaired can make inferences about what they cannot clearly see. And, because of my philosophical training, I am confident (some would say overconfident) in my ability to make correct inferences concerning God's existence. But after years of searching and researching, I have come to believe that the inferential evidence concerning God's existence is, at least at the present time, ambiguous. One consequence of this is that I am an agnostic. I don't believe with any confidence that God exists, nor do I believe with any confidence that God does not exist. Though I won't be terribly surprised if I one day meet my maker, I also take seriously the possibility that I have no maker, that nature is a closed system. And so I find myself sitting on the fence between theistic and atheistic belief, waiting – indeed hoping – to be pulled over to one side or the other.

As suggested by the personal nature of my comments so far, this paper will be a sort of case study or case self-study of divine hiddenness. How does God, if she exists, hide from *me*? The advantage of this approach is that sometimes particulars matter. When I say that the evidence concerning God's existence is ambiguous, what sort of evidence am I talking about? Is it ambiguous because it is largely absent or because it is present but vague? Or is it neither absent nor vague but still ambiguous because there are ample amounts of clear evidence on both sides? Also, what exactly do I take the evidence to be and how do I assess its strength? Finally, do I believe that theism and its denial are equally probable? Or do I believe that no precise probability judgment about God's existence can be made? By answering these questions, I hope to put some flesh on the claim that God, if she exists, hides from me behind ambiguous evidence. This in turn will permit a more focused examination of the implications of that ambiguity. Should ambiguous evidence lead one to take a leap of faith? Or should it make one an atheist, either because theism starts with a very low probability or because, as J. L. Schellenberg claims, the ambiguity of the evidence is *"itself* a consideration that tips the scales towards atheism"[1]? I will argue that ambiguous evidence provides a justification for agnosticism rather than for theistic leaping or atheistic tipping. I will also address the question of what this means on a practical level. What sort of religious behavior, if any, would be appropriate for someone whose agnosticism is justified by ambiguous evidence? In short, how should I practice my agnosticism?

I. The Ambiguity of the Evidence

Many people are agnostics because they believe there are no good arguments for or against God's existence. I believe there are several good arguments for theism and several good arguments for naturalism and hence against theism. By naturalism I mean the view that the physical universe is a closed system in the sense that nothing that is neither a part nor a product of it can affect it. In other words, naturalists deny the existence of "supernatural" entities – nonnatural entities that can affect nature. How can there be both good arguments for theism and good arguments for naturalism? The short answer is that, although these arguments support their conclusions, none of them proves conclusively that a perfect supernatural person exists or that there are no supernatural beings. But then what sort of arguments are they? An example will help answer this question.

Suppose you enter a room in which there are two very large glass jars, each filled with hundreds of red and blue jelly beans. A very high percentage of the beans in the first jar are red, while a very high percentage of the beans in the second jar are blue. You are certain that the lid of one of the two jars can be removed, while the lid of the other one is securely glued in place and so cannot be removed without breaking the jar. But you cannot tell by looking which is which, and you have no idea what procedure was used to determine which jar to glue shut. Suddenly the lights go out, you hear someone open one of the jars and remove a bean. Then you hear the person replace the lid and shake both jars. The lights come back on, and you observe that the bean that was removed is red. You also know that the person who drew the bean could not have intentionally picked a red bean – it was a random draw. A prize is offered if you can determine whether the bean came from the first jar or the second.

Of course, you lack conclusive proof here; the bean could have come from either jar. But the fact that the bean is red is some evidence favoring the hypothesis that it came from the first jar over the hypothesis that it came from the second jar. This fact raises the probability of that hypothesis because it is more likely that a bean drawn randomly from the first jar will be red than that a bean drawn randomly from the second jar will be red.

Now suppose the lights go out again, four more beans are drawn, and they are all red too. Since you now have five red beans, all drawn from the same jar, you have a very strong cumulative case for the position that the beans are coming from the first jar – that the second jar is the one that is glued shut. You still do not have conclusive proof. But each of the five red beans raises the probability of this position, and all five together make the position highly probable. Suppose, however, that the next five beans drawn are all blue. The evidence provided by these blue beans for the hypothesis that the beans are being drawn from the second jar offsets the evidence provided by the red beans for the hypothesis that they are coming from the first jar. Thus, one should no longer believe that the beans are being drawn from the first jar. Nor should one believe they are coming from the second. The only reasonable thing to do at this point is to suspend judgment on the issue.

The evidence I have for and against theism and naturalism is similar to the evidence in this example and not (given my blurred religious vision) to the evidence provided by actually seeing one of the jars being opened. None of it proves conclusively that naturalism or theism is true. But some of it raises the ratio of the probability of theism to naturalism and some of it lowers this ratio. Certain facts are more likely to obtain if God exists than if nothing supernatural exists. These facts are evidence favoring theism over naturalism. And other facts are more likely to obtain if nothing supernatural exists than if God exists. These facts favor naturalism over theism.[2]

Let us begin, then, to examine the relevant facts, keeping in mind that I cannot in the space I have here fully develop and adequately defend the arguments for and against theism I find convincing. Instead, I will just sketch these arguments. Though this will (to say the least) oversimplify, it will suffice to make clear precisely what sort of ambiguity I have in mind when I claim that the evidence concerning God's existence is ambiguous.

A. Cosmological Evidence

We learned prior to the twentieth century, not only that the earth is not the center of the universe, but also that the universe is much older than humans, indeed much older than any life. One could argue that these facts support naturalism over theism. For although theism doesn't entail that humans hold a spatially or temporally privileged position in the universe, such a position is slightly more likely on theism than on naturalism, and thus the discovery that human beings hold no such position is some evidence, though very weak, favoring naturalism over theism.[3]

A metaphysically more crucial cosmological issue is whether or not the universe is infinitely old. Historically speaking, naturalists have favored the view that it is. For if the universe has always existed, then, despite its contingency, no explanation of its existence is really necessary. That there be no such explanation is crucial for naturalism, since any such explanation could not appeal to the universe itself and so would have to be a supernaturalistic one. Though there was never any strong evidence for an infinitely old universe, the seeming stability of the universe and the growing evidence that natural laws govern its operations were, prior to the twentieth century, taken to support the naturalistic view. Recently, though, this cherished idea has come under scientific attack. We now have some cosmological evidence (namely, evidence for certain models of the big bang theory) that the universe had a beginning.[4] Since the universe is more likely to have had a beginning on theism than on naturalism (since a cause for such a beginning is available if theism is true), it follows that any cosmological evidence for such a beginning is, potentially at least, evidence favoring theism over naturalism.[5] How strong this evidence is depends on how strong the cosmological evidence in question is. I believe some theistic philosophers (and some scientists) overestimate the strength of this evidence. I also believe that, to the extent that the evidence supports a beginning of the universe *with* time rather than *within* time, the support provided by this evidence for theism is weakened. But these are long stories I won't tell here.[6] On the whole, I believe that twentieth century cosmology supports theism over naturalism.

B.   *Intelligent Life and Its Evolution*

Another fact supporting theism over naturalism is the existence of intelligent life. Once again, twentieth-century science puts us in a new position. We currently have considerable evidence for the conclusion that such life depends on a variety of physical constants having the precise values they have. For example, if the rate of expansion of the universe, the balance of matter to antimatter shortly after the big bang, and the values of the strong and weak nuclear forces had been even slightly different, our universe would have been lifeless. So the existence of intelligent life is much less probable on naturalism than on theism, which assumes the existence of a being who is capable of fine tuning the universe for life and who, being a morally perfect person, might very well have good reason to produce intelligent life. Granted, one might have expected something more impressive than humans. And it is a real possibility that what we call the universe is actually just one part of a much larger system – the real universe – that contains indefinitely many subsystems like ours, almost all of which have different cosmic constants than our universe and no life. But we lack any convincing evidence that this is so; thus, the argument from intelligent life still has considerable force.[7]

This force is to some extent counterbalanced, however, by what we know about the development of intelligent life. Although there is still much to learn about the mechanisms that drive evolution, the fact that evolution has occurred is beyond reasonable doubt. By "evolution" here I mean the claim that all relatively complex living things are the more or less gradually modified descendants of relatively simple single-celled organisms. If naturalism is true, then evolution is very likely to be true. Given that complex life has not always existed, evolution is the only plausible way to account for its existence in a naturalistic universe. If, on the other hand, theism is true, then God might have created life through evolution or he might have created each species independently, or he might have used some combination of evolution and special creation. So while evolution is compatible with theism – it doesn't prove that theism is false – it is no more likely on theism than a variety of other alternatives, alternatives that are incompatible with naturalism. Thus, evolution is more likely on naturalism than on theism and hence raises the ratio of the probability of naturalism to the probability of theism.[8] This partially offsets the force of the argument from intelligent life, but only partially – that argument seems to me to be much more impressive than the argument from evolution for naturalism.

C. Free Will and the Brain-dependence of Consciousness

The importance of free will for theism has long been recognized, especially in connection with the problem of moral evil. But here I wish to discuss what role it can play in positive apologetics. If free will (of the sort required for moral responsibility) and causal determinism are incompatible and we are morally responsible for some of our actions, then we have incompatibilist or "libertarian" free will. Such free will is more likely on theism than on naturalism for two reasons.

First, on theism, which entails that God is morally perfect, one has reason to believe that our actions are not the inevitable consequences of natural laws and antecedent conditions chosen by God. For that would mean that God is the ultimate sufficient cause of every morally wrong action we perform. More importantly, it would mean that any relationship we might have with God, indeed any response at all that we make to God, would be the result of divine manipulation.

Second, it is hard to make sense of libertarian free will unless substance dualism is true – unless human beings are a composite of a physical body and a non-physical mind. And the existence of such minds is much more likely if theism is true than if naturalism is true. For on naturalism, everything in our universe, including human beings, is or is the product of physical processes, and hence the existence of immaterial substances attached to bodies – bodies that evolved from nonconscious life – would be extremely surprising. On theism, however, an immaterial mind exists independently of the physical universe. Thus, theism presupposes a radical metaphysical dualism and thus makes it much more likely than naturalism does that, like God's mind, human minds are immaterial substances. Thus, evidence for the existence of such substances is evidence favoring theism over naturalism.[9]

Of course, most naturalists would reject this argument from libertarian free will because they do not believe we have libertarian free will. Most of them are compatibilists and thus do not believe that moral responsibility proves the existence of libertarian free will. Yet I can't help but wonder if the only reason most naturalists find compatibilism so appealing is that their naturalism combined with a belief in moral responsibility points them down that path. I myself am less sure of the existence of moral responsibility than I am of the falsity of compatibilism.

Once again, however, this theistic evidence is offset by naturalistic evidence. Just as evidence for the existence of immaterial minds favors theism over naturalism, so too evidence for their nonexistence favors naturalism over theism. And thanks, once again, to contemporary science, specifically neuroscience, a wealth of such evidence exists. It is now known that conscious states of all sorts, and even the very integrity of our personalities, are dependent to a very high degree on physical processes occurring in the brain. Although neuroscientists have not, in my opinion, proven that brain states and mental states are identical, they have discovered overwhelming evidence for an invariable correlation between the two. In short, nothing mental (and human) happens unless something physical happens.

This extends even to our deepest sense of self and to the most entrenched parts of our character and personality. For example, in the advanced stages of Alzheimer's disease, a patient who had previously been a kind gentle person may become violent and aggressive towards others – this in addition to being incontinent, totally confused, and unable to remember anybody, including the patient's closest family members. All this is caused by the loss of neurons and by the presence of neurofibrillary tangles. The greater the damage to the brain, the more severe the symptoms and the more we will be inclined to believe that the person in question has been destroyed by the disease. While all of this is *compatible* with substance dualism, it is very strong evidence for the position that human consciousness and personality are properties of brains or nervous systems or bodies rather than properties of immaterial substances.[10]

And, as I have already said, this supports naturalism over theism because the non-existence of immaterial human minds is much more likely on naturalism than on theism.

D. Good and Evil

Another fact supporting naturalism over theism is that pain and pleasure are systematically connected to the biological goal of reproductive success. For example, it is no accident we find a warm fire on a cold night pleasurable and lying naked in a snow bank painful. Maintaining a constant body temperature increases our chances of (temporary) survival and thereby increases our chances of reproducing. I could give countless other examples, but the connection between pain and pleasure and reproductive success and the systematic nature of that connection is so striking that additional examples aren't really needed.

What is needed is an explanation of why this connection is much more probable on naturalism than it is on theism. On naturalism, one would expect this connection. For if naturalism is true, then there are no supernatural beings that care how much pain or pleasure we feel. Thus, one would expect pain and pleasure to play the same biological role that so many other parts of organic systems play, especially since they are so well suited to play that role. On the assumption that theism is true, however, one would be far less sure about what to expect. For pain and pleasure have a specific sort of moral significance that other parts of organic systems do not have. And we have no reason at all to believe that God's moral purposes for pain and pleasure would permit their functioning like other parts of organic systems. Indeed, it would be quite a coincidence if they did. Thus, the fact that pain and pleasure are systematically connected to reproductive success is much more likely on naturalism than on theism and so is evidence favoring naturalism over theism.[11]

Another part of the so-called "evidential problem of evil" is the fact that our world contains an abundance of tragedy.[12] I remember reading about a little girl whose mother was taking her to see her grandmother for the first time. A van lost control and hit the girl's car, killing her mother and permanently paralyzing the girl from the neck down. Months later the girl was told her birthday was coming up and she would get some new toys. Her response was that she didn't care, because she wouldn't be able to play with them with her own hands. So far as we can tell, no good comes from tragedies like this, or at least no good comparable to the harm done by them. Indeed, so far as we can tell, an omnipotent being could have prevented this and countless other tragedies in thousands of ways without robbing us of our free will, or of opportunities to develop moral character, or of any other significant good. Also, notice that a world in which pain and pleasure play the biological role they do need not be a world in which tragedies like this occur daily – so tragedies add something new to the case against theism.

Of course, it is possible there is some good reason (perhaps a reason too complicated for humans to understand) for God to permit tragedies. So tragedies don't conclusively disprove God's existence. But their existence is clearly much more probable on naturalism than on theism. After all, we know of good reasons to prevent such evils (we wouldn't hesitate to stop them if we could). And while there might be reasons beyond our ken to permit them, it's at least as likely that there are additional reasons beyond our ken to prevent them. So their occurrence is much less likely on theism than on naturalism.

One might object that this evidence for naturalism is offset by the good in the world, which is more likely on theism than on naturalism. For example, theism is supported by the fact that the universe contains an abundance of beauty. The fact that the parts of the universe constructed by humans are not for the most part beautiful shows that there's nothing about physical objects that makes them inevitably beautiful. Thus, a beautiful universe, especially one containing beings that can appreciate that beauty, is clearly more likely on theism than on naturalism and so is evidence favoring theism over naturalism.[13] I agree that beauty supports theism, but maintain that the overall pattern of good and evil in the world is much more probable on naturalism than on theism. For beauty seems to be the only exception to the general rule that the advantages for theism of biologically gratuitous goods are counterbalanced by corresponding biologically gratuitous evils and by the limited amounts or apparently random distribution of such goods. Indeed, even the argument from beauty is partially offset by the fact that, while the universe is saturated with visual beauty, it is not saturated with auditory, tactile or other sensory beauty. So the ability of theism to explain beauty and our enjoyment of it is a relatively small advantage for theism. Arguments from evil against theism are much more powerful than the argument from beauty in favor of theism.

E. Religious Experience

Though I myself am not fortunate enough to have powerful religious experiences, the experiences of others can provide me with some evidence favoring theism over naturalism. For certain religious experiences are, I believe, both cross-cultural and very naturally interpreted as experiences apparently of God. And surely these "theistic experiences" are more likely to occur on the assumption that theism is true than on the assumption that naturalism is true.[14]

While this argument has some force, certain facts about the distribution and effects of theistic experiences favor naturalism. First, not everyone has them and those who do typically have a prior belief in God or extensive exposure to a theistic religion. Given that theistic experiences occur, this sort of distribution is just what one would expect on naturalism, while it is surprising on theism. Second, the subjects of theistic experiences pursue a variety of radically different religious paths, none of which bears abundantly more moral fruit than all of the others. This is also much more likely if these experiences are all delusory than if some or all are veridical and hence is much more likely on naturalism than on theism. Finally, many people do not seem to feel God's comforting presence when tragedy strikes. This fact is much more probable on naturalism than on theism.

To see how this last point adds to the evidence favoring naturalism over theism provided by tragedies, suppose God has good reasons humans cannot understand to permit tragedies. Then he would be like a father who must take his young daughter to the hospital for painful medical treatments without being able to explain to her why those treatments are necessary. But what does a good father do in these circumstances? He stays with his daughter, comforting her and thereby reassuring her of his love.[15] Thus, even given the existence of a God who is justified in permitting tragedies, the fact that so many victims of tragedies do not feel God's comforting presence is still surprising. Once again, the theist must settle for showing that this fact is compatible with theism. Once again, the theist will point out that there might be some good reason we don't know about for God to let us suffer alone. The point remains, however, that the frequent lack of experiences apparently of God's presence when tragedy strikes is much more likely on naturalism than on theism and hence is evidence supporting naturalism over theism.

F. Weighing the Evidence

The preceding discussion should make it clear I don't agree with agnostics who claim the evidence is ambiguous because it is absent or vague. I believe there is plenty of clear evidence, but the clear evidence for theism is offset by clear evidence for naturalism. I don't believe, however, that the evidence on each side is perfectly balanced, so that as a whole it has no effect on the ratio of the probability of theism to the probability of naturalism. Rather, I find it very difficult to make such a judgment because I find it very difficult to compare the strength of the various pieces of evidence. This is not to say no such comparisons can be made. For example, I believe the abundance of tragedy in the world is much stronger evidence against theism than the abundance of beauty is for it. The same can be said about the systematic connection between pain and pleasure and reproductive success. I also believe the cosmic coincidences that make intelligent life possible are stronger evidence for theism than evolution is against it. But I am unable to judge the relative strength of, for example, the argument from pain and pleasure and the argument from intelligent life. And because of this, I am unable to judge whether the conjunction of all of the facts I have considered is more probable on theism or on naturalism. So I'm left with a variety of arguments on each side, but no clear answer to the question "which side is supported by the stronger arguments?"

Notice that such a predicament is hardly unusual or restricted to metaphysical issues. We frequently find ourselves unable to make an overall judgement about the probability of an hypothesis because we are unable to determine whether the (clear) evidence for it is stronger than the (clear) evidence against it. This may occur when trying to decide whether a suspect is guilty of a crime, or when wondering who will win a football game, especially early in the season. In such circumstances, one must suspend judgement, not because one lacks clear evidence nor because one believes the evidence on each side is perfectly balanced. Rather, one must suspend judgment because it is not clear which side, if any, is supported by the stronger evidence.

II.   The Implications of Ambiguity

A.   Leaps of Faith

Many who might agree with me that the evidence concerning God's existence is ambiguous would nevertheless reject my position that such ambiguity justifies an agnostic stance, maintaining instead that ambiguous evidence calls for a (pragmatically justified) leap of faith. While I do think such ambiguity calls for religious practice of a certain sort (I will explain this in Section II.D), and while it is possible such practice might ultimately lead to belief by leading first to new evidence, belief itself is, at least for me, too passive to be a part of such practice. Given how I see the evidence, it would be just as impossible for me to believe with confidence that God exists as it would for me to believe that the jelly beans are being drawn from the first jar after five red and five blue beans have been drawn. So willing or not, I'm unable to take a leap of belief. Nor am I sure such a leap would count as faith. For the ability to believe with confidence when one also believes the evidence doesn't warrant such confidence is an intellectual vice, and faith is supposed to be a virtue.

B.   The Prior Probability of Theism

Another objection to my claim that agnosticism is justified by ambiguous evidence is that this claim is based on questionable assumptions about the prior probabilities of theism and naturalism – about how probable theism and naturalism are independent of the evidence. A closer examination of my analogy to the jars of jelly beans will help to expose these assumptions. In that example, the fact that five red beans and five blue beans were drawn justifies suspending judgement about which jar is the source of the beans. We have already seen one disanalogy between this example and the evaluation of theistic and naturalistic metaphysics: In the case of the jelly beans, each piece of evidence is equally strong because the ratio of red to blue jelly beans in each jar doesn't noticeably change from one draw to the next, and the ratio of red to blue jelly beans in the first jar is the same as the ratio of blue to red jelly beans in the second jar. I claimed above that this disanalogy is not crucial because in the metaphysical case the inability to make precise judgments about the relative strength of the different pieces of evidence on each side can also provide prima facie justification for an agnostic stance. There are, however, two more disanalogies that threaten to undermine my prima facie case for agnosticism. Each of these concerns judgments of prior probability.

The first disanalogy arises because, in the jelly bean example, the two hypotheses being compared are clearly equally probable prior to drawing any beans. Recall that in that example, nothing is known about what procedure was used to determine which jar is glued shut and which is not. If we change the example, so that the procedure is known, then an equal number of red and blue beans need not imply that one should suspend judgment. For example, suppose a lottery with 1000 tickets was used, with ticket #1 being the only ticket that would result in the first jar being glued shut. Then five red beans and five blue beans won't justify suspending judgement. Rather, one should believe with considerable confidence that the second jar is glued shut – that the beans are being drawn from the first jar.[16]

What about the metaphysical case? Do theism and naturalism start out equally probable before considering the evidence? It's far from clear they do, for, unlike the two jelly bean hypotheses, they are very different sorts of claims. Theism asserts the existence of a specific sort of supernatural being, while naturalism denies the existence of all supernatural beings. This means that, if the claim that something exists and the claim that nothing exists are equally probable prior to considering the evidence, then naturalism has a higher prior probability than theism.[17] But this is a big "if." Though many people have the intuition that the "burden of proof" is on the theist because theism makes a positive existential claim, it is not easy to prove that this is so.

Another disanalogy is that, in the jelly bean example, there are only two jars, and it is assumed that all of the beans are being drawn from one of the two. If there were 1000 jars with a variety of different mixtures of red and blue beans, then the fact that the evidence is ambiguous between the first two jars wouldn't justify suspending judgment. Rather, it would justify rejecting both hypotheses, for each hypothesis would start and end with a very low probability. What about the metaphysical case? Many hypotheses are alternatives both to theism and to naturalism. The fact that all of these are supernaturalistic hypotheses is often taken as a reason for thinking they are a greater threat to theistic belief than to naturalistic belief. But this assumes both that naturalism starts out at least as probable as supernaturalism and that theism is not overwhelmingly more probable prior to considering the evidence than all of its supernaturalistic competitors. And both of these assumptions are also questionable.

My own view is that, independent of the evidence, neither theism nor naturalism is overwhelmingly more probable than the other and each is much more probable than any alternatives. This means that the way the evidence affects their overall probability is closely analogous to the way the evidence affects the overall probability of the two hypotheses in the original jelly bean example. I don't have the space here to fully develop and defend my reasons for holding this view. But I will at least try to sketch those reasons.

My starting point is a strong and admittedly controversial conviction that idealism and (hard) materialism are false. Reality has (at least) two parts, the physical (or ontologically objective) and the mental (or ontologically subjective), and neither is reducible to the other (though one might be merely a property of the other). Next, it is very likely, I believe, that either the mental world ultimately explains the physical or vice versa. One world is very probably a product of the other. Prior to considering the evidence, I see no reason to prefer one of the two options here. Like the two jelly bean hypotheses, they are parallel claims, equal in content and simplicity, and thus equally probable initially. Therefore, prior to considering the evidence, each has a probability of close to $\frac{1}{2}$.[18]

What does this tell us about the prior probabilities of naturalism and theism? First, if the physical world provides an ultimate explanation of the mental, then naturalism has a high prior probability. For the view that the mental world is ultimately a product of the physical makes supernaturalism a bizarre view, to say the least. Second, if the mental world provides an ultimate explanation of the physical, then theism does not have a very low prior probability. For anti-realist views according to which human minds create the physical world have, I believe, an extremely low prior probability. And, as Swinburne has argued, atheistic or deistic or quasi-theistic hypotheses entailing the existence of supernatural minds are much less simple than theism and for that reason much less probable intrinsically.[19] To suppose that the creator of the universe is a perfect person and so has unlimited power and knowledge is simpler and hence intrinsically more probable than to suppose, for example, that such a being can create some things but not others or has knowledge of some facts but not others. And a being of unlimited power and knowledge is unlikely to be influenced by nonrational desires and hence is likely to do whatever she knows to be best overall, i.e. morally best.

It follows, then, both that theism and naturalism are much more probable prior to considering the evidence than any alternative hypothesis and that neither has an overwhelmingly higher prior probability than the other. Independent of the evidence, each has a probability of less than one half, but neither has a probability of very close to zero. Perhaps this is why I have so many epistemic peers who take each seriously. Further, if this conclusion is correct, then a look at the evidence concerning theism and naturalism is absolutely essential. For it follows from this conclusion that, if the evidence strongly favored theism or strongly favored naturalism, then theism or naturalism would be highly probable. Thus, my agnosticism depends on my belief that the evidence concerning theism and naturalism is ambiguous.

C. The Stability of Agnosticism

J. L. Schellenberg doesn't deny that ambiguous evidence provides prima facie justification for an agnostic stance. He holds instead that such justification will be defeated as soon as one recognizes the evidential implications of such ambiguity. This is because ambiguous evidence implies that reasonable nonbelief in theism exists, and the existence of reasonable nonbelief is itself strong evidence against theism. Indeed, Schellenberg goes so far as to say that, when agnostics claim that the question of God's existence cannot be settled on evidential grounds, they are describing an impossible state of affairs, because "Any apparent inconclusiveness in the evidence must . . . *itself* be taken as a consideration (evidentially) justifying the conclusion that God does not exist."[20] So Schellenberg believes my position on the fence is unstable. Reflection on the evidential implications of my reason for sitting up there should pull me over to the atheistic side.

A theist might counter that ambiguous evidence, as opposed to strong evidence against theism, is actually evidence for theism,[21] because ambiguity is more likely when someone controls what evidence is available, and such control is entailed by theism but not by naturalism. Suppose, for example, we know that, if the jelly beans are being taken from the first jar, then they are being drawn by someone who *might* not want us to know which jar the beans are coming from, while if they are being taken from the second jar, then they are definitely being drawn randomly. Then an equal number of red and blue beans is actually evidence that the beans are coming from the first jar, and the strength of this evidence increases as the number of draws increases while still maintaining roughly an even split between red and blue beans.

One (but by no means the only) crucial issue involved in this debate between Schellenberg and those who would try to put a theistic spin on ambiguous evidence is the issue of just how likely it is that God would want to prevent all forms of reasonable nonbelief, including agnostic forms. I'll have a little to say about this in the next section. But for now let's assume that reasonable nonbelief of any sort is much less likely on theism than on naturalism. Does it follow that ambiguous evidence is evidence favoring naturalism over theism? Not yet, because ambiguous evidence has other implications besides reasonable nonbelief. (For example, as I shall argue in the next section, it makes theistic practice reasonable.) And these other implications may be more likely on theism than on naturalism. But let's ignore this possibility and assume that ambiguous evidence itself is much more likely on naturalism than on theism and so is strong evidence favoring naturalism over theism. Does it follow that my agnostic stance is unstable?

Again, the answer is "no." The answer would be "yes" if it could be shown that, prior to considering the evidential significance of ambiguous evidence, naturalism and theism are equally probable. But, as I argued above, this cannot be shown. No precise comparison of the probabilities of naturalism and theism can be made because no precise judgements about the relative strength of the different pieces of evidence can be made. Adding this single new piece of evidence doesn't change this. There remains significant evidence on both sides, the relative strength of which is hard to assess. And this implies that agnosticism remains the only reasonable stance.[22]

D. Agnostic Practice

In his book *Belief* H. H. Price quotes the Agnostic's Prayer, "O God, if there be a God, save my soul, if I have a soul." He claims that, despite the derision poured on this prayer, it is actually "a perfectly sensible prayer for an agnostic to offer."[23] Of course, agnostics need not – indeed, they probably should not – make the conditional nature of their prayers explicit. For, as Price points out, what they are doing when they pray and engage in other religious behavior is a sort of imaginative exercise, "something like what an actor does when he throws himself into his part."[24] Though they do not believe, their attitude is very similar to belief in many ways. Price justifies such agnostic religious practice on the grounds that it is the only way a non-believer can test the claim, which he takes to be essential to a theistic world view, that every human being has spiritual capacities that, when developed, will result in experiences that support the basic propositions of theism.

My own view is a bit different than this. I don't believe that "seek and ye shall find (in this life)" is an essential part of a theistic world view. Since, however, I regard God's existence as a *real* possibility, I whole-heartedly agree with Price that it is reasonable – indeed, I would say rationally required – for me to behave differently than I would if I were an atheist. For example, I ought to pray – unlike the atheist, I believe there just might be a God listening. More generally, I ought to do what I can to cultivate or at least prepare for a relationship with God. Also, it is not unreasonable for me to spend a considerable amount of my time looking for new evidence and reexamining old evidence both for and against theism. If I were an atheist, then I wouldn't bother to search for evidence for or against God's existence, because I wouldn't expect to find any confirming evidence and I wouldn't need any more disconfirming evidence.[25]

What will be the consequences of agnostic religious practice? It may or may not lead to belief, even on the assumption that God exists. Indeed, it may or may not lead to belief (in this life), even on the assumption that it leads to (or prepares one for) a closer relationship with God. Religious practice is very difficult for an agnostic, and for some there may be value in that difficulty. After all, human beings are psychologically very complex, to say the least. And it is well known that belief is not strongly correlated with sanctification. Thus, if theism is true, then I seriously doubt that the moral and spiritual development of every single human being is best served by belief in this life. And if such doubt is justified, then perhaps reasonable nonbelief in some forms is not as unlikely on theism as Schellenberg thinks.

III.   Questioning the Ambiguity

I must confess that at times the ambiguity of the evidence seems to me to be just a little too neat, a little too perfect. It seems almost contrived, as if the beans aren't being drawn randomly. But if this is so, then who *is* drawing the beans? Is it me? Am I manufacturing an apparent ambiguity for myself, either by refusing to recognize clear differences in the strength of different pieces of evidence or by refusing to take seriously supernaturalistic alternatives to theism? And am I doing this in order to rationalize a strong desire to sit on the fence that has nothing to do with evidence? Further, if the answer to these questions is "yes," then what accounts for my desire to sit on the fence? Is it the result of subconsciously rejecting God, thereby making me unable to see that the evidence favoring theism is much stronger than the evidence favoring naturalism? Or do I sit on the fence because I am horrified by the possibility that the suffering of innocents has no purpose and no compensation, and so I refuse to recognize what seems perfectly obvious to so many of my fellow philosophers, that belief in God is just silly superstition or, at best, understandable self-deception. I hope and even believe that my assessment of the evidence is the result of an open mind rather than a closed or tender heart. But if this is so, then is the ambiguity of the evidence just an unfortunate coincidence? Or is it designed, not by me, but by a God whose policy is, "Don't find me, I'll call you . . . when the time is right"? I don't know the answers to these questions. So for now I will sit on the fence, lost perhaps but still looking, leaning perhaps but not leaping, listening I hope, but not yet hearing.[26]

Notes

1. *Divine Hiddenness and Human Reason* (Ithaca: Cornell University Press, 1993), p. 212.
2. Two technical points about the probability judgments I will be making need to be mentioned. First, what we ultimately want to know about the relevant facts is whether their *conjunction* favors theism or favors naturalism. And these facts are not "independent." In other words, knowing that one obtains affects the probability of the others (either given theism or given naturalism). Thus, using the symbol "Pr(f/h)" to stand for the probability that f is true given that h is true, the relevant rule of mathematical probability can be expressed as follows: $Pr(f_1\&f_2\& \ldots \&f_n/h)$ $= Pr(f_1/h) \times Pr(f_2/f_1\&h) \times \ldots \times Pr(f_n/f_1\&f_2\& \ldots \&f_{n-1}\&h)$. Notice that on the right side of this equation, the probability of each fact f_i is assessed on the assumption, not just that h is true, but also that $f_1, f_2, \ldots$, and f_{i-1} are all true. I won't make this explicit when I discuss the various individual facts that favor either theism or naturalism, but it is important not to forget that it is implicit. Otherwise, one might wonder why I ignore certain facts that are clearly much more probable on one of the two hypotheses than on the other. The reason in many cases is that those facts are not much more probable *given some fact I do mention*, so they don't add anything new to the case in question. A second technical point is that, since the facts I discuss are *known* facts and so have a probability of close or equal to one either on naturalism or on theism, whenever I make a claim that some fact is more probable on one of the two hypotheses, I should be understood to be making a claim about the "antecedent" probability of the fact in question – about its probability independent of the observations or testimony upon which our knowledge of all of the various facts I consider is based. Notice that this sort of abstraction is also implicit in my jelly bean example. Once one sees that the bean drawn is red, its probability of being red on either of the two hypotheses is close or equal to one. Why, then, do I claim that it is more likely to be red if it was taken from the first jar than if it was taken from the second jar? Because what I mean by this claim is that it is "antecedently" more likely to be red, given that it came from the first jar. In other words, the probability of its being red, independent of the observation upon which my knowledge of its being red is based, is greater on the assumption that it came from the first jar than on the assumption that it came from the second jar.
3. This argument was suggested to me by Bruce Hauptli.
4. For a detailed presentation of this scientific evidence, as well as two philosophical arguments for a beginning of the universe, see William Lane Craig, *The Kalam Cosmological Argument* (Harper & Row Publishers, 1979). For serious debate about this evidence, see William Lane Craig and Quentin Smith, *Theism, Atheism, and Big Bang Cosmology* (Oxford University Press, 1993).
5. I say "potentially" here because the general principle, "if e is evidence favoring h_1 over h_2 and f is evidence for e, then f is evidence favoring h_1 over h_2" is false. This is because f might have other implications that favor h_2 over h_1 or f might support either a part of e that is not more likely on h_1 or a particular way of e's being true that is not more likely on h_1. None of these conditions applies in this case. To the extent that the evidence we have for a beginning of the universe is evidence for a beginning *with* time rather than *within* time, the third condition threatens. But even a beginning with time is, I believe, more likely on theism than on naturalism.

6. I tell some of these stories in "A Critique of the *Kalam* Cosmological Argument," in *Philosophy of Religion: An Anthology*, third edition, ed. Louis P. Pojman (Wadsworth Publishing Co., 1998), pp. 42–7. I also argue there that philosophical arguments for a beginning of the universe do not succeed.

7. For a detailed statement of this sort of design argument, see John Leslie, *Universes* (Routledge, 1989). Leslie's argument is an argument against naturalism, but not in his opinion an argument for theism. I disagree with this opinion (for reasons implicit in Section II.B).

8. For a detailed statement of this argument from evolution, see Section II of my "Evolution and the Problem of Evil," in *Philosophy of Religion: An Anthology*, pp. 219–230.

9. Again, the potential defeaters for inferences like this mentioned in note 4 do not apply in this case. Nor do they apply in other cases in this paper in which I use this sort of inference.

10. This argument was inspired by (and the Alzheimer's example was borrowed from) Paul Edwards' argument against survival after death. See his "The Dependence of Consciousness on the Brain," in *Immortality*, ed. Paul Edwards (Macmillan Publishing Co., 1992), pp. 292–307.

11. I develop this sort of argument in detail in two articles: "Pain and Pleasure: An Evidential Problem for Theists," *Noûs* 23 (1989), 331–350; "Evolution and the Problem of Evil," Section III.

12. Atheistic arguments from tragedy are worked out in detail in numerous articles. My favorite is William L. Rowe, "The Evidential Argument From Evil: A Second Look," in *The Evidential Argument From Evil*, ed. Daniel Howard-Snyder (Indiana University Press, 1996), pp. 262–85.

13. For a full statement of the argument from beauty, see F. R. Tennant, *Philosophical Theology*, vol. II (Cambridge University Press, 1930), pp. 89–93. See also Richard Swinburne, *The Existence of God* (Oxford University Press, 1979), pp. 150–1.

14. For a detailed statement of an argument like this, see Swinburne, Ch. 13. I believe Swinburne and many other theistic philosophers overestimate the strength of this sort of argument. See my "God and Perceptual Evidence," *International Journal for the Philosophy of Religion* 32 (1992), 149–165.

15. William L. Rowe emphasizes the absence of God's felt presence in times of tragedy as part of a defense of his argument from evil. See his "The Evidential Argument From Evil: A Second Look," p. 276.

16. Of course, in this new example, the evidence is not, strictly speaking, ambiguous, because the procedure is itself evidence that the beans are being taken from the first jar. Here, "prior probability" means "probability prior to the evidence *under consideration*" (that is, prior to considering the ten beans that were drawn) rather than "prior to considering *any* evidence." If, however, I have not left out any significant evidence favoring theism or naturalism over the other, then the issue of the prior probabilities of theism and naturalism will be tantamount to the issue of how probable they are independent of all evidence. The probability of an hypothesis prior to all evidence is sometimes called its "intrinsic" or "a priori" probability, though for a variety of reasons the former term is, I believe, preferable.

17. This is because any specific existential claim entails but is not entailed by the claim that something exists and so is intrinsically *less* probable than the claim that something exists, while the denial of any specific existential claim is entailed by, but does not entail, that nothing exists and so is intrinsically *more* probable than the claim that nothing exists.

18. One might object here that I am relying on the notorious "principle of indifference." For a defense of that principle properly understood, see George N. Schlesinger, *The Sweep of Probability* (South Bend: University of Notre Dame Press, 1991), ch. IX.
19. Swinburne, ch. 5.
20. Schellenberg, p. 212.
21. Paul Tidman suggested this view when he commented on an earlier version of this paper, but I cannot recall how (or if) he argued for it.
22. Schellenberg himself suggested this criticism of his own argument to me. Notice that a parallel criticism would block attempts to draw a theistic conclusion from the premise that ambiguous evidence is more likely on theism.
23. (Allen & Unwin, 1969), p. 484.
24. Ibid., pp. 484–485.
25. One might raise the Pascalian objection that, since the reward of finding God is infinite, even the atheist should join the search. This objection makes an assumption I find implausible, namely, that, if God exists, then belief (in this lifetime) is required for salvation.
26. I am grateful to Andrew J. Cortens, Kai Draper, Jamie M. Ferreira, C. Douglas Geivett, Bruce Hauptli, J. L. Schellenberg, and Paul Tidman for helpful comments. I am also grateful to Daniel Howard-Snyder for suggesting I write a paper about the role played by divine hiddenness in my own religious life.

11

The Silence of the God Who Speaks

NICHOLAS WOLTERSTORFF

Silence is of many sorts. There's the silence of the countryside on a still winter's night, when all the animals are sleeping and all the insects hibernating. There's the silence of Amsterdam on the eve of the fifth of May, when the entire old city halts for fifteen minutes to memorialize those who fell in the war and were silenced. There's the silence of the mute, and the silence of rocks, hills, and valleys. There's the silence in music, silence as essential to the music as the sounds. There's the silence of the audience chamber when the imminent entrance of the queen is announced. And there's the hush of the cosmos that the psalmist enjoins when he announces: "The Lord is in his holy temple, let all the earth keep silence before him."

The silence of which I will be speaking is unlike all of those. It's the silence of the biblical God – the biblical God being a God who is not only capable of speaking but has on many occasions spoken. More specifically, I will be speaking of the *biblical* silence of the biblical God. The biblical silence of God is the nonanswering silence of God. It's like the silence of the parent who doesn't answer when the child asks "Why? Why did it happen? Where were you?" It's the silence which the poet of Psalm 83 pleads with God to break: "O God, do not keep silence; do not hold thy peace or be still, O God!"

1. Biblical Silence

The Bible – both the Hebrew Bible and the Christian Bible – represents God as having spoken. In addition, there's a long tradition within both Judaism and Christianity of regarding the Bible itself as a medium of divine speech. When I began composing this essay, I had just finished putting the final touches on a book of philosophical reflections on the claim that God speaks. *Divine Discourse*, I titled it. I argued that if we take speaking to consist in the performance of what J. L. Austin called *illocutionary actions*, then there is nothing incoherent or impossible in the claim that God speaks – that is, *literally* speaks. Nothing incoherent or impossible in the claim that God performs such actions as commanding, assuring, promising, asserting, and so forth. The silence of God is not an ontologically necessitated silence. It's not like the silence of the rocks and the hills, of which it is only metaphorically true that they speak. If God were impersonal – the "ground of being" or something of that sort – then God's silence would be ontologically necessitated. The silence of the biblical God is the silence of a God who speaks.

Though the biblical God – by which I mean, God as represented in the Bible – though the biblical God does indeed speak, nonetheless, on most matters, God chooses not to say anything. Most matters God leaves it to us to find out about, by observation and inference. And that's wonderful. Who wants to be told everything? The silence of God – the *biblical* silence of God – does not consist in the fact that on many matters, God says nothing.

The biblical silence of God is the failure or refusal of God to answer a question put to Him. Though not the failure or refusal to answer any question you please, however. Some of the questions put to God are questions which, given what God has already said, are misguided questions. Questions that one wouldn't ask if one has heard and genuinely listened to what God has already said. The biblical silence of God is the nonanswering silence of God in the face of those questions which take into account what God has already said.

There are many such questions, and of many sorts. I shall focus all my attention on just one sort. The sort I have in mind are questions which we find ourselves incapable of answering on our own. At least, we have been unsuccessful thus far in answering them on our own. Yet they are questions to which the person who believes in the biblical God wants an answer with all one's soul. They are questions which, unanswered, put biblical faith at risk. The risk has proved too great for many; faith has succumbed. Yet God does not answer the questions. Strange and disturbing. Though one poses the questions in the context of having listened to God, to ask them is to find oneself standing alongside the psalmist before the non-answering silence of God.

2.   Locating the Silence

Let me begin by locating the sort of questions I have in mind, thus locating the silence. Strange forked creatures, we human beings: animalic persons, personic animals. Persons indeed, but also animals. Animals indeed, but also persons: creatures endowed with consciousness and free agency, reflective of God, meant to enjoy and tend the earth and to live in fellowship with other persons, both those of our own kind and God. Placed in a spatio-temporal physical world along with lots of other forms of life, including other kinds of animals.

Upon inspecting this curious forked creature which he had made, God pronounced the workmanship good; by which God no doubt meant, in part, that our design-plan was a good one for our situation. Inspection completed and passed, God sent us on our way with various instructions for conduct, and a blessing: May you flourish, said God. May you flourish as a species. When one reads the report of God's blessing of humanity in the context of the other Genesis blessings, that's the natural interpretation. But as the Bible proceeds it becomes clear that the Genesis report of God's blessing of humanity had a latent meaning. What God had in mind was not just that we flourish as a species but that we flourish as individual members of the species. That we each live until "full of years" – the three score years and ten built into our design plan; and that during those years we flourish. Flourish *qua* the animalic persons, the personic animals, that we were created as being. And flourish in the earthly and social environment in which we have been placed. In Genesis, God was not pronouncing a blessing on disembodied souls about to enter an immaterial heaven.

But things have gone awry, terribly awry, with respect to God's creating and providential intent for these creatures. The divine experiment has not worked out: the experiment of creating this species of forked creatures, placing and maintaining the species in this physical universe along with other forms of life, giving the species instructions for conduct, and doing this creating and maintaining with the intent that each member of the species should flourish on earth in society until full of years. The blessing has not been fulfilled. Some do not flourish; some do not live until full of years; some neither flourish nor live until full of years.

Prominent among the things which have gone awry in human existence are life duration and suffering. The lives of many do not endure as they were meant to endure. And suffering does not serve the function it was meant to serve. Neither do affection and volition function as they were meant to function; they do not measure up to God's instructions. But on this occasion, I shall concentrate on the malfunctioning of suffering.

To see in what way suffering malfunctions, we must reflect on the nature of suffering and on its *proper* function. For it does indeed have a proper function. In turn, to reflect on those matters we must attend to a dimension of our constitution so deep and pervasive that neither ordinary speech nor the language of psychology and philosophy provide us with a conceptuality apt for describing it. My best will thus be fumbling. Let me take *joy*, or synonymously for my purposes, *delight*, as the opposite of suffering.

Built into the constitution of all of us are two distinct systems of suffering and delight. "System" is an inept word for what I wish to point to; but I can think of none better. One of these systems pertains to experience; the other pertains to belief. Let me begin with that system of suffering and delight which pertains to experience.

Pass quickly before your mind's eye samples of human experience in all its rich variety: sensations, moods, perceptions, emotions, desires, pains, believings, and so forth. And then notice this fundamental fact about our way of having such experiences: Though some are such that our having them is a matter of indifference to us, many are ones we *like* having, and many others we *dislike* having. Many of our experiences are, as it were, valorized, charged – some positively, some negatively – while others remain neutral, with the charges coming in varying degrees of intensity, from intensely positive to intensely negative. There is thus in the life of each of us a continuum of valorization, with each of our experiences having a place on the continuum. As one moves out from the neutral center toward the positive end, one reaches a point where everything beyond is experienced joyfully. As one moves out from the neutral center toward the negative end, one reaches a point where everything beyond is experienced sufferingly.

Physical pain, for example, is experienced by most of us most of the time with a negative charge. When that charge is sufficiently intense, we experience it sufferingly; we suffer from the pain. Apparently, though, there are cases in which even fairly intense physical pain is experienced with a positive charge. I do not have in mind those cases in which a person puts up with some pain – may even be glad to have it – because she believes that some good will ensue; such cases bring belief into the picture, and we will get to that shortly. Rather I have in mind those cases in which the person just likes having the pain. This makes clear that we must beware of identifying strong negative valorization with pain. Though we sometimes speak of suffering as pain, to speak thus is to speak metaphorically. A good deal of suffering, even of experiential suffering, has nothing to do with pain; witness those who suffer from mental depression. And conversely, as we have just seen, pain can be experienced with a positive rather than a negative charge.

We regularly speak of someone suffering *from* the pain, of someone's suffering being *caused by* mental depression, of someone getting delight *from* the music, and so forth. In short, we regularly use causal language, and causal-sounding language, to describe the relation between suffering or delight, on the one hand, and the experience of pain, mental depression, or hearing music, on the other. But we must not think of the connection between suffering or delight, and some experience, as the connection of efficient causality; for the suffering which we describe as "caused" by pain is not a sensation *in addition to* the pain sensation, causally evoked by it. The only sensations are the pain sensations. When the operative system is the experiential system, then suffering and joy are, as it were, adverbial modifiers of the states and events of consciousness which are the experiences. They are not distinct experiences but *ways of having* experiences. Pain and depression are among the experiences that we normally have sufferingly; the perception of art and the taste of good food are among the experiences that we often have joyfully. Suffering is an existential No-saying to some experience; delight, an existential Yes-saying.

What I have been describing thus far is just one of the two systems of suffering and delight which I claimed to identify in us human beings – the *expe-*

riential system. Let us move on to consider the other system – that which pertains to belief, the *belief* system. When I learned of the death of my son, I was cast into suffering. What caused my suffering was not his death; for in the interim between his death and my learning of it, I did not suffer. What caused my suffering was my coming to believe that he was dead. If things had gone in the opposite way, if I had come to believe that he was dead when he was not, then too I would have been cast into suffering by my belief that he was dead, not by his death; for in this case there would not even have been his death. So our beliefs have the power of casting us into suffering; and they have that power whether or not they are true.

Yet what I suffered over was not the experience of my actively believing that my son was dead; it was, rather, that my son was dead. And that was not an experience of mine. It wasn't even an object of my experience; it was something of which I had only a belief. It's *what I believed to be the case* that I suffered over, not my experiential state of *believing* it. I suffered over that which was the content of my belief, namely, that my son was dead, not over my believing it. The suffering which occurs when the experiential system is operating is the suffering which consists of sufferingly having some experience. By contrast, the suffering which occurs when the belief system is operating is an emotion caused by coming to believe something, the emotion having as its object that which one believes to be the case.

It's true that there are cases in which we sufferingly or joyfully experience a believing. People wracked by religious doubt who finally come to believe confidently in their salvation not only rejoices over their salvation; they also experience rejoicingly their confident believing. But my case was not like that. My suffering was not my existential No-saying to my *believing* that my son was dead, but my existential No-saying to his being dead.

We are all created with these two systems of valorization. They're part of the design plan of our constitution. And in all of us, this part of our design plan gets activated by our life in this world. Sometimes my throat does actually feel unpleasantly parched. Sometimes I do actually feel unpleasantly hungry. Sometimes I do actually feel a distinctly unpleasant burning sensation in my finger. Just as one cannot imagine a human being whose constitution does not incorporate those two systems, so one cannot imagine a human life here on earth in which these two systems of our constitution are not activated in such a way as to yield not only positively but negatively valorized experiences, and beliefs concerning occurrences about which the person feels negatively.

And now for the point about proper functioning. Being constituted as we are in this regard serves our flourishing as animalic persons in the world in which we are placed. That we need water, food, and intact flesh if we are to remain alive is a direct consequence of our animalic constitution. Accordingly, it's conducive to our endurance as animalic persons that we have feelings of thirst when in need of water, feelings of hunger when in need of food, feelings of pain when our flesh gets burned, and that we experience these sensations negatively. In some cases we experience them with such intense negativity that we *suffer* from parched throat sensations, *suffer* from hunger pang sensations, *suffer* from burn sensations. Our endurance as animalic persons would be vastly more precarious than it is if we didn't experience thirst, hunger, and the pain of burned flesh, or if we didn't experience them negatively.

The examples I have given, of the proper functioning of unpleasantness and suffering, were all taken from the animalic side of our existence; examples of the same point from the personal side of our existence can also easily be given. Our dislike of loneliness leads us to establish families and communities. Our dislike of intellectual bewilderment leads us to pursue knowledge. Our dislike of disappointment over unachieved goals leads us to try harder. And our dislike of a wide range of things makes them candidates for functioning as means of appropriate punishment and chastisement.

The conclusion is unavoidable that suffering in particular, and negative valorizations in general, often serve our flourishing as the animalic persons that we are. Of course the person suffering doesn't *like* the suffering. But that's exactly the point. We draw back from the experiences we dislike, do what we can to alleviate and forestall them. It's the combination of our being so constituted as to feel pain upon being burned and our not liking that pain which makes it much easier for us to survive than would otherwise be the case; witness the precarious existence of those rare human beings who do not feel such pain. The suffering serves our flourishing.

Dislike and suffering are existential No-saying to that from which and over which we suffer. But when a human being placed in this world has a constitution which includes such capacities for existential No-saying as ours typically does, we must pronounce a judgmental Yes on that aspect of our constitution itself. For we cannot imagine creatures such as ourselves flourishing, or even surviving, in environments such as ours without such capacities as we have for existential No-saying. Part of what God found good about the way God created us was surely that we were capable of suffering. The point is made with poetic eloquence by Karl Barth in his discussion of *das Nichtige*:

We must indicate and remove a serious confusion which has been of far reaching effect in the history of theology. . . . [T]here is a positive as well as a negative aspect of creation and creaturely occurrence. . . . Viewed from its negative aspect, creation is as it were on the frontier of *das Nichtige* and orientated towards it. Creation is continually confronted by this menace. . . . Yet this negative side is not to be identified with *das Nichtige*, nor must it be postulated that the latter belongs to the essence of creaturely nature and may somehow be understood and interpreted as a mark of its character and perfection. . . . [I]n creation there is not only a Yes but also a No; not only a height but also an abyss; not only clarity but also obscurity; not only growth but also decay; not only opulence but also indigence; not only beauty but also ashes; not only beginning but also end; not only value but also worthlessness. . . . [I]n creaturely existence . . . there are hours, days and years both bright and dark, success and failure, laughter and tears, youth and age, gain and loss, birth and sooner or later its inevitable corollary, death. . . . Yet it is irrefutable that creation and creature are good even in the fact that all that is exists in this contrast and antithesis. In all this, far from being null, it praises its Creator and Lord even on its shadowy side, even in the negative aspect in which it is so near to *das Nichtige*. *Church Dogmatics* III/3, pp. 296–7.

All true. Yet to say it once again, things have gone terribly awry with respect to the function of suffering in our lives – and with respect to life duration. It was and is the intent behind God's creation and maintenance that with the constitution God gave us we would each and all flourish until full of years in the environment in which God placed us. But with reference to that intent, things have gone terribly awry. Sometimes a person's constitution itself becomes disordered in such a way that the person doesn't flourish; one lives in severe depression or intractable pain. More often, the fit between our constitution and our environment does not serve our flourishing. The food I need to maintain my animal existence isn't available; so I die long before full of years, suffering intensely from starvation. You fall. If you merely break an arm, that doesn't significantly inhibit your flourishing, since the break soon heals and the suffering caused by the break nicely exemplifies the design plan functioning properly. Life would be far more precarious than it is if breaking bones produced no pain. But if your fall brings about your early death, I can expatiate as long as I have breath on the fact that this is just a natural consequence of your doing what you did with the animal body that you have in the physical universe which is ours; that doesn't address the fact that things have gone awry with reference to God's intent that you should live until full of years. Again, rather than flourishing in the company of your fellow human beings you may be subjected to indignity and even torture. Your human constitution operating in your social and physical environment does not bring about your flourishing until full of years.

The divine experiment has not worked out: the experiment of creating these forked creatures with the constitution that they have, placing them in this physical and social situation, and doing that, as well as maintaining and instructing them, with the intent that each and every one should flourish until full of years. Suffering and life duration have gone agonizingly awry with reference to that intent.

Why have they gone awry? The very speech of God invites us to pose the question. Invites us to pose the question for this case and for that case; and for all the cases in general. Why was the life of this person snuffed out when young? Why did that person suffer years of intractable suffering that not only went beyond all proper functioning but from which nothing redemptive could any longer be extracted? Why all this brevity of life and why all such suffering? But no answer is forthcoming. Listen as we may, we hear no further speech. Only silence. Nonanswering silence.

3. Objection: The World has Been Misdescribed

Most philosophers and theologians in the Christian tradition would deny that I have rightly located the silence of God. My location of the silence is predicated on the claim that things have gone awry with reference to God's creating and maintaining intent – in particular, that suffering and life duration have gone awry. They would insist that that is not so.

Some would say that I have misdescribed the world. I said that in this world of ours we are confronted – not just now and then but over and over – with malfunctioning suffering and suffering which we prove incapable of making redemptive. The tradition of "soul making theodicy," initiated by Irenaeus, would deny this. Let me quote Calvin as an example. He says in one passage that

Whether poverty or exile, or prison, or insult, or disease, or bereavement, or anything like them torture us, we must think that none of these things happens except by the will and providence of God, that he does nothing except with a well-ordered justice (*Institutes* III,viii,11).

Coming to the surface in this passage is Calvin's inclination toward radical occasionalism – toward the view that God is the only true causal agent in reality. As to the character of God's agency, Calvin was persuaded that God acts always out of justice or love. Thus we get this other passage:

All the suffering to which human life is subject and liable are necessary exercises by which God partly invites us to repentance, partly instructs us in humility, and partly renders us more cautious and more attentive in guarding against the allurements of sin for the future (Commentary on Genesis 3:19).

The thought is clear: All suffering is sent by God. Partly out of retributive justice, but mainly *out of love*. Suffering is God's gift to us: God's medicine, God's surgery. We don't like the medicine and the surgery; who does like medicine and surgery? But suffering is for our moral and spiritual welfare. It prods us, provokes us, into reorienting and deepening our moral and spiritual selves. The experience of suffering may even, in mysterious ways, provide us with the material *necessary* for such deepening. As I put it in a passage in my *Lament for a Son*:

Suffering is the shout of 'No' by one's whole existence to that over which one suffers – the shout of "No" by nerves and gut and gland and heart to pain, to death, to injustice, to depression, to hunger, to humiliation, to bondage, to abandonment. And sometimes, when the cry is intense, there emerges a radiance which elsewhere seldom appears: a glow of courage, of love, of insight, of selflessness, of faith. In that radiance we see best what humanity was meant to be. . . .

In the valley of suffering, despair and bitterness are brewed. But there also character is made. The valley of suffering is the vale of soul-making (96–7).

Soul-making theodicy points to something deep and true. Yet if we judge ourselves answerable to the biblical speech of God, then we cannot accept its claim that, with reference to God's creating and maintaining intent, suffering and life duration have not gone awry in our world – cannot accept its assumption that only our affections and volitions have gone awry. It may well be that the suffering of a parent over the death of a child provides opportunity for the spiritual growth of the parent, or that the wrong-doing of the parent merits some suffering. But what about the child? What about the benediction God pronounced over the child: May you flourish until full of years? Or to move to a totally different scale: It may well be that the suffering of the survivors of the Jewish Holocaust provided an opportunity for their spiritual growth, or that their wrong-doing merited suffering. But what about the victims? What about the benediction God pronounced over each and every one of them: May you flourish until full of years?

Soul-making theodicy speaks only of the survivors, not of the victims. Either that, or it links victims with survivors by saying that the chastisement or opportunity for spiritual growth provided to the survivors outweighs in its goodness the evil of the early death and suffering of the victims. In so speaking, it displays its obliviousness to that "each-and-every" note in the biblical speech of God. The biblical God is not a nineteenth century English utilitarian concerned only with the greatest flourishing of *the greatest number*. The God who kills children for the sake of the chastisement or spiritual growth of parents, the God who kills millions of Jews for the sake of the chastisement or spiritual growth of the survivors, is a grotesque parody of the biblical God. And should someone suggest that the early death of the child represents the punishment of the child for the child's own sins, and that the early death of the victims of the Holocaust represents the punishment of the victims for the victims' own sins, we must, emboldened by God's own book of Job, reject this suggestion as blasphemy against the justice of God and grotesquely libelous of those we loved.

4. Objection: The Divine Intent Misdescribed

To suggest that God trades off the suffering and early death of victims for the opportunity provided to survivors for chastisement or spiritual growth is to imply that I have not so much misdescribed the world as misdescribed the

divine intent. Probably that is the more common objection to the picture I have
drawn.

The most common form of the objection holds that it is essential to distinguish between, on the one hand, God's creating and maintaining intent, and
on the other hand, God's desires. Nothing goes awry with reference to God's
intent. Yet it would be profoundly mistaken to say that God is indifferent as
between a life of seventy seconds and a life of seventy years, indifferent as
between a life of malfunctioning and unredemptive suffering and a life absent
of such. God desires, for each and every human being, that that human being
flourish on earth in the community of persons until full of years.

From this point onward, the objection is developed along two distinct lines.
Call the one, the *Leibnizian* position. The Leibnizian holds that what must be
distinguished from God's creating and maintaining intent is God's *ceteris
paribus* desires. With reference to God's intent, everything happens exactly as
God's plans: early death, unredemptive suffering, everything. Nonetheless it
remains true that God desires, *other things being equal*, that each human being
flourish on earth in the community of persons until full of years. But other
things are not equal – so much so that it's not possible for God to bring about
a world in which that *ceteris paribus* desire is satisfied for each and every
human being. We can be assured that in choosing to create this actual world,
from among all possible worlds, God was choosing the best possible – or if
there isn't any best possible, that God was choosing as good a world as any.
But the only reasonable conclusion, given the nature of God and the way the
world is, is that any such world incorporates trade-offs; not even God can
achieve everything that God desires, other things being equal. That's why we
cannot equate what God desires *ceteris paribus* with God's creating intent.
Though suffering and life duration certainly go awry with reference to the
former, nothing goes awry with reference to the latter.

Call the other way of developing the objection, the *free will* position. The
person who embraces this position holds that suffering and life duration, and
other things as well, go awry with reference to God's *actual* desires, not just
with respect to God's *ceteris paribus* desires. Not, though, with reference to
God's creating and maintaining intent; on this central point he agrees with the
Leibnizian. The root of the disagreement between the two lies in the fact that
the person espousing the *free will* position holds – as the name suggests – that
human beings are created capable of free agency. There are, in turn, two different ways of working out the free will position, depending on whether one
holds that God can and does know in advance what agents will freely do in
such-and-such situations, or denies that.

The *Molinist* holds that God does know this; and that God uses that knowledge to select, from among all the possible worlds, this actual world of ours
to create and maintain. Everything happens according to the foreknowledge
of God. But not everything happens because God brings it about; some of it

happens because of the free agency of created persons. Though God knew in advance what Hitler would freely do, nonetheless it was not God who perpetrated the holocaust but Hitler, along with his henchmen and underlings. And God profoundly disapproved of Hitler's actions. With reference to God's desires and commands for those creatures capable of free agency, volitions and affections have gone profoundly awry; as the consequence of that, in turn, very much suffering and life duration have gone awry. Yet nothing has gone awry with reference to God's creating intent. For as on the Leibnizian position, the only reasonable conclusion, given the nature of God and the world, is said to be that God at creation was confronted with no option but to make trade-offs. Among the good-as-any worlds available to God for creating, there was none in which it was both true that human beings were free to make significant choices between good and evil, and true that each and every human being flourished on earth in the community of persons until full of years. The course of the world makes clear that God regards free agency as something of enormous value. But the fact that God tolerates the evil of our choices for the sake of our freedom by no means implies that God approves of that evil. God disapproves of it: *actually* disapproves of it, not just *ceteris paribus* disapproves.

The Bañezian, by contrast, denies that God could know in advance what a person capable of free agency would freely do in such-and-such a situation. Accordingly, assuming that God does sometimes allow persons capable of free agency actually to act freely, we cannot think of this actual world of ours as selected by God from among all the possible worlds. Its realization does not represent the unfolding of a plan chosen by God before the foundations of the world. That's not to say that the world as it develops is constantly surprising God; though one cannot know what an agent *will* freely do in such-and-such a situation, often one can know what he or she is *likely* to do. Nonetheless, whereas providence on the Leibnizian and Molinist views consists basically of maintenance, on the Bañezian view it requires a considerable degree of intervention if God is to bring about as good a world as any that God is capable of bringing about. The counterpart to God's creating intent in the Leibnizian and Molinist views is, in the Bañezian view, the combination of God's creating and providential intents. By reference to that intent, nothing goes awry – even though very many of the actions of free agents and the consequences thereof go radically contrary to God's actual desire and command.

Three ways of working out the same idea: Though things go awry with reference to God's desires and commands, nothing goes awry with reference to God's creating and maintaining intent. The history of the world simply exhibits the trade-offs already built into the divine intent.

But if we judge ourselves answerable to the biblical speech of God, we can no more accept this position than that of soul-making theodicy. Again it is especially the "each-and-every" note in God's self-characterizing speech which goes unheard – or perhaps in this case not so much unheard as consciously rejected. Let's be sure that we rightly hear that "each-and-every" note. There's no problem, as such, with trade-offs in the life of a single person: no problem as such with the fact, for example, that I suffer from the consequences of my own free agency. I say, "no problem as such"; as a matter of fact, the suffering caused by physical and mental disease in our world often goes far beyond what could possibly be redemptive. The problem inherent in the Irenaean position, as in the Leibnizian articulation of it, is that the divine intent is regarded as using the suffering and early death of *one* person as a means for the chastisement or spiritual growth of *another*; and the problem inherent in the free will position is that the divine intent is regarded as allowing the suffering and early death of *one* person as a means for the chastisement or spiritual growth of *another*; and the problem inherent in the free will position is that the divine intent is regared as allowing the suffering and early death of *one* person for the sake of the unencumbered free agency of *another*. It is this using of one person for the good of another that the person who judges himself or herself answerable to the biblical speech of God cannot accept as belonging to the divine intent.

Or, given the working of laws of nature in our world and the consequences of free agency, must we concede that God doesn't really pronounce over each and every person the creational and providential benediction: May you flourish on earth in the community of persons until full of years? Must we concede that that's an unsustainable interpretation of the biblical speech of God – for the reason that that benediction could not possibly be fulfilled in a world with free agency and laws of nature such as ours, and that God would know that, and accordingly would not pronounce such a benediction?

I think we should not concede this. It's thinkable, indeed, that a lot more knowledge about laws of nature than we actually have might force us to make that concession, as would a lot more knowledge about the relation between divine and human agency. But in our current state of relative ignorance, there is, so far as I can see, no such rational compulsion. Though the point is certainly relevant: a fundamental principle for the interpretation of divine discourse is that God does not say what entails or presupposes falsehood.

The root of the difficulty, for the person who judges himself or herself answerable to the biblical speech of God, is that the God of the Bible has told us too much. If we hadn't been told that it was God's intent that we should live until full of years, then no problem. If we hadn't been told that it was God's intent that we should flourish, then no problem. If we hadn't been told that it was God's intent that we should flourish here on earth in the community of persons, then no problem. If we hadn't been told that it was God's intent that each and every one of us should flourish until full of years, then no problem. It's the speech of the biblical God that leads us to see that suffering and life-duration have gone awry with reference to God's creating and maintaining intent. If we could dispense with answering to that speech, it would be possible to devise a point of view which fits together such suffering and brevity of life as we find in our world with the divine intent; many have done exactly that.

5.   Living in the Silence

Suffering and life duration have gone awry with reference to God's creating and maintaining intent. To acknowledge that is to have the question well up irresistibly: Why? Why this untimely death? Why that unredemptive suffering? Why any untimely death and why any unredemptive suffering?

We cannot help but ask. Yet we get no answer. None that I can discern. We confront nonanswering silence. We confront the biblical silence of the biblical God. We shall have to live in the silence.

What will such living be like? If we have all this while judged ourselves answerable to the speech of God in determining the questions we put to God, then we shall likewise judge ourselves answerable to the speech of God as we live in the silence of God.

In the first place, we shall endure in holding on to God, and shall engage in the practices of devotion whereby such holding on is accomplished, expressed, and nurtured.

Secondly, we shall join with God himself in keeping alive the protest against early death and unredemptive suffering. Till breath dies within us we shall insist that this must not be. We shall reject all consolation that comes in the form of urging us to accept untimely death, all that comes in the form of urging us to be content with unredemptive suffering. We shall endure in our existential No to untimely death; we shall forever resist pronouncing No on our existential No to untimely death. We shall endure in our existential No to unredemptive suffering; we shall forever resist pronouncing No on our existential No to unredemptive suffering. In the stories we tell of humanity's dwelling on earth, we shall not forget untimely death and unredemptive suffering; We shall keep the memory alive so as to keep the protest alive. And in the stories we tell of our own lives, we shall not disown our suffering but own it. There will be more to our stories than that; but there will be at least that.

Thirdly, we shall hope for the day, await the occasion, and seize the opportunity to own our own suffering redemptively. We shall struggle to wrest good from this evil – "to turn it to our profit" – while still saying No to untimely death and unredemptive suffering.

And lastly, whenever and wherever we spot an opening, we shall join the divine battle against all that goes awry with reference to God's intent. We shall join God in doing battle against all that causes early death and all that leads to unredemptive suffering: disease, injustice, warfare, torture, enmity. The self-characterization of the biblical God is not that of a God who passively accepts things going awry with reference to his intent but that of a God who does battle; and is not that of a God who weakly struggles in a failing cause but that of a God whose cause will triumph. It is in that cause that we shall join, as God's co-workers. In his discussion of *das Nichtige* Karl Barth makes the point far more eloquently than I myself could possibly make it:

> The incredible and real mystery of the free grace of God is that He makes His own the cause of the creature. . . . There is a grain of truth in the erroneous view that in virtue of His Godhead God himself has absolutely done away with *da Nichtige*, so that for Him it is not only *das Nichtige* but nothing. In Him there is room only for its negation. And as the Creator He has effected this negation once and for all. In creation He separated, negated, rejected and abandoned *das Nichtige*. How, then, can it still assail, oppose, resist and offend Him? How can it concern Him? But we must not forget the covenant, mercy and faithfulness of God, nor should we overlook the fact that God did not will to be God for His own sake alone, but that as the Creator He also became the covenant Partner of his creature. . . . Why is this so? Because, having created the creature, He has pledged His faithfulness to it. . . . That is to say, He whom *das Nichtige* has no power to offend is prepared on behalf of His creature to be primarily and properly offended and humiliated, attacked and injured by *das Nichtige*. . . . Though Adam is fallen and disgraced, he is not too low for God to make Himself his Brother, and to be for him a God who must strangely contend for his status, honor and right. For the sake of this Adam God becomes poor. . . . He lets a catastrophe which might be quite remote from Him approach Him and affect His very heart. . . . He does this of His free grace. For He is under no compulsion. He might act as the erroneous view postulates. He might remain aloof and detached from *das Nichtige*. . . . He might have been a majestic, passive and beatific God on high. But He descends to the depths, and concerns Himself with *das Nichtige*, because in His goodness He does not will to cease to be concerned for His creature. . . . He would rather be unblest with His creature than be the blessed God of an unblest creature. He would rather let Himself be injured and humiliated in making the assault and repulse of *das Nichtige* His own concern than leave His creature alone in this affliction. . . . There are few heresies so pernicious as that of a God who faces *das Nichtige* more or less unaffected and unconcerned and the parallel doctrine of man as one who must engage in independent conflict against it. *Church Dogmatics* III/3, 356–60

I add, in closing, that it is at the very point on which Barth speaks so eloquently that biblical faith is most severely tried. Is it really true that God will win? Can we trust the struggle's outcome when we don't know the struggle's cause? Or wouldn't it help to know the cause?

Bibliography

PAUL K. MOSER

Adams, Marilyn. "Redemptive Suffering." In *Rationality, Religious Belief, and Moral Commitment*, eds. Robert Audi and William Wainwright, pp. 248–70. (Ithaca: Cornell University Press, 1986).

Allen, Diogenes. *Three Outsiders: Pascal, Kierkegaard, Simone Weil.* (Cambridge, MA: Cowley Publications, 1983).

Anderson, Robert. *The Silence of God*, 9th ed. (London: Hodder and Stoughton, 1911).

Babolin, Albino. "Deus Absconditus: Some Notes on the Bearing of the Hiddenness of God Upon Butler's and Pascal's Criticism on Deism." In *Joseph Butler's Moral and Religious Thought*, ed. C. Cunliffe, pp. 29–35. (Oxford: Oxford University Press, 1992).

Balentine, Samuel E. *The Hidden God: The Hiding of the Face of God in the Old Testament.* (Oxford: Oxford University Press, 1984).

"A Description of the Semantic Field of the Hebrew Words for 'Hide'." *Vetus Testamentum* **30** (1980): 137–53.

"Isaiah 45: God's 'I am,' Israel's 'You Are'." *Horizons in Biblical Theology* **16** (1994): 103–20.

Barcroft, Janet. "The Eclipse of God: A Jewish-Christian Perspective." *Christian Jewish Relations* **17** (1984): 20–9.

Barth, Karl. *Church Dogmatics, Volume II: The Doctrine of God*, pp. 179–204. (Edinburgh: T. and T. Clark, 1957).

Bloom, John A. "Why Isn't the Evidence Clear?" In *Evidence for Faith: Deciding the God Question*, ed. J. W. Montgomery, pp. 305–46. (Dallas: Probe Books, 1991).

Benor, Ehud Z. "Meaning and Reference in Maimonides' Negative Theology." *Harvard Theological Review* **88** (1995): 339–60.

Bergmann, Michael. "Skeptical Theism and Rowe's New Evidential Argument from Evil." *Noûs* **35** (2001): 278–96.

Bolle, Kees W. "Secrecy in Religion." In *Secrecy in Religions*, ed. K. Bolle, pp. 1–24. (Leiden: Brill, 1987).

Bouyer, Louis. "Deus Revelatus ut Absconditus." In *Newman's Vision of Faith*, chap. 3. (San Francisco: Ignatius Press, 1986).

Brown, David. "Butler and Deism." In *Joseph Butler's Moral and Religious Thought*, ed. C. Cunliffe, pp. 7–28. (Oxford: Oxford University Press, 1992).

Brueggemann, Walter. "The Hiddenness of Yahweh." In *Theology of the Old Testament*, pp. 333–58. (Minneapolis: Fortress, 1997).

Buber, Martin. *The Eclipse of God.* (London: Victor Gollancz, 1953).

Butler, Joseph. "Upon the Ignorance of Man." In *The Works of Joseph Butler*, ed. S. Halifax, Vol. II, pp. 190–202. (Oxford: Oxford University Press, 1840).

Byrne, Peter. "Review of *Divine Hiddenness and Human Reason*, by J. L. Schellenberg." *Religious Studies* **29** (1993): 570–1.

Clines, David. "Quarter Days Gone: Job 24 and the Absence of God." In *God in the Fray*, eds. Tod Linafelt and Timothy Beal, pp. 242–58. (Minneapolis: Fortress Press, 1998).

Coburn, Robert C. "The Hiddenness of God and Some Barmecidal Surrogates." *Journal of Philosophy* **57** (1960): 689–711.

Colombo, Joseph A. "God as Hidden, God as Manifest: Who Is the Subject of Salvation in History in Liberation Theology?" *Journal of Religion* **71** (1991): 18–35.

Cornelison, Robert T. "Losing Oneself to Gain Oneself: Rethinking God in a Narcissistic Age." *Union Seminary Quarterly Review* **52** (1998): 67–84.

Dales, D. J. *Living Through Dying*. (Cambridge: Lutterworth, 1994).

De Vaux, Roland. "The Presence and Absence of God in History According to the Old Testament." In *Concilium, Vol. 50: The Presence of God*, eds. P. Benoit, R. Murphy and B. van Iersel, pp. 7–20. (New York: Paulist Press, 1969).

Digby, Thomas. "On Unobservability and Detectability." *Religious Studies* **18** (1982): 509–11.

Dillenberger, John. *God Hidden and Revealed: The Interpretation of Luther's Deus Absconditus and Its Significance for Religious Thought*. (Philadelphia: Muhlenberg Press, 1953).

Dilley, Frank B. "Fool-Proof Proofs of God?" *International Journal for Philosophy of Religion* **8** (1977): 18–35.

Dinan, Stephen A. "The Tantalizing Absence of God." In *Religions and the Virtue of Religions*, ed. T. Druart, pp. 87–98. (Washington, DC: American Catholic Philosophical Association, 1992).

Dowey, Edward. *The Knowledge of God in Calvin's Theology*. (New York: Columbia University Press, 1965).

Doyon, Jacques. "Présence et Absence de Dieu dans la Theologie de D. Bonhoeffer." *Science et Esprit* **32** (1980): 73–81.

Drange, Theodore. *Nonbelief and Evil*. (Amherst, NY: Prometheus Press, 1998).

Duquoc, Christian, ed. *Where is God? A Cry of Human Distress*. (London: SCM Press, 1992).

Farmer, Herbert H. "God's Way of Hiding Himself." In *The Healing Cross*, pp. 76–85. (London: Nisbet, 1938).

The World and God, chaps. 13–14. (London: Nisbet, 1935).

Ford, David. *Self and Salvation: Being Transformed*. (Cambridge: Cambridge University Press, 1999).

Friedman, Richard E. *The Disappearance of God*. (New York: HarperCollins, 1996).

"The Hiding of the Face: An Essay on the Literary Unity of the Biblical Narrative." In *Judaic Perspectives on Ancient Israel*, ed. J. Neusner, pp. 207–22. (Philadelphia: Fortress Press, 1987).

"The Biblical Expression 'Mastir Panim'." *Hebrew Annual Review* **1** (1977): 139–47.

Gerrish, Brian. *Grace and Reason: A Study in the Theology of Luther*, chap. 5. (Oxford: Oxford University Press, 1962).

"To the Unknown God: Luther and Calvin on the Hiddenness of God." *Journal of Religion* **53** (1973): 263–93.

Grislis, Egil. "Martin Luther's View of the Hidden God: The Problem of the Deus Absconditus in Luther's Treatise De Servo Arbitrio." *McCormick Quarterly* **21** (1967): 81–94.

Gunderson, Keith. "Are There Criteria for 'Encountering God'?" In *Faith and the Philosophers*, ed. John Hick, pp. 57–8. (New York: St. Martin's Press, 1964).

Hall, Douglas John. *Lighten our Darkness*. (Philadelphia: Fortress Press, 1976).

Hanson, Norwood Russell. "Why I Do not Believe." *Continuum* **5** (1976): 89–105.

Haught, John. *God After Darwin*. (Boulder, CO: Westview Press, 2000).

Mystery and Promise. (Collegeville, MN: Liturgical Press, 1993).

Heller, Jan. "Hiding of the Face." *Communio Viatorum* **1** (1958): 263–6.

Henry, Douglas. "Does Reasonable Nonbelief Exist?" *Faith and Philosophy* **18** (2001): 75–92.

Herzog, Frederick. "Towards a Waiting God." In *Future of Hope*, ed. F. Herzog, pp. 51–7. (New York: Herder and Herder, 1970).

Heschel, Abraham Joshua. "The Hiding God." In *Man Is Not Alone*, chap. 16. (New York: Noonday Press, 1951).

Hick, John. *An Interpretation of Religions: Human Responses to the Transcendent*. (London: Macmillan, 1989).

Faith and Knowledge. (Ithaca: Cornell University Press, 1966).

Horst, Pieter Willem van der. "The Unknown God (Acts 17:23)." In *Knowledge of God*, ed. R. Broek, pp. 19–42. (Leiden: Brill, 1988).

Howard-Snyder, Daniel. "The Argument from Divine Hiddenness." *Canadian Journal of Philosophy* **26** (1996): 433–53.

"Review of *Divine Hiddenness and Human Reason*, by J. L. Schellenberg." *Mind* **104** (1995): 430–5.

"The Argument from Inscrutable Evil." In *The Evidential Argument from Evil*, ed. D. Howard-Snyder, pp. 286–310. (Bloomington: Indiana University Press, 1996).

"Seeing Through CORNEA." *International Journal for the Philosophy of Religion* **32** (1992): 25–49.

Human, Dirk J. "Psalm 44: 'Why do you hide your face, O God?!'" *Skrif en Kerk* **19** (1998): 566–83.

Jocz, Jakob. "The Invisibility of God and the Incarnation." *Canadian Journal of Theology* **4** (1958): 179–86.

John of the Cross. "The Dark Night." In *John of the Cross: Selected Writings*, eds. K. Kavanaugh and E. E. Larkin, pp. 155–209. (New York: Paulist Press, 1987).

Johnson, Luke T. "Seeking God While God Is Near." *Christian Century* (1990): 828.

Kasper, Walter. *The God of Jesus Christ*, trans. M. O'Connell, pp. 123–30. (New York: Crossroad, 1986).

Keller, James A. "The Hiddenness of God and the Problem of Evil." *International Journal for Philosophy of Religion* **37** (1995): 13–24.

Kierkegaard, Søren. *Concluding Unscientific Postscript*, eds. and trans. H. V. Hong and E. H. Hong. (Princeton: Princeton University Press, 1992).

Kiernan-Lewis, Del. "Review of *Divine Hiddenness and Human Reason*, by J. L. Schellenberg." *The Journal of Religion* **75** (1995): 295.

Kinlaw, Jeffrey C. "Determinism and the Hiddenness of God in Calvin's Theology." *Religious Studies* **24** (1988): 497–509.

Kitamori, Kazoh. "The Pain of God and the Hidden God." In *Theology of the Pain of God*, pp. 105–16. (Richmond, VA: John Knox Press, 1965).

Lacy, Larry. "Review of *Divine Hiddenness and Human Reason*, by J. L. Schellenberg," *International Journal for Philosophy of Religion* **40** (1996): 121–4.

Lane, Belden C. "A Hidden and Playful God." *Christian Century* **104** (1987): 812–13.

Lewis, Joe O. "Gen 32: 23–33, Seeing a Hidden God." In *Proceedings of the Society of Biblical Literature*, pp. 449–57. (Atlanta: Scholars Press, 1972).

Lucas, J. R. "Doubt: A Sermon." In *Freedom and Grace*, pp. 120–5. (London: SPCK, 1976).

Luther, Martin. "The Bondage of the Will." In *Martin Luther: Selections*, ed. John Dillenberger, pp. 190–2. (Garden City, NY: Anchor, 1961).

Macquarrie, John. In *Search of Deity*, chap. 14. (New York: Crossroad, 1985).

Maitzen, Stephen. "Review of *Divine Hiddenness and Human Reason*, by J. L. Schellenberg." *The Philosophical Review* **104** (1995): 153–6.

McGrath, Alister E. *Luther's Theology of the Cross: Martin Luther's Theological Breakthrough*, chap. 5. (Oxford: Blackwell, 1985).

McKim, Robert. "The Hiddenness of God." *Religious Studies* **26** (1990): 141–61.

"Review of *Divine Hiddenness and Human Reason*, by J. L. Schellenberg." *Faith and Philosophy* **12** (1995): 269–77.

Religious Ambiguity and Religious Diversity. (New York: Oxford University Press, 2001).

Mesle, Robert C. "Does God Hide from Us? John Hick and Process Theology on Faith, Freedom and Theodicy." *International Journal for Philosophy of Religion* **24** (1988): 93–111.

Michalson, Carl. "The Real Presence of the Hidden God." In *Faith and Ethics: The Theology of H. Richard Niebuhr*, ed. P. Ramsey. (New York: Harper, 1957).

Moore, Gareth. "Tradition, Authority and the Hiddenness of God." In *Philosophy and the Grammar of Religious Belief*, ed. T. Tessin, pp. 134–60. (New York: St. Martin's Press, 1995).

Moroney, Stephen K. *The Noetic Effects of Sin*. (Lanham, MD: Lexington Books, 2000).

Morris, Thomas V. "The Hidden God." *Philosophical Topics* **16** (1988): 5–21.

"The Hidden God." In *Making Sense of It All: Pascal and the Meaning of Life*, pp. 85–108. (Grand Rapids: Eerdmans, 1992).

"Agnosticism" *Analysis* **45** (1985): 219–24.

Moser, Paul K. *Why Isn't God More Obvious?* (Atlanta: RZIM, 2000).

"Does Divine Hiddenness Justify Atheism?" In *Contemporary Debates in Philosophy of Religion*, ed. Michael Peterson. (Malden, MA: Blackwell, forthcoming).

"On Two Arguments from Hiddenness for Atheism." In *Contemporary Debates in Philosophy of Religion*, ed. Michael Peterson. (Malden, MA: Blackwell, forthcoming).

"Divine Hiding." *Philosophia Christi* **2** (2001): 439–55.

"A God Who Hides and Seeks." *Philosophia Christi* **2** (2001): 467–73.

Moule, C. F. D. "Revelation." In *The Interpreter's Dictionary of the Bible*, vol 4, pp. 54–8. (New York: Abingdon Press, 1962).

Murray, Michael J. "Coercion and the Hiddenness of God." *American Philosophical Quarterly* **30** (1993): 27–38.

Mundle, W. "Hide." In *The New International Dictionary of New Testament Theology*, ed. Colin Brown, pp. 214–20. (Grand Rapids: Zondervan, 1976).

Neher, Andr. "Silence and the Hidden God in Prophecy." In *Fifth World Congress of Jewish Studies*, ed. A. Shinan, Vol. 3, pp. 259–63. (Jerusalem: World Union of Jewish Studies, 1972).

Oakes, Robert A. "Religious Experience, Sense-Perception and God's Essential Unobservability." *Religious Studies* **17** (1981): 357–67.

O'Hagan, Timothy. "Charles Taylor's Hidden God." *Ratio* **6** (1993): 72–81.

Oman, John. *Grace and Personality.* (Cambridge: Cambridge University Press, 1917).

Otto, R. *The Idea of the Holy.* (Oxford: Oxford University Press, 1923).

Padgett, Alan G. "Review of *Divine Hiddenness and Human Reason*, by J. L. Schellenberg." *Philosophical Books* **35** (1994): 208.

Pascal, Blaise. *Penseés*, trans. A. J. Krailsheimer. (London: Penguin, 1966).

Paulson, Steven D. "Luther on the Hidden God." *Word and World* **19** (1999): 363–71.

Penelhum, Terence. *Butler*, chap. 8. (London: Routledge, 1985).

    "Butler and Human Ignorance." In *Joseph Butler's Moral and Religious Thought*, ed. C. Cunliffe, pp. 117–40. (Oxford: Oxford University Press, 1992).

    "Faith and Ambiguity." In *Reason and Religious Faith*, chap. 6. (Boulder, CO: Westview Press, 1995).

    God and Skepticism: A Study in Skepticism and Fideism, pp. 62–159. (Dordrecht: Reidel, 1983).

    "Reflections on the Ambiguity of the World." In *God, Truth and Reality: Essays in Honour of John Hick*, ed. A. Sharma, pp. 165–75. (New York: St. Martin's Press, 1993).

    "Skepticism and Fideism." In *The Skeptical Tradition*, ed. M. Burnyeat, pp. 287–318. (Berkeley: University of California Press, 1983).

Pettit, Peter A. "Christ Alone, The Hidden God, and Protestant Exclusivism." *Word and World* **11** (1991):190–8.

Pilkington, Christine. "The Hidden God in Isaiah 45:15 – A Reflection from Holocaust Theology." *Scottish Journal of Theology* **48** (1995): 285–300.

Platt, David. "Divinity as a Given." *International Philosophical Quarterly* **27** (1987): 381–92.

Pratney, W. A. *The Thomas Factor.* (Old Tappan, NJ: Revell, 1989).

Price, H. H. "Faith and Belief." In *Faith and the Philosophers*, ed. John Hick, pp. 3–37. (New York: St. Martin's Press, 1964).

Rahner, Karl. *Theological Investigations: Experience of the Spirit: Source of Theology*, trans. D. Morland, chap. 14. (New York: Seabury Press, 1979).

Richardson, Alan. "The Death of God: A Report Exaggerated." In *Religion in Contemporary Debate*, pp. 102–20. (Philadelphia: Westminster Press, 1966).

Rolfe, James A. "The Hidden God." *Faith and Freedom* **44** (1991): 43–52.

Roth, John. "The Silence of God." *Faith and Philosophy* **1** (1984): 407–20.

Rouquette, Jean. "The 'Hidden' and the 'Manifest' in the New Testament." In *Concrete Christian Life*, ed. C. Duquoc, pp. 44–6. (New York: Herder, 1971).

Rowe, William. "Religious Experience and the Principle of Credulity." *International Journal of Philosophy of Religion* 13 (1982): 85–92.

"Skeptical Theism: A Response to Bergmann." *Nous* 35 (2001): 297–303.

Schellenberg, J. L. *Divine Hiddenness and Human Reason.* (Ithaca: Cornell University Press, 1993).

"Response to Howard-Snyder." *Canadian Journal of Philosophy* 26 (1996): 455–62.

"Does Divine Hiddeness Justify Atheism?" In *Contemporary Debates in Philosophy of Religion*, ed. Michael Peterson. (Malden, MA: Blackwell, forthcoming).

"Hiddenness Concealed: A Reply to Moser." In *Contemporary Debates in Philosophy of Religion*, ed. Michael Peterson. (Malden, MA: Blackwell, forthcoming).

Scherer, Paul. *When God Hides.* (New York: Harper, 1934).

"The God Who Leaves Man Alone." In *The Place Where Thou Standest*, pp. 17–22. (New York: Harper, 1942).

Schlesinger, George N. "The Availability of Evidence in Support of Religious Belief." *Faith and Philosophy* 1 (1984): 421–36.

Schoen, Edward L. "Perceiving an Imperceptible God." *Religious Studies* 34 (1998): 433–55.

Schroeder, Edward H. "Encountering the Hidden God." *Areopagus* 6 (1993): 26–9.

Sontag, Frederick. "The Mysterious Presence" [Knowing an Unknown God]. *Asia Journal of Theology* 5 (1991): 151–62.

Swinburne, Richard. *Revelation.* (Oxford: Clarendon Press, 1992).

The Existence of God, chap. 11. (Oxford: Clarendon Press, 1979).

Providence and the Problem of Evil, chap. 11. (Oxford: Clarendon Press, 1998).

Taubes, Susan Anima. "The Absent God." *Journal of Religion* 35 (1955): 6–16.

Taylor, Barbara Brown. *When God is Silent.* (Boston: Cowley, 1998).

Terrien, Samuel. *The Elusive Presence.* (New York: Harper, 1978).

Thielicke, Helmut. *The Hidden Question of God*, trans. G. W. Bromiley. (Grand Rapids: Eerdmans, 1977).

How to Believe Again, pp. 162–6. (Philadelphia: Fortress, 1972).

The Silence of God, trans. G. W. Bromiley. (Grand Rapids: Eerdmans, 1962).

Tracy, David. "The Hidden God: The Divine Other of Liberation." *Cross Currents* (1996): 5–16.

von Rad, Gerhard. *Old Testament Theology*, trans. D. Stalker, Vol. II, pp. 374–82. (New York: Harper and Row, 1965).

Wainwright, Geoffrey. "Recent Continental Theology: Historical and Systematic" [review article]. *Expository Times* 97 (1986): 267–72.

Wainwright, William J. *Reason and the Heart.* (Ithaca: Cornell University Press, 1995).

Williams, Clayton E. "The Silence of God." In *Best Sermons, Vol. X: 1966–1968*, ed. G. P. Butler, pp. 179–86. (New York: Trident Press, 1968).

Williams, Rowan. "The Dark Night." In *A Ray of Darkness*, pp. 80–4. (Cambridge, MA: Cowley, 1995).

Wolpe, David. "Hester Panim in Modern Jewish Thought." *Modern Judaism* 17 (1997): 25–56.

Yaryan, Elaine A. "Dark Night of the Soul: Evil or the Shadow of God?" *Ashland Theological Journal* 24 (1992): 1–13.

Index of Names

Index of Subjects